Axel Honneth

Axel Honneth

A Critical Theory of the Social

Christopher F. Zurn

polity

First published in 2015 by Polity Press

Polity Press
65 Bridge Street
Cambridge CB2 1UR, UK

Polity Press
350 Main Street
Malden, MA 02148, USA

ISBN-13: 978-0-7456-4903-0
ISBN-13: 978-0-7456-4904-7(pb)

A catalogue record for this book is available from the British Library.

Library of Congress Cataloging-in-Publication Data

Zurn, Christopher F., 1966–
    Axel Honneth / Christopher Zurn.
        pages cm. – (Key contemporary thinkers)
    Includes bibliographical references.
    ISBN 978-0-7456-4903-0 (hardback : alk. paper) – ISBN 978-0-7456-4904-7 (pbk. : alk. paper)   1. Honneth, Axel, 1949-   2. Social sciences–Philosophy.   3. Sociology–Philosophy.   4. Critical theory.   I. Title.
    B63.Z87 2015
    301.092–dc23
                            2014023353

Typeset in 10/11.5 Palatino
by Toppan Best-set Premedia Limited
Printed and bound in the United Kingdom by Clays Ltd, St Ives PLC

For further information on Polity, visit our website:
politybooks.com

In memory of Michelle

Contents

Contents

Abbreviations

CoP	*The Critique of Power: Reflective Stages in a Critical Social Theory*
FR	*Freedom's Right: The Social Foundations of Democratic Life*
PoIF	*The Pathologies of Individual Freedom: Hegel's Social Theory*
R	*Reification: A New Look at an Old Idea*
RoR	*Redistribution or Recognition? A Political-Philosophical Exchange*
SAaHN	*Social Action and Human Nature*
SfR	*The Struggle for Recognition: The Moral Grammar of Social Conflicts*

1

Introduction

1992 saw the publication in Germany of an influential new book combining diverse lines of research across philosophy, psychology, history, sociology, and political theory by the theorist Axel Honneth. By the time its English translation was published in 1995 as *The Struggle for Recognition: The Moral Grammar of Social Conflicts* (abbreviated hereafter as SfR), it was clear that a major new voice in the tradition of critical theory had arrived. The book not only forwarded a number of important original claims but, more importantly, provided a new research paradigm – centered on the keystone concept of intersubjective recognition – for revitalizing interdisciplinary social theory with emancipatory intent. With *Struggle for Recognition*, it became clear, moreover, that there was a successor third-generation critical theorist in the tradition of the Frankfurt School (Anderson 2011), one who could claim to legitimately carry on the broad heritage of the first generation – especially Theodor Adorno and Max Horkheimer – and of the second generation – especially Jürgen Habermas – while at the same time advancing a new, insightful critical social theory sensitive to the changed sociopolitical circumstances of advanced western democracies at the end of the twentieth and beginning of the twenty-first centuries.

The aim of the book before you is to give a general overview of the crucial claims and arguments of Honneth's new critical social theory, as well as assessing some of the substantive controversies surrounding them. This is by no means a complete treatment of everything Honneth has written, nor does it provide an exhaustive appraisal of all of the critical debates on his work. In fact, it will often need to foreshorten important issues and skirt lightly over or even ignore significant detail in the service of usefully concise summary. The intention is thus more modest: a clear, introductory exposition of the core theses of Honneth's own original theory, presented along with balanced assessments of its strengths and weaknesses in the light of prominent alternatives. This introductory chapter provides a brief biography of Honneth (1.1), a preview of the chapters indicating Honneth's crucial theoretical contributions and themes (1.2), and a frame for grasping those contributions in a broader intellectual context of major philosophical, social, and political theories (1.3).

1.1 A Brief Biography

Axel Honneth was born in 1949 in Essen, Germany, and graduated in 1969 from secondary school through the *abitur* (university entrance exams), also in Essen.[1] The son of Horst Honneth, a medical doctor, and Annemarie Honneth, he grew up in a bourgeois milieu, though becoming increasingly disaffected with it while witnessing the new upward mobility amongst the working class in his coal-mining region and taking part in the cultural and political ferment of the late 1960s and early 1970s – Bob Dylan has long been a touchstone for him. From 1969 until 1974, in addition to involvement with the student movement and progressive political parties, he studied a variety of subjects at a variety of locations. He immersed himself in philosophy, sociology, and German literature at the universities in Bonn and Bochum, earning a master's degree in philosophy at Bochum in 1974. He then did postgraduate and doctoral work at the Institute of Sociology at the Free University of Berlin from 1974 until 1982. In 1980, during his doctoral studies and growing out of courses he and his co-author Hans Joas had been teaching, Honneth and Joas published an extraordinarily useful and insightful book: *Social Action and Human Nature* (SAaHN). It outlined the relationship between various theories of social action found in the social sciences and diverse nineteenth- and twentieth-century traditions in philosophical anthropology, that is, philosophical theories of human nature. His doctoral dissertation, submitted in 1983, was written under the directorship of Urs Jaeggi on the competing theories of power found in first-generation critical theory (especially in the work of Adorno and Horkheimer) and the work of French post-structuralist Michel Foucault. The dissertation's six chapters were subsequently combined with three further chapters on power in the work of Jürgen Habermas and published by the prestigious Suhrkamp Verlag as a monograph in 1985, later translated into English with the title *Critique of Power: Reflective Stages in a Critical Social Theory* (CoP).

From 1982 to 1983, he had a grant to do research under Jürgen Habermas at the Max Planck Institute for the Study of the Scientific-Technical World in Starnberg. (This is the extraordinary research institute that Habermas was the director of from 1971 until 1983, bringing together some of the brightest researchers in philosophy, sociology, linguistics, social psychology, economics, and other social sciences, an environment which enabled Habermas to develop his massive two-volume magnum opus, *The Theory of Communicative Action* (Habermas 1984, 1987)). In the hierarchical world of German academics, each full professor has significant authority over a cadre of lower-status academics, ranging from doctoral students and research assistants to assistant professors and senior research fellows. Accordingly, in 1983, when Habermas again took up his chair in philosophy at Goethe University in Frankfurt, Honneth also moved to Frankfurt, becoming *Hochschulassistent* in philosophy under Habermas. In 1990, Honneth completed his *Habilitationsschrift* – a major work that qualifies one to move up the academic ladder, often referred to as a second doctoral dissertation. It was titled "Kampf um Anerkennung" (Struggle for Recognition). As noted above, the German publication of a greatly expanded version of this work in 1992 and its translation into English in 1995 (SfR) set the world on notice that a major new research paradigm in critical social theory had arrived.

After his *Habilitation* in Frankfurt, and a year as a fellow at the Institute for Advanced Studies in Berlin (the *Wissenschaftskolleg*), Honneth took up a position as C3-professor (roughly equivalent to the American "associate professor") in philosophy at the University of Konstanz from 1991 to 1992. He was quickly promoted to C4-professor (roughly equivalent to the American "full professor") when he took up a position in political philosophy at the Free University of Berlin, remaining in Berlin from 1992 until 1996. In 1996, he returned to Frankfurt as C4-professor of social philosophy, a position he has retained until the present. In addition, in 2001 he took up his current position as director of the Institute for Social Research. Since 2011, he has split his time between Frankfurt and New York City, where he is a professor of humanities at Columbia University. Throughout his career, Honneth has given many prestigious lectures, won several awards and honors, and held many visiting academic positions around the world: McGill University in Montreal, Canada, Kyoto University in Japan, the New School in New York, University of Amsterdam in the Netherlands, Boston College in the United States, the Ecole des Hautes Etudes et Sciences Sociales in Paris, Dartmouth College in the United States, and the Université de Paris (Sorbonne).

Honneth has been a particularly productive scholar and public intellectual, producing a raft of books and articles not only expounding his own unique form of critical social theory, but also insightfully interpreting, selectively appropriating, and critiquing the work of other major thinkers. Bare numbers give at least a sense of the prodigious quantity of his efforts: some seven original monographs, seven further collections of his own essays, twenty-one edited books of work by others, more than 220 journal articles and book chapters, and more than fifty newspaper pieces. As this book could not hope to deal with this mass of material in a systematic way, I have chosen instead to focus on what I consider the core elements of his mature critical social theory. This entails lightly treating or disregarding here much that is of deep theoretical interest in Honneth's corpus, an oversight hopefully justified by relative brevity and clarity. In particular, this book focuses most intently on what I consider the two core works of Honneth's mature corpus –1992's *The Struggle for Recognition* and 2011's *Das Recht der Freiheit*, translated in 2014 as *Freedom's Right: The Social Foundations of Democratic Life* (FR) – while also treating other key works, including his 2003 co-authored book debating Nancy Fraser *Redistribution or Recognition? A Political-Philosophical Exchange* (RoR), his Tanner Lectures of 2005 *Reification: A New Look at an Old Idea* (R), and various essays and other works that are crucial to his mature critical theory.[2]

1.2   Honneth's Themes

1.2.1   Critical social theory

As I indicated above, Honneth's central aim is to produce an accurate, convincing, and insightful *critical social theory*.[3] One way to understand what such a theory consists of would be to trace its lineage through major intellectual precursors and influences – e.g., Kant, Fichte, Hegel, Feuerbach, Marx, Nietzsche, Durkheim, Freud, Mead, Dewey, Weber, Lukács, Parsons – and through the substantive work of major practitioners who explicitly understand themselves as producing critical social theory – e.g., Max Horkheimer, Theodor Adorno, Herbert Marcuse, Jürgen Habermas, Karl Otto Apel, Seyla Benhabib, Thomas McCarthy, Nancy Fraser, Rainer Forst, Axel Honneth. Another way to understand critical social theory, however, is to define it rather broadly as "interdisciplinary social theory with emancipatory intent."[4] That would then rightly include not only Frankfurt School theorists but also a broader range of critical theories, including feminism, critical race theory, critical legal studies, postcolonial theory, queer theory, and post-structuralism.

The basic idea of critical theory is to carry out the charge that Marx set for a new journal in 1843: the "the self-clarification (critical philosophy) of the struggles and wishes of the age."[5] Such a theoretical elucidation starts from a *description* of current society, a description which must be not only accurate but also particularly attuned to any and all explicit and implicit struggles occurring within contemporary social relations. But description alone is not enough, for self-clarification also requires a satisfactory *explanation* of why the present situation is as it is – almost surely including historical explanations of how it has come to be so – and why these are the particular struggles and dreams of current social actors. These descriptive and explanatory tasks can only be fulfilled by integrating research across a diverse range of social sciences: sociology, history, psychology, economics, political science, law, etc. – hence the "interdisciplinary social science" portion of my formula.

Producing an empirically accurate, integrated social scientific picture of the present is sufficient to fulfill the tasks of traditional social theory. But to be *critical*, such a theory must also have a *practical* purpose: namely, an interest in furthering reason-governed human freedom and well-being, in overcoming unjustifiable or unreasonable forms of constraint or oppression – in short, an "emancipatory interest." Rejecting the notion that we must simply accept current social reality as given, no matter what its problems, Max Horkheimer insists, in his canonical 1937 article, that: "critical theory maintains: it need not be so; man can change reality; and the necessary conditions for such change already exist" (Horkheimer 1992: 227). Of course, change simply for the sake of change is not acceptable; critical theory must also articulate *evaluative standards* for distinguishing progressive and regressive changes, assessing whether the status quo is acceptable or not, and evaluating the moral adequacy of measures taken to further progressive social change. Horkheimer again: "the self-knowledge of present-day man is…a critical theory of society as it is, a theory dominated at every turn by a concern for reasonable conditions of life" (Horkheimer 1992: 198–9). In summary, then, critical social theory is interdisciplinary social theory with an emancipatory intent: it aims to describe and explain current social reality, with particular attention to the actual conflicts and aspirations of contemporary social actors aiming at human emancipation in such a way that theory can help to both morally evaluate contemporary conflicts and contribute to progressive social change.

Honneth's particular brand of critical social theory is rooted in contemporary social struggles for recognition and social freedom. He focuses, as we will see, on quite a broad range of different types of sociopolitical conflicts, ranging from feminist struggles for anti-patriarchal family relationships, to gay and lesbian fights for equal legal rights, to workers' struggles for decent working conditions and egalitarian social justice, and more. His descriptive and explanatory social theory is built around the history, structure, and dynamics of struggles for adequate recognition and increased freedom. Successful struggles end up changing a society's current recognition order by institutionalizing new forms of intersubjective practices that afford social actors the recognition and conditions of freedom they rightfully deserve. Further, the theory's normative standards are constructed out of the moral "grammar" or deep structure of recognition claims. Finally, the theory aims practically to aid in the furtherance of more expansive and morally justified relations of undistorted social recognition and social freedom. Intersubjective recognition provides, then, the "immanent transcendent" for Honneth's theory: it guides interdisciplinary social theory to those emancipatory impulses which are found immanently in present social relations and simultaneously transcend those relations by pointing beyond unjust impediments to full human freedom. The building blocks of Honneth's new paradigm of critical social theory are laid out in the following chapters of the book, of which I give a brief preview here.

1.2.2   Individuals' struggle for recognition

The first main building block of Honneth's theory is an account of personal identity, rooted in social psychology, moral theory, and philosophical anthropology. It aims to answer the question: how do persons develop and maintain their identity, their sense of themselves as practical, moral beings with unique characteristics and distinctive places in the social world? The basic answer Honneth proposes is: individuals only become who they are in and through relations of mutual recognition with others. In short, persons gain subjectivity only intersubjectively. Only when individuals receive positive acknowledgment from others of their own personal traits, standing, and abilities can individuals begin to see themselves as others do and thereby gain an efficacious sense-of-self. Mutual recognition, according to Honneth, characterizes a whole range of intersubjective relations: between parents and children, between lovers and friends, between legal subjects, between participants in labor markets, between commodity consumers and producers, between fellow citizens, between men and women, between members of different ethnicities and races, between members of various civil society organizations, between democratic actors, and so on.

Further, because individuals fundamentally depend on such recognition for the construction and maintenance of their very identity – their sense of themselves as distinct and worthy persons – there is a basic moral demand to be recognized appropriately by others and fundamental moral obligations to recognize others appropriately built into the very structures of intersubjectivity. Honneth provides a typology of different forms of mutual recognition and their role in developing different types of practical identity. As we will see, he focuses in particular on: the importance of relations of care and love for the development of basic self-confidence; legal relations and rights for the development of self-respect; and relations of solidarity for the development of self-esteem. This three-part account of different kinds of recognition is then the basis for Honneth's moral philosophy, where different types of relationships are shown to involve different kinds of interpersonal entitlements and obligations.

Notwithstanding this underlying ideal "moral grammar" built into interpersonal relationships, individuals' expectations of appropriate moral recognition are often violated through inappropriate or destructive forms of misrecognition and nonrecognition: physical abuse, denial of rights, exclusion, denigration, disdain, etc. In fact, as Honneth often points out, it is negative emotional experiences of such disrespect, when our expectations of appropriate recognition are violated, that provide the motivations for struggles to overcome misrecognition – whether those struggles are local and interpersonal (chapter 2) or society-wide and group-based (chapter 3).

1.2.3 Social struggles for recognition

The second main building block of Honneth's critical social theory is an account of social reproduction and social change, rooted in sociology, history, and social and political philosophy. The key idea is that social practices and institutions are integrated and reproduced through specific regimes of recognition. However, those regimes are not timeless orders, but change over history. Even as Honneth regards the basic grammar of intersubjective recognition as part of the fabric of the human condition, the particular roles, expectations, and concrete forms of recognition change through time and differ across distinct societies. Consider, for instance, the massive changes in the roles and obligations of men, women, and children within families – and the very definition of family – over the last two hundred years. On Honneth's account, these changes should be understood as transformations in our society's particular recognition order. Furthermore, the central claim of his historical reconstruction is that such massive changes are driven specifically by struggles for recognition by social actors and groups, struggles motivated by negative experiences of misrecognition. For when members of groups experience misrecognition epidemically – when they notice that all similarly situated persons are subject to the same unjustified forms of disregard or mistreatment – the potential exists for social movements aiming to change an insufficient status quo toward a more just recognition order.

This descriptive and explanatory social theory is also a critical theory, since Honneth proposes to measure change against evaluative standards of progress and regress. He builds a political philosophy out of the three-pronged analysis of recognitional morality, showing how different types of justice claims are made to the broader society by different types of social struggles for expanded or more appropriate recognition. As we will see, he proposes two key measures of progress: inclusion and individualization. Put very simply, societies are better when their recognition regimes lessen discrimination and exclusion on the one hand, and acknowledge the distinctiveness of individuals across more dimensions of personality on the other. These criteria, formulated into a "formal conception of ethical life," can also be used to evaluate the claims of various social and political movements. Recognition theory thus fulfills the various tasks of critical social theory: describing how societies are integrated and reproduced, explaining a significant cause of social change, assessing the value of such change against the normative standard of undistorted recognition relations, and practically orienting social actors and movements as they further the project of human emancipation and individual self-realization.

1.2.4   Diagnosing social pathologies

As described so far, it will seem that Honneth's project is overly idealistic and optimistic, even if its foundational social phenomena are agonistic struggles among individuals and groups. But this is a misimpression, for Honneth is deeply concerned to present a critique of the present. Such a critique requires normative standards for evaluating what is worthwhile and what problematic – hence the need to develop a social theory that can ground its own moral standpoint. But such a critique then uses that critical social theory to diagnose the present.

Chapter 4 reconstructs Honneth's social diagnoses of the present, a third main building block of his theory. I take this to be one of the most distinctive and unique of Honneth's contributions: his attempt to systematically develop a social philosophy oriented toward the diagnosis of contemporary social pathologies, to be carried out in the light of his developed theory of recognition. As Honneth characterizes such social philosophy, "its primary task is the diagnosis of processes of social development that must be understood as preventing the members of society from living a 'good life'" (Honneth 2007f: 4). Alongside clarification of the methodological demands of social diagnosis, the bulk of the chapter is concerned with elucidating four of the specific substantive diagnoses that Honneth has developed, attending to the modern pathologies of invisibilization, instrumental rationalization, reification, and organized self-realization. Two other significant diagnoses – of the pathologies of economic maldistribution and of overly individualized understandings of freedom – are taken up in chapters 5 and 6 respectively. Without previewing all of that content here, suffice it to say that, in this aspect of his project, Honneth shows himself to be an insightful diagnostician of the present, as well as a worthy contributor to the inheritance of the Frankfurt School.

1.2.5 Recognition and markets

In one of the more extraordinary exchanges between contemporary critical theorists, Honneth and Nancy Fraser published *Redistribution or Recognition?* in 2003, an exchange of views about the adequacy of the recognition paradigm for conceptualizing economic relations, contemporary capitalism, and diverse struggles for social justice. Chapter 5 presents Honneth's theory of contemporary capitalism in RoR, Fraser's various critiques of that theory, and an evaluative assessment of Honneth's actual and potential responses to those critiques. As we will see, this debate is both methodological and substantive.

In part, it is a debate about what kind of intellectual tools are best suited to a critique of contemporary political economy and to carrying on the tradition of critical social theory. Fraser's basic conviction is that misrecognition and maldistribution are two different kinds of social injustice, with different causal factors and dynamics, and therefore different (and potentially competing) remedies. In contrast, Honneth proposes that economic injustices of many kinds, including unjust economic distributions, must be understood as constitutively connected to a society's underlying recognition order. In particular, Honneth is insistent that critical theory should not adopt fundamentally different tools for analyzing economic and recognitional injustices, but should account for changes in political economy in terms of changes in a society's recognition order.

But this is not merely a methodological debate, for Fraser is convinced that a focus on recognition alone is practically unwise, encouraging us to overlook, ignore, or displace economic injustices, often in favor of a politics centered solely on more symbolic and reputational harms. As I try to show in the chapter, there is a natural, but misleading association of recognition theory solely with social movements focused on identity-based forms of injustice, that is, injustice affecting persons on account of "who they are": female, nonwhite, immigrant, homosexual, and so on. In fact, Honneth's substantive concerns have always been wider than this, and he has consistently tied his recognition theory to issues of political economy: the division of labor, the nature of work and working conditions, the role of unions and corporations, levels of income and wealth inequality, the risk-mitigating function of welfare-state interventions in the economy, the rapid progress of neoliberal privatization, and so on.

1.2.6 Social freedom and recognition

The final building block of Honneth's critical theory is a full-blown social theory by way of an account of the central institutions of modern western societies: friendship, romantic love, the family, morality, law, the labor market, the consumer economy, the democratic public sphere, and the constitutional state. First published in German in 2011, *Freedom's Right* is an original and monumental book, attempting nothing less than a contemporary re-actualization of Hegel's 1820 ambitious project in *Philosophy of Right* (Hegel 1991). However, this is not achieved in a highly abstract philosophical discourse of pure concepts, but through an empirical history and analysis of those actually effective social movements that have increasingly shaped modern society's institutions around the ambitious demands of promoting individual freedom. While *freedom* is in fact the keyword of the book, Honneth has not abandoned the notion of *recognition*. Instead, he argues that real freedom – what he calls "social freedom" – can only be achieved in and through social institutions that sustain and promote appropriate relations of mutual recognition. We might say that while 'recognition' is the key to the transhistorical grammar of moral struggles, 'social freedom' is the key ambition of recognition struggles in modern society.

Because of the extraordinary scope, detail, and philosophical depth of FR, chapter 6 focuses on three thematic complexes. First is Honneth's distinctive theory of human freedom. To begin, he claims that freedom is, simply, the paramount value of modern life, the one which all other values are arranged around. He argues further that negative and reflexive conceptions of freedom – freedom as non-interference and freedom as setting one's own ends, respectively – are limited and inadequate. His alternative conception of social freedom insists that individuals' actions gain their value and purpose when they fit into a cooperative scheme of social activity. For Hegel and for Honneth, persons are free only when they can be "at home" in their social world: when their own unique motives and intentions can be meaningfully realized in a context of accommodating social roles and obligations.

A second theme of the new book is that the major institutions of modern life – personal relationships, markets, and public political spaces – should be understood as spheres of social freedom. In part, this is an empirical claim: the history of the major private, economic, and political institutional spheres of modern western societies is interpreted as arising out of diverse social struggles aiming to secure expanded social freedom. But it is also a moral claim, for social freedom forms the basis for a moral justification of each of the institutional spheres. The particular practices, social roles, and obligations of friendship, romantic love, the family, morality, law, the division of labor, the consumer economy, the political public sphere and the constitutional state are all justified only to the extent that they facilitate and promote the realization of social freedom for all individuals. And, finally, it is a critical claim: the significant deficiencies and achievements of contemporary institutions, their progressive and pathological aspects, are to be diagnosed in terms of the degree to which social freedom is facilitated, impeded, or frustrated. Thus social freedom is the backbone of Honneth's new, institutionally based critical social theory.

The chapter focuses thirdly on various methodological innovations and problem areas raised in Honneth's ambitious new project. Particular attention is given to FR's accounts of social integration, value consensus, progress in history, and the diagnosis of the present, as well as the bold claim that a philosophical theory of justice must be developed out of a concrete, empirical social analysis. Although *Freedom's Right* heralds a major deepening of Honneth's critical social theory, it is not a departure from his long-standing emphases on the constitutive character of intersubjective recognition for social reality and the potentially dynamic energies of social movements for emancipatory transcendence of the limits of current society.

1.3 Intellectual Contexts

An important aspect of Honneth's work is that – as do many other German theorists – he develops his own theory through appreciation and critique of the work of other theorists. This presents a sometimes formidable challenge for new readers, as Honneth's writings presume significant familiarity with the texts and authors being interpreted, often assuming real knowledge of most of the great thinkers of the eighteenth through twenty-first centuries. Furthermore, it can sometimes be hard to distinguish when Honneth is merely reporting the ideas of others, is also endorsing those ideas or, more subtly, is taking a hint or latent suggestion from another's text and polishing it into an original component of his own theory. To be sure, such distinctions get easier the more one knows of Honneth's own theory, but the challenges remain even for the initiated. One aim of this book, therefore, is to present a summary of Honneth's theory that can be readily grasped by readers without presuming such specialized knowledge and interpretive facility. Thus the book largely avoids exegesis of the full breadth of what Honneth himself draws upon: three centuries of western philosophy, sociology, political science, law, cultural theory, literature, psychology, economics, and history.

The point of this current section, then, is simply to post a few road signs to some of the most prominent of those traditions for Honneth as a way of locating his *oeuvre* in its intellectual contexts.[6] In the end, the best way to explore the connections between Honneth's thought and its intellectual contexts is, simply, to read his own writings on the relevant thinkers. They are not only remarkably subtle and insightful interpretations of his predecessors and contemporaries; they are also unmatched for revealing what is living and vibrant therein for contemporary philosophy and social theory.

1.3.1 From Kant to Hegel

Honneth's theory of recognition has antecedents detectable in ancient Greek theories of friendship, in Renaissance humanist revivals of classical thought, in Scottish and English moral sentiments theory of the eighteenth century, and especially in Rousseau's groundbreaking insistence on the essentially *social* character of human personality (Neuhouser 2010). Nevertheless, the most influential single thinker on Honneth is undoubtedly Hegel, whose thought forms the cornerstone of Honneth's two core works, SfR and FR. Of course, Hegel himself was deeply indebted to Kant, as is Honneth, though in ways less explicitly acknowledged.[7]

One fundamental aim Kant and Hegel share is to vindicate the universality and justifiability of the great Enlightenment ideals of reason, progress, freedom, equality, democracy, solidarity, and justice. Honneth is likewise deeply committed to these ideals, but follows Hegel's lead rather than Kant's as to how to conceptualize and justify them. What I mean by this can be seen in three transformations in Hegel's treatment of these ideals, transformations central to Honneth's own project. The first transformation is the conceptualization of these ideals in *intersubjective* and *social* terms, rather than in subjective and individual terms. Rather than adopting the Kantian strategy of finding the faculties of reason and the demands of morality within the minds of isolated thinkers, Hegel seeks reason and morality in the space of social interactions between persons. It is hard to overemphasize how important the turn toward intersubjectivity is for Honneth – as we will see in every chapter of this book, it is quite simply at the core of all the concepts of his critical social theory, including the key notions of mutual recognition and social freedom.[8]

A second Hegelian transformation is the move from the timeless to the historical. For not only does Hegel propose taking reason and morality out of the solitary minds of individuals, but he argues that their particular shape, structure, and content is not eternal, transcending all epochs, as Kant claims, but instead develops over time, in and through human history. The strategy for vindicating the ideals must shift then as well. Rather than advancing a priori arguments from pure reason, Hegel (and Honneth) advance teleological, developmental arguments. Our current ideals of reason and morality are not simply the ones we happen to be stuck with, but are justifiable (to the extent they are) because they can be shown to have resulted from a progressive process of learning, error correction, and refinement. In short, our ideals are worthy only as a result of human progress.

A third Hegelian transformation is to take the central Kantian moral and political ideals – of respect for individual autonomy, categorical duties to others as moral equals, and justice through individual rights and the social contract – and place them in a specific historical context – modern ethical life. In part, putting morality into ethical life means acknowledging that our particular moral and political ideals are historical ideas, found paradigmatically in contemporary western societies, and developed as progressive transformations of older ideas. For instance, our prioritization of freedom and individuality over communal obligations and conformity is not a result of the formal demands of pure, timeless, abstract reason itself, but a fact about our own modern values and concrete mores. In part, it also means that abstract formal reasoning about our duties must be understood in a broader context of substantive evaluation and ethically significant practices and institutions. Finally, putting morality into ethical life also means acknowledging with Kant the force of moral rules and just laws, but with Hegel seeing the force of such rules and laws as itself derived from the worth of them to what we as humans value. While morality surely makes obligatory demands on us as Kant emphasizes, those demands are seen in the Hegelian vision as justified only because obeying such demands ultimately facilitates what we value as worthy and good in the first place. In short, on the Hegelian transformation that Honneth embraces, the right is embedded in the good.

1.3.2 Marx, Nietzsche, and Freud

Marx, Nietzsche, and Freud together stand for a generally critical and suspicious stance toward overweening philosophical claims for the powers of human reason, each in their own way seeking to deflate the pretensions of rationality, reasoned morality, subjectivity, self-transparency, conscious self-direction, and reasoned social organization.[9] Such deflation was achieved by showing how these supposed attributes of Enlightened cognizers were actually illusions, and how some other factors beyond reason actually determine the shape and content of rationality, morality, consciousness, intentionality, and social organization. Of course the *real* drivers of human phenomena – the real, explanatory causal factors – are different according to each thinker's own theory. For Marx, it is a society's particular mode of economic material production that is the real explainer of human phenomena; for Nietzsche, it is the schemes of meaning that have maximized feelings of power and vitality; for Freud, it is the organization and dynamics of unconscious libidinal drives in the psyche. Whatever the real is for each thinker, however, the key claim is that the surface appearances of reason, morality, and subjectivity are not to be trusted as revealing the way things actually are. The (three different) conceptions of the real then count as the "Others" of reason.

Even as Honneth's work is certainly neither aimed at, nor resulting in, a thoroughgoing debunking of reason, morality, and self-consciousness – his project is after all Hegelian – he nevertheless displays throughout his writings a real sensitivity to the importance of remaining skeptical and critical of the pretensions of rationality, self-transparency, and self-determination (exemplary here is Honneth 1995a). And the influence of Marx, Nietzsche, and Freud on his writings is clearly detectable, even if often in the background.

Marx is unsurprisingly the least in the background since the Frankfurt School tradition is a major part of so-called "western Marxism." Honneth's earliest essays from 1980 and 1981 critique his mentor Habermas's theory for insufficient attention to the deep ways in which class cleavages and everyday experiences of work in late capitalist societies may influence moral categories and provoke social struggles (Honneth 1995g, 1995j). Further, by 1989, it is clear that Honneth intends his theory of recognition as a replacement for Marx's theory of labor, all in order to better fulfill Marx's more general intentions of connecting social theory to a critical theory of emancipation (Honneth 1995b). Finally, central Marxist concerns are also expressed in Honneth's work: the importance of a society's political–economic relations; the nature and value of work; the existence of class-based domination; the injustice of massive economic inequality; and the capitalist pathologies of ideology, alienation, reification, and commoditization.

Nietzsche's influence on Honneth is more indirect. While Honneth is certainly not carrying out a Nietzschean program of skeptical irrationalism or revaluation of all existing values, I would suggest that Honneth is deeply influenced by the Nietzschean theme of the politics of interpretation. As we will see, for Honneth, struggles for recognition revolve centrally around the meanings, symbols, concepts, and values that collectively make up a particular society's recognition order. Consequently, a struggle against misrecognition or distorted recognition is often, practically speaking, a struggle to revalue contemporary meanings, interpretations, and values in order to change institutions and practices.

Finally, Freud's influence on Honneth is substantial, though usually mediated through later generations of psychoanalytic research, particularly object relations theory.[10] As we will see especially in the next chapter, more recent psychoanalytic research is absolutely central to Honneth's work. Emotions are at the center of his intersubjectivist theory of the self and individual identity development, and that theory is aimed at a central topic of psychoanalysis: the conditions of healthy psychological development and an undistorted ego identity. But psychoanalytic themes are also central to his social and political theories of interpersonal and familial relations, of political culture and democratic interaction. Love and solidarity are, after all, both central categories for his political theory of justice, as we'll see in chapter 6. And of course, Honneth stresses the importance of morally reactive emotions

– such as indignation, shame, guilt, and sympathy – as motivators for social struggles.

1.3.3 The Frankfurt School

Honneth's overarching aim is to produce a critical social theory: an interdisciplinary social theory aiming to diagnose the emancipatory perils and potentials of the present. Although Hegel is the single theorist with the greatest influence on Honneth, it is clear that the Frankfurt School – that diverse group of intellectuals collected around the Institute for Social Research (Institut für Sozialforschung) in Frankfurt am Main, Germany – has had an equal if not greater role in the development and nature of Honneth's thought.[11] After all, it was the first generation – most prominently Theodor Adorno, Max Horkheimer, and Herbert Marcuse – who gave the name "critical theory" to the intellectual endeavor that Honneth explicitly aims to continue. And Honneth's work is deeply influenced by his mentor, the leading second-generation Frankfurt School critical theorist Jürgen Habermas – Germany's preeminent public intellectual and most influential philosopher and sociopolitical theorist of the last fifty years.

Although Honneth's theory of recognition has been broadly influential across many research paradigms, he sees his work as carrying on the Frankfurt School tradition, albeit with quite different tools than those of the first two generations. His second published article, from 1979, is on Habermas's critique of Adorno (Honneth 1979). His first book, *The Critique of Power*, published in German in 1985 and subtitled *Reflective Stages in a Critical Social Theory*, provides an intellectual history of the Frankfurt School (and Foucault) that also builds a new critical theory out of the strengths and weaknesses detected in predecessors' theories. This intention has continued in his writings up to the present; for instance, he considers the recent essays in *Pathologies of Reason: On the Legacy of Critical Theory* (2009 [2007]) a positive argument for the "timeliness of Critical Theory" (vii).

Beyond his own publications, moreover, Honneth has been the driving force behind the revivification of the Institute for Social Research in Frankfurt and its work in producing empirical social science with an emancipatory intent.[12] Since becoming the director of the Institute in 2001, he has brought in new researchers and funding, developed empirical research programs,[13] edited a dedicated book series from Campus Verlag of Institute work entitled "Frankfurt Contributions to Sociology and Social Philosophy," now in eighteen volumes (the first volume in the series: Honneth 2002b), and begun an excellent new academic journal *WestEnd: Neue Zeitschrift für Sozialforschung* (New Journal for Social Research), subtitled, in a deliberate echo of the original 1930s' Frankfurt School journal, *Die Zeitschrift für Sozialforschung*.

Honneth has also argued for a specific conception of what is distinctive about the Frankfurt School brand of social philosophy. "Social philosophy" according to Honneth is a broad tradition – including not only Frankfurt School theorists, but also Rousseau, Hegel, Marx, Nietzsche, Durkheim, Weber, Lukács, Freud, Plessner, Arendt, and Foucault – where theory aims to diagnose misdevelopments in society, that is, social pathologies (Honneth 2007f). The Frankfurt School is that specific form of social philosophy which has consistently focused on social pathologies of *reason* or *rationality* (Honneth 2009d).

> Through all their disparateness of method and object, the various authors
> of the Frankfurt School are united in the idea that the living conditions
> of modern capitalist societies produce social practices, attitudes, or per-
> sonality structures that result in a pathological distortion of our capaci-
> ties for reason.... They always aim at exploring the social causes of a
> pathology of human rationality. (*Pathologies of Reason*: vii)

Another distinctive theme of Frankfurt School theory, according to Honneth, has been a central commitment to building theory around a point of "immanent transcendence," something *within* actual society that simultaneously points *beyond* it. The basic idea is that the various elements of critical theory – the analysis of society, the diagnosis of pathologies, the justification of evaluative standards, and so on – must all be systematically connected to something found in actual, everyday social life, something that also points to a better, more emancipated, and reasonable form of life.[14] As Honneth puts the idea: "within the given relations, an element of practice or experience must always be identifiable that can be regarded as a moment of socially embodied reason insofar as it possesses a surplus of rational norms or organizational principles that press for their own realization" (RoR: 240). Different varieties of Frankfurt School theory can be seen as embracing different elements of immanent transcendence: the workers' movement for Horkheimer et al. before World War II; aesthetic and mimetic experience for Adorno after the war; language and public communication for Habermas; and struggles for recognition and social freedom for Honneth.[15]

A third, and crucial, theme unites the work of Habermas and Honneth: the turn to *intersubjectivity*. Whereas the first generation of the Frankfurt School seemed to be always searching for some form of undamaged subjectivity as a critical point of reference, both Habermas and Honneth decisively turn toward undamaged intersubjectivity – intact forms of social interaction – as the critical reference point of immanent transcendence. For instance, the American pragmatist George Herbert Mead's startlingly original empirical arguments that humans actually come to have an understanding of themselves only in and through social interactions with others are a touchstone for both

Habermas and Honneth. To be sure, Habermas focuses on the rational structure of language itself – for instance, in his claim that every speech act raises simultaneously three validity claims to truth, moral rightness, and sincerity. Honneth undoubtedly endorses the broad Habermasian argument that "the moral potential of communication is the engine of social progress and at the same time also indicates its direction" (RoR: 242). But he intends, as we will see, to find the inherent, progressive normative content that points toward emancipation in the very structures of social interaction – specifically in the diverse practices of reciprocal recognition – rather than in the structures of language, as does Habermas. To put it simply, whereas Habermas prioritizes undistorted intersubjective language, Honneth looks to undistorted intersubjective recognition.[16]

1.3.4 French social theory

French social theory has seen a renaissance since the end of World War II, and Honneth has been an insightful reader and interpreter of much of it. The work of the preeminent French post-structuralist Michel Foucault has received the most systematic attention, especially early in Honneth's corpus; later references become less frequent. There is a chapter on Foucault in his early co-authored book on philosophical anthropology (SAaHN: 129–50), and Foucault's theory of power receives sustained critical attention across three chapters in Honneth's first monograph (CoP: 99–202). The social theory developed by the phenomenologist Jean-Paul Sartre later in his life in order to analyze colonialist domination also receives appreciative treatment, particularly since that theory is built around struggles for recognition (SfR: 145–59). In addition, other prominent French social theorists have been the object of individual essays and sporadic references: the structural anthropologist Claude Lévi-Strauss (Honneth 1995i), the phenomenologist of embodiment Maurice Merleau-Ponty (Honneth 1995c), the psychoanalyst of social imaginaries Cornelius Castoriadis (Honneth 1995h), the sociologist of cultural power Pierre Bourdieu (Honneth 1995d), and the sociologists of moral beliefs Luc Boltanski and Laurent Thévenot (Honneth 2012c). Finally, we can point to two more programmatic essays from the mid-1990s that explicitly come to terms with post-structuralist critiques of the ideal of the autonomous subject (Honneth 2007b) and of the ideal of universal morality (Honneth 2007e). The latter essay also contains explicit treatment of the ethical thought of Jacques Lacan, Jean-François Lyotard, and Jacques Derrida.

However, it is difficult to accurately assess how *influential* all of this has been on the core conceptions and arguments of Honneth's own theory. In many ways, he is explicitly sympathetic to much of the empirical and concrete social analysis that these thinkers have produced. They are important touchstones for exploring themes such as the hidden suffering caused by modern social life; the fragility of subjectivity and autonomy; our persistent lack of self-transparency, self-knowledge, and self-control; the ethical importance of particularized care, concern, and benevolence toward the singular and unique other; the central role of distinct webs of symbolic and evaluative meanings and understandings for practices and institutions of social interaction; and, especially, the many ways in which the social is a field of inelimi-nable confrontation, conflict, and disagreement. But at the same time Honneth never endorses the skeptical and relativistic conclusions that are often taken to follow from post-structuralist theories. Indeed, rather than embracing such denials of reason, truth, and moral progress – for instance, Foucault's picture of social history as simply one contingent historical organization of power/knowledge regime after another, or Bourdieu's reductionist account of norms as mere symbolic currency in a relentlessly strategic competition for cultural capital – Honneth in fact joins the project of vindicating such ideals, the project that stretches from Kant through Hegel and on to Habermas. In the end, it is perhaps safest to say that Honneth is surely an admirer of the empirical social insights of much French social theory, even as he is emphatically not in agreement with the skeptical methodological and normative consequences it is usually taken to have.

1.3.5   Political philosophy

Debates in normative political philosophy, especially those begun after the 1971 publication of John Rawls's groundbreaking *Theory of Justice* (Rawls 1971), form an important context for Honneth's work. A good way to get a sense of the distinctiveness of his project is to see how it resonates and contrasts with other contemporary political philosophies, both ideal and critical.

The clearest contrast with Honneth's project – and with all critical social theories – is provided by ideal political philosophies. The basic aim of such philosophies is to articulate and justify ideal principles of justice, rightness, legitimacy, and so on. The justified principles are usually understood as true and perfect *simpliciter*, that is, true for all time and perfect in the sense of there being nothing better or more ideal. In other words, ideal political philosophy focuses first – and often only – on explicating and defending the ideal normative standards for any perfect society. This is the primary aim, for instance, of John Rawls's celebrated theory of justice as fairness. Rawls's work is directed almost entirely at developing "strict compliance theory": "I shall assume that . . . the nature and aims of a perfectly just society is the fundamental part of the theory of justice" (Rawls 1971: 9). The idea here is that we must first possess perfect principles of justice and the like – justified as true by pure moral/philosophical arguments – before we can go on, in a second and derivative step, to do "non-ideal" or "partial compliance theory." Only then do we move into the messy and opaque world of social reality, delicately but not directly applying some of our ideal principles, in suitably modified and qualified ways, in order to attempt to deal with the "pressing and urgent matters... that we are faced with in everyday life" (Rawls 1971: 9). Unfortunately, as a matter of fact about intellectual life, such pressing and urgent matters often receive short shrift in the actual debates that dominate political philosophy, as theorists focus almost entirely on matters of ideal theory alone.

There are many other contemporary examples of such ideal political philosophies beyond Rawls's own liberal egalitarianism, ranging across other forms of liberal egalitarianism (e.g., Ronald Dworkin), social contract theory (David Gauthier), libertarianism (Robert Nozick), socialism (G. A. Cohen), utilitarianism (Peter Singer), and many more. Clearly, Honneth's theory resonates with the substantive concerns of many of these theories, if not all. Like consequentialism, it is concerned with human well-being; like social contract theory and liberal egalitarianism, it sees individual freedom as the preeminent value; like socialism, it is concerned that economic arrangements facilitate the self-realization of all persons. But its method for understanding these substantive concerns is quite different.

The opening sentence of *Freedom's Right* directly critiques the methods of ideal political philosophy: "One of the major weaknesses of contemporary political philosophy is that it has been decoupled from an analysis of society and has thus become fixated on purely normative principles" (FR: 1). In contrast and following Hegel, Honneth proposes that "a theory of justice must be based on social analysis" (FR: 1). According to this conception, political thought ought to begin with the institutional reality of actually existing society, elucidate the basic underlying values that serve as the integrative glue of those institutions, demonstrate that those institutions are themselves legitimate to the extent they fully facilitate those values, and thereby contribute to a critique of existing institutions when they insufficiently or imperfectly embody and facilitate those values. In short, rather than approaching existing society with values that are philosophically justified independently of existing reality, political theory should be immanently constructed out of the actual values that integrate a given society.[17]

Of course, an ideal theorist might object that we cannot take existing values as justifiable simply because they exist – that would be to court the danger of endorsing any and every status quo social consensus, no matter how unattractive or horrific. Agreeing that this is a real danger, Honneth's theory attempts to show, in a deeply Hegelian manner, that modern society's values and central institutions are in fact legitimate since they are historically superior to older values and institutions. In particular, as we will see in chapter 6, the central institutions of society – personal relationships, the economy, and democratic public life – are themselves justified because they more adequately facilitate the realization of the social freedom and appropriate recognition of each person than did earlier institutional orders. Although Honneth has only recently stressed this in FR, it is clear that his philosophy has proceeded this way at least since SfR, according to which "processes of social change are to be explained with reference to the normative claims that are structurally inherent in relations of mutual recognition" (SfR: 2). Thus methodologically, Honneth's project has been consistently distinct from ideal political philosophy: a normative reconstruction of actually existing practices and institutions, attuned to the ways in which they facilitate or frustrate the values of mutual recognition and social freedom.

We should also note that such a method implies a very deep interdependence between empirical social analysis and normative analysis, rather than the traditionally strict division of labor between social science and philosophy, between empirical and normative issues. For while Honneth's normative analysis gains its content – immanently justified values – from existing social reality, his social theory sorts and organizes the mass of social phenomena according to those very same immanent values. Ideal political philosophy, by contrast, strictly separates its own issues of the elaboration and justification of perfect ideals from various empirical questions that are the proper province of (supposedly value-free) social sciences. As a critical social theorist, Honneth envisions an inevitably tight connection between interdisciplinary social theory and its emancipatory intent.

While liberal egalitarianism, libertarianism, and utilitarianism have been the dominant traditions in the last fifty years of political philosophy – usually pursued as ideal political philosophy – there are a host of alternative types of political thought that have arisen distinct from this mainstream. Such "critical political theories," to coin a phrase of convenience, have focused on substantive issues often shunted aside by mainstream theories or have pursued alternative theoretical methodologies. We can further contextualize Honneth's work by seeing how many of their focal concerns overlap and intersect with his.

Honneth's work resonates with central themes of communitarianism: the critique of social atomism in contemporary societies, of unbridled egoistic individualism leading to social anomie and feelings of alienation. Communitarians such as Alasdair MacIntyre, Michael Sandel, Charles Taylor, and Michael Walzer engaged in a sustained back and forth with Rawls and other liberal political philosophers – itself an update of disputes in political philosophy between Hegel and

Kant. In fact, Honneth originally framed his project through these debates. For instance, the capstone idea in SfR – the idea of a "formal conception of ethical life" – is itself developed as a solution to the cul-de-sac that Honneth argues both liberals and communitarians had arrived at in their debate (Honneth 1995f). Unsurprisingly, Honneth and many communitarians pursue theories of justice through social analysis and are methodologically indebted to Hegel, even as the substance of Honneth's theory of justice – preeminently concerned with freedom – is much more left-Hegelian than the usually more conservative right-Hegelian prioritization of collective goods by communitarians.

With socialism and Marxism, Honneth shares several central concerns: with exploitation and alienation of employees in unbridled, deregulated labor markets, and with the ways market structures can undermine the normative content of personal relationships and the democratic public sphere. To be sure, quite unlike Marxism, Honneth does not reject capitalism wholesale, seeing market relations rather as structured by inherent moral content and as potential spheres for the realization of individuals' social freedom when properly institutionalized.

Recognition theory has often been strongly associated with multiculturalism, perhaps largely due to the powerful influence of Taylor's essay on the politics of recognition (Taylor 1994, originally published 1992). Indeed, Honneth shares multiculturalism's central concern with problems of cultural denigration and marginalization – and shares its key philosophical claim that individual self-respect and self-esteem are indissociably connected to social structures of recognition. However, it is quite misleading to reduce the broad diversity of what Honneth understands as recognition struggles to merely cultural battles over "identity politics" and state policies accommodating multicultural differences. As we will see, Honneth's aim in theorizing recognition and freedom is much broader than this, attempting to delineate the moral grammar of modern family life, law and rights, constitutional democracy, the workplace, economy, and so on.

Feminist social movements, furthermore, are cited by Honneth as examples of salutary and successful struggles for expanded recognition and social freedom, and his recognition theory provides useful normative categories for analyzing the diversity of much feminist politics (Zurn 1997). While Honneth is surely no radical calling for the overthrow of the sex–gender system, he clearly counts many of the signal aims and (partial) achievements of feminism as progressive: overcoming gender-specific discrimination in various spheres of life, deactivating the moral denunciation of sexuality, increasing open communication and negotiation within families, overcoming the unequal gendered distribution of care work, securing laws against rape, abuse and domestic violence, seeking the full legal and political equality of men and women, and movements against the feminization of poverty.

Honneth's theory finally has broad resonances with the recent revival of democratic theories, especially theories of deliberative democracy and civic republicanism. Like deliberative democrats from John Dewey to Jürgen Habermas, Honneth stresses the epistemic and reflexive features of democratic interaction. When political interaction is based on communication and the exchange of reasons, its reflexive character enables social learning, where new knowledge is generated from free and open discussions amongst the broadest selection of affected persons. That is why Honneth's theory of democracy, like those of Hannah Arendt and Habermas, places so much emphasis on the necessity for vibrant, healthy, and diverse public spheres that can facilitate broad debate and discussion. A healthy democratic public sphere promises not only increases in knowledge but also functions as a sensing medium for problems and injustices experienced in everyday life. Further, as civic republican theories consistently point out, political apathy threatens the realization of politics as a cooperative attempt to fulfill the ideals of equal citizenship and self-rule. Like civic republicans, Honneth is also convinced that some more substantial cultural and symbolic ties must be shared by democratic consociates than their merely abstract identities as legal equals. Both argue, for instance, that the solidarity needed for an equitable sharing of the burdens and benefits of social cooperation requires some substantial culturally imbued sense of collective mission and belonging above and beyond mere membership in a given polity.

But like Dewey's political philosophy, Honneth's also prioritizes a capacious conception of *democratic ethical life*, that is, a form of life with inclusive and cooperative modes of solving problems and coordinating interactions across many social spheres, not only in the formal spheres of electoral politics and government (Honneth 2007c). Thus, unlike Habermas's democratic theory which is focused more narrowly on constitutional government and the production of law, Honneth's vision pushes toward a broader form of democracy – democratic ethical life – where a democratic political sphere is systematically joined to emancipated, democratic families and, a socialized market.[18] As he puts the point at the end of his most recent book:

> The social system of democratic ethical life thus represents a complicated web of reciprocal dependencies, where the realization of freedom in one sphere of action depends on the realization of the principles of freedom underlying the other spheres. Free market participants, self-aware democratic citizens and emancipated family members...mutually influence each other, because the properties of the one cannot be realized without the other two. (FR: 330–1)

Perhaps the best way to summarize the distinctiveness of Honneth's project is to characterize it as a broad social philosophy rather than a narrow moral or political philosophy. Although moral obligations and formal legal structures are part of its purview, Honneth's theory also investigates other central spheres of modern social life: family, friendship, marriage, the labor market, the consumer economy, civil society, and the public sphere. And unlike moral and political philosophies which begin with beliefs and shared intuitions about normative principles, Honneth's social philosophy begins with normative principles that are actually already embedded in extant social practices and institutions. Like Aristotle and Hegel, Honneth is convinced that "intersubjectively practiced customs and not cognitive beliefs are what define the homestead of morality" (FR: 7); hence his insistence on the method of reconstructive social analysis. Further, the theory is not just about the obligations of interpersonal morality or the demands of justly distributing goods through political communities – but about the fabric of intersubjective relations since those both make possible and impede freedom and self-realization. Individual freedom worth having is rooted in the social institutions of intersubjective socialization and reciprocal recognition characteristic of modern societies. Said in Hegel's terms, the particular form of individual human agency – individual autonomy – that morality and justice are designed to protect is itself embedded in, and the historical result of, modern ethical life. Finally, such a broad social philosophy goes beyond an articulation and justification of normative principles, and even beyond a straightforward application of such principles. Continuing the Frankfurt School heritage of critical theory, Honneth also insists that social philosophy must develop theoretical tools sufficient for diagnosing various social misdevelopments, disorders, and pathologies, even when such social problems are not yet acknowledged or experienced as such. The point then of a social reconstruction of the history and current configuration of our society's ethical life is not to reconcile ourselves with it but to critically appropriate its unfulfilled normative promise in the service of an emancipatory future. "Critical theorists share with their audience... a space of potentially common reasons that holds the pathological present open to the possibility of transformation through rational insight" (Honneth 2009d: 40).

2

Individuals' Struggle for Recognition

2.1 The Intersubjectivist Turn

This chapter presents the first building block of Honneth's critical theory: an intersubjectivist theory of how individuals develop a practical identity, a sense of themselves as interacting, moral beings with unique characteristics and distinctive places in the social world.[1] The aim is an account of how individuals come to have an understanding of themselves as individuals in a milieu of social interaction, that is, as persons oriented both by general norms, values, principles and goals, and by their own particular beliefs, ambitions, and needs. Honneth's guiding intuition is that one can find in the concept of *intersubjective recognition* an underlying normative structure that explains the practical growth and development of individuals. Not only that but the very same infrastructure of intersubjective recognition is connected to the practical growth and development of societies. So the division between this chapter and the next is somewhat artificial, even as it may aid clarity. For the point of studying the intersubjective constitution of individual practical identity is to put it to systematic use in a critical social theory.

Honneth's moral and social theories are founded upon the thesis that personhood is essentially constituted intersubjectively. The key claim is that we only become who we are through our interactions with others. This thesis has received many different interpretations over the past two centuries of philosophy, psychology, and sociology, and Honneth puts his distinctive stamp on it with his theory of recognition. *Struggle for Recognition* develops that theory through detailed interrogations of the work of German philosopher Hegel, American pragmatist social-psychologist George Herbert Mead, and British object relations psychologist Donald Winnicott. For Honneth, what ties all of these theorists together is the idea that when individuals struggle to gain various forms of positive recognition of their different characteristics, abilities, and achievements from their interaction partners, they are at the same time becoming who they are as moral, ethical, socially interacting agents. Through intersubjective recognition, they are engaged in the process of self-realization with respect to their practical relation-to-self.

Habermas's communicative theory of individual development is also quite influential, in the background, for Honneth. Habermas's theory is that persons become who they are through the intersubjective acquisition of communicative competence – that is, the ability to be a responsible actor in the social world through linguistic communication. He formulates the intersubjectivist thesis as the claim that *individuation* – the processes of becoming an individual person with a distinct identity – occurs only *in and through socialization* – the processes of learning how to navigate the diverse aspects of the social world and becoming an agent capable of competently interacting with others. As he puts it: "Individuation is pictured not as the self-realization of an independently acting subject carried out in isolation and freedom but as a linguistically mediated process of socialization and the simultaneous constitution of a life-history that is conscious of itself....Individuality forms itself in relations of intersubjective acknowledgement and of intersubjectively mediated self-understanding" (Habermas 1992: 152–3). If we were to change the words "linguistically mediated" in this Habermas quote to "recognition mediated," I believe it would accurately represent the central intersubjectivist intuition fueling Honneth's theory. In other words, Honneth shifts the central medium of intersubjective life from language to practical attitudes of acknowledgment.

Honneth traces the specific recognitional interpretation of the intersubjectivist thesis back to the earliest "Jena period" writings (1801–1806) of the young Hegel, though similar ideas can be found in the earlier work of Fichte.[2] Hegel's basic paradigm is the struggle for recognition, within which individuals gain a sense of what and who they are only through comprehending and internalizing their interaction partner's recognition of their own autonomous subjectivity. For Hegel, there are decisive differences between an intersubjectivist starting point and one focused around a fully formed subject capable of independent thought and action, a starting point characteristic of modern philosophy beginning with Descartes and carrying through the rationalists and the empiricists and on to Kant's transcendental project. While the philosophical perspective of the former starting point is essentially dialogical – the focal phenomena are persons communicating and meaningfully reacting to one another's meaningful communications – the latter's perspective is essentially monological – one single mind focused upon its own inner world and the phenomena to be observed there. Consider Descartes's *Meditations on First Philosophy*: there the subject's solipsistic self-reassurance as an independent, thinking being is the first and foundational certainty; any further certainties – including the independent existence of other people – must be grounded upon the existence of the cogitating ego. According to the Cartesian picture, one is an independent subject first and only subsequently a potential member of a community of other subjects. In contrast, Hegel's intersubjectivist conception of personhood suggests that one only becomes a thinking, self-aware subject by being one amongst others, by being able to take up the perspective of one's *alter* toward oneself, and by engaging with others in an ongoing process of self-reassurance through one's internalization of the recognition of others. Thus, for Hegel, the essential features and capacities of human individuals cannot be understood through a solitary subject's introspection, but can only be comprehended and articulated by attending to the intersubjective processes of mutual recognition through which socialization and individuation occur.

In the practical domains of moral, political, and social philosophy that Honneth is particularly interested in, the shift to the standpoint of intersubjectively constituted subjectivity represents an important change from the model dominant in modern western moral and political theory: the subjectivity model of a fully formed rational and egoistic individual agent calculating the best means to self-preservation. Honneth points to Machiavelli as inaugurating the modern subjectivist tradition in social thought, and to Hobbes as carrying it forward in its most pure form through the development of modern social contract theory. In Hobbes's account, the individual is pictured as having a given set of beliefs about the natural and social world, a given set of more or less idiosyncratic desires, and the ability to rationally calculate which course of action will be most effective in realizing the individuals' desires, given the state of the world and the likely dispositions and actions of other persons. Moral obligations and social order are then supposed to arise from the fact that each individual realizes that it will be in his or her own rational self-interest to contract away some discretion and power in return for the benefits of a rule-governed set of obligations and a social order backed by the coercive threats of a centralized state with a monopoly on the legitimate use of power. In short, both the rightness of the moral order and the legitimacy of the state are supposed to arise from the identical instrumental and solipsistic reasoning of mutually antagonistic individuals, each of whom are vulnerable to the violence of others in a perpetual war of each against all. Morality and justice are thereby derived as dictates of strategic reasoning arrived at in identical fashion by isolated, anonymous, antagonistic, adult individuals.

In contrast, on the Hegelian intersubjectivist model, morality organically grows out of the very infrastructure of social relations since one can only become an individuated and competent individual through socialization into different forms of interpersonal regard, acknowledgment, and recognition. Only by taking up the perspective of others on oneself can one begin to develop a sense of who one is, of one's beliefs, desires, needs, inclinations, values, and ideals. The perspectives of others, further, are themselves shaped in culturally specific ways through a society's institutions, practices and customs. Thus individuals develop by internalizing and understanding a socially specific and morally saturated set of perceptions, expectations, and attitudes. Only from the standpoint of a mature, fully socialized individual, capable of autonomous thought and action, can one then take up a reflective stance toward the specific institutions, practices, and customs of one's society, evaluating them to see whether and to what extent they are justified and considering how to change them if they are not. The fully formed practical self that Hobbes presupposes as the origin of morality is, on the Hegelian model, always already a product of substantial socialization into a morally and ethically meaningful set of social relations. It is from the point of view of intersubjectivity and not of the isolated subject, then, that we are to understand and evaluate the structure and content of our moral, social, and political life.[3]

Honneth, following Habermas and others, argued at first that, as a matter of the history of ideas, this radical intersubjectivist turn in practical philosophy is most clearly articulated and carried through in Hegel's early writings and that, in fact, in his later, more famous works Hegel often returns to a kind of philosophy of subjectivity with metaphysical ambitions that is no longer philosophically tenable. Furthermore, it is only in the early Hegel that Honneth originally found the outlines of a defensible social theory structured around different forms of recognition. This interpretation of Hegel's career largely explains the initially surprising fact that, with approximately one third of SfR dedicated to Hegel, readers will find no sustained treatment, and barely a mention, of the very famous passages on the master–slave dialectic in Hegel's *Phenomenology* that are most renowned in other scholarly literature for focusing on intersubjective struggles for recognition (Hegel 1977: 111–19). (A 2008 essay finally takes on these famous passages (Honneth 2012e.)) More recently, Honneth has revised his original interpretation, becoming more favorable to Hegel's later writings – including attempting a re-actualization of Hegel's late *Philosophy of Right* in PoIF and FR. Honneth now contends that fully intersubjective recognition is at the heart of Hegel's corpus from beginning to end (*The I in We*: viii). Whatever the case, Hegel's intersubjectivist turn decisively influenced later nineteenth- and twentieth-century developments in philosophy and social theory.

Crucially for Honneth's purposes, the early Jena-period Hegel provides the key distinctions between three forms of intersubjective recognition – love, legal relations, and solidarity – corresponding to three forms of practical self-understanding – self-confidence, self-respect, and self-esteem – that form the basis for Honneth's critical social theory of recognition. Similar analyses and distinctions can be found in the social psychology developed by Mead a hundred years after Hegel, and in the quite different psychodynamic psychology developed by Winnicott another fifty years on. Honneth in effect takes the quite significant overlap of Hegel's, Mead's, and Winnicott's theories of recognition as empirical confirmation of the claims that Hegel originally advanced in a tentative and speculative manner. Honneth's theory thus performs a kind of inter-translation between the very different approaches, methods, vocabulary, and focal problems found in the three main theorists he draws on.

2.2   Self-Confidence and Love

The first of three distinct forms of recognition Honneth distinguishes in SfR is *love*, and it is essential to the individual's development of basic *self-confidence*. It is important to note that the concept of love Honneth employs is quite broad: "Love relationships are to be understood here as referring to primary relationships insofar as they – on the model of friendships, parent–child relationships, as well as erotic relationships between lovers – are constituted by strong emotional attachments among a small number of people" (SfR: 95). In a sense, Honneth proposes using Winnicott's psychoanalytic theory of the mother–infant relationship, developed out of careful observation of many parent–child pairs, as empirical confirmation of Hegel's account of adult erotic love, developed from speculative philosophical premises. (Mead's theory of practical identity development has comparatively little to say about this first form of recognition.) The key idea that Honneth uses to link Winnicott and Hegel is that love is a form of mutual recognition between intimates whereby one comes to know oneself and to be oneself only in and through a specific form of emotional support from another. Hence, Hegel's speculative idea of love as "being oneself in another" can be confirmed in psychological research when it is translated into the vocabulary of object relations psychoanalysis. The overall account can be clarified under three areas of claims: (2.2.1) the substantive analysis of love relationships, (2.2.2) the connection between love and the development of self-confidence, and (2.2.3) the account of the specific form and harms of disrespect corresponding to intimate relations.

2.2.1 Love

Honneth's substantive analysis of the distinctive practical self-relation that is developed through love is indebted to psychoanalysis, which takes the mother–infant relationship as a paradigm of love. Freud's original theory of psychosexual maturation is not inherently intersubjective, but is instead focused on the dynamics of a set of inner drives that the child has and how those drives get expressed, reshaped, inhibited, or redirected as the child grows and faces new situations in the world. However, an influential branch of psychoanalytic theory, starting in the mid-twentieth century and termed "object relations theory," expanded beyond Freud's intrapsychic focus on drives to an intersubjective focus on the system of mutual relations between the developing child and its parents.[4] (As developed in Winnicott and others, the term "object" refers to the parent and "subject" to the child; further, the significant other of the child doing the parenting is invariably referred to as the "mother," a practice I reluctantly follow here even though a father or other nonbiological parent could also fulfill the role.)

According to object relations theory, there is an original *symbiosis* between baby and mother: neither understands themselves as fully distinguished from the other, as fully individuated beings over against the other. Rather, both the mother and infant, in a significant sense, feel the needs, desires, disappointments, and joys of the other as though they were their own. (In Hegel's account of love, this feeling of symbiotic unity is experienced by two adults through the de-individuating union of sexual ecstasy.) The development of this relationship occurs precisely through the mutual negotiation of each away from the feelings of original symbiosis and toward a state where each can understand itself as a separate and distinct being, with its own separate physical and emotional existence. Thus, in one dimension, each goes from dedifferentiated symbiosis toward individuation. However, this individuation only occurs in a healthy and productive manner if accompanied all along by mutual emotional support, where each is willing to set aside some self-regard in order to acknowledge and support the other's expression of embodiment, needs, and emotions. Of course, the vast differences in maturity and previous degree of individuation between mother and infant mean different forms and amounts of support and sacrifice for each. On the one side, the mother must support the baby with an unconditional, trustworthy background of steady care and love in order to enable the baby to begin to understand its corporeal urges and emotions as its own urges and emotions. On the other side, the baby must provide a kind of emotional attachment so that the mother will be provided with the trusted space in which she can differentiate herself, her needs, and her emotions from those of her baby. Therefore, parent–infant love can be described as a system of *mutual recognition*, where each acknowledges the other as a vital, living, embodied physical being with its own particular urges and emotions, through a steady background of emotional support that allows for the healthy individuation of each away from the original state of felt symbiosis.[5]

In Winnicott's analysis, the development of this system of emotional intersubjectivity is described as a process of negotiating a balance between attitudes of symbiotic self-sacrifice for the other and individual self-assertion. As the child matures and the relationship progresses, the baby grows from a stage of absolute dependency on the mother to lesser degrees of dependency, and this is achieved through renegotiating the structures of intersubjectivity between them, a renegotiation which is full of difficulties and challenges for each. In particular, Winnicott points to the ways in which the infant must overcome its original sense of being able to control all in its world, including its mother, and begin to realize that the mother has a physical and emotional existence independent of its own. And the mother likewise must struggle to assert her own independence even in the face of the evident needs and desires of the child. Because of the particularly strenuous emotional dynamics of this process of mutual individuation, another object relations psychoanalyst, Jessica Benjamin, has aptly described love as a *struggle* for mutual recognition (Benjamin 1988). Even as each must realize its independence from the other in order to grasp itself as its own person, this is only possible to the extent to which a strong bond of emotional attachment supports this mutual independence. Only the unconditional support of the mother's expression of needs and emotions allows the infant to recognize its needs and emotions as its own. While the infant desires to return to the symbiotic merging it originally experienced and dissolve the boundaries, it must refract its love through the realization that there are in fact boundaries between the mother and it, that both indeed are separate creatures with their own particular forms of embodiment, needs, and desires. As Honneth puts the point, "it is only... in the form of a struggle... that the child realizes that he or she is dependent on the loving care of an independently existing person with claims of her own" (SfR: 101).

Hegel analyses a similar set of dynamics in erotic love. Here is a struggle for mutual recognition of each other's affective particularity, that is, of the set of contingently given body, emotions, needs, desires, fantasies, and so on that distinguish each from other persons. In mature sexual relations between adults, persons are able to know themselves emotionally – as unique sources of personal and particular needs and desires – in and through loving physicality with the other, and this is reciprocal in that each knows that the other knows him or her self in the other. In the family for Hegel, parents and children also "recognize each other reciprocally as living, emotionally needy beings" (SfR: 18) and they do so in the mode of emotional comprehension of the other. Love in all these forms of relationships, then, involves the intersubjectively shared knowledge of this knowing-oneself-in-the-other, and this enables each individual to trust fundamentally that the other is there for one. In particular, one's given affective particularity is first confirmed in the love relationship where each knows the other as a particular emotional self. Recognition from an other is then required to be able to grasp oneself as an individuated self with given needs and desires.

2.2.2 Self-confidence

The payoff of this substantive analysis of love, from the perspective of Honneth's broader theory, is that love is critical for one pillar of practical identity: self-confidence. Both Hegel's and Winnicott's accounts support the crucial claim that intersubjective recognition in the mode of love is a necessary and irreplaceable condition for the development of healthy self-confidence. And further, basic self-confidence is a necessary and irreplaceable fundamental for the development of the two other major modes of practical self-relation: self-respect and self-esteem. Because the development of a multifaceted practical identity is necessary not only for self-realization but also for broader social interaction, it will even turn out that love is crucial for social and political participation.

"Self-confidence" (like "self-respect" and "self-esteem," to be explained shortly) should be understood as a technical term. Thus Honneth's use of "self-confidence" should not be confused with ordinary notions of it, such as a positive attitude toward one's own abilities, traits, performances, and so on. (In fact, this ordinary sense of self-confidence is more closely related to Honneth's notion of self-esteem.) Rather, as used here, self-confidence refers to a very basic sense of the stability and continuity of one's self as a differentiated individual with particular needs and emotions. This basic confidence must also extend to the stability and continuity of the world outside, focused particularly on the social world of significant and anonymous others. Along with this stability is the sense of being able to autonomously control one's own body, to be able to direct one's physical and vital nature according to one's own impetus. This kind of a foundational sense-of-self also involves the ability to trust oneself, to be able to be relaxed in the face of the various eruptions of emotions one experiences within oneself, to be able to be alone with oneself without basic anxiety or a sense of the alien character of one's own needs and drives. According to the distinct accounts of love given by both object relations psychoanalysis and Hegel, the development of this kind of basic self-confidence is only possible against a steady background of unconditional emotional support from trusted others. According to Winnicott, it is only the mother's love of the infant that allows it to differentiate itself from the mother and begin to trust in the stability of its own ego, all the while knowing that it is not emotionally cut off from others in the world. "In becoming sure of the 'mother's' love, young children come to trust themselves, which makes it possible for them to be alone without anxiety" (SfR: 104). Successful reciprocal recognition in the form of love – what Winnicott terms "good-enough mothering" – involves a balance between boundary creation and boundary dissolution achieved through emotional support that enables both the child and the mother to establish basic self-confidence in the stability of themselves and their intersubjective worlds.

Because it is so fundamental to personal identity – an individual without self-confidence in the relevant sense has no stable ego identity over time with a settled sense of his or her own embodied and affective particularity, a sense sufficiently differentiated from the particularity of others – self-confidence functions as a baseline requirement for a healthy practical relation-to-self. Higher forms of normative self-regard such as self-respect and self-esteem are simply impossible to realize in any fulsome sense in the absence of healthy self-confidence. Thus the recognition relationship of love has a kind of priority over the forms of recognition granted through rights and social solidarity. As will be seen below, self-respect and self-esteem are essential for individual participation in higher forms of social life. Therefore, self-confidence is, as Hegel himself hypothesized, a necessary precondition for both political citizenship and social participation. Surprisingly, then, it turns out that the relation of reciprocal recognition whereby one's emotional and embodied particularity is reaffirmed through the affective support of intimate others is foundational for social relations generally. This is in stark contrast to the individualistic assumptions of traditional forms of liberal and social contract theory which simply presuppose atomistic and asocial, instrumentally calculating rational actors, each looking out for their own interests with no intrinsic concerns for or emotional connections to others, and generally unaffected by ties of emotional and affection with particular others.[6]

2.2.3   Violating physical integrity

The indispensability of self-confidence can also be grasped by considering the specific form of misrecognition corresponding to appropriate love. Here Honneth is not as interested in the pathologies of love relations as psychoanalysts often are. Rather, he takes rape and torture – fundamental, willful violations of one's physical integrity – as paradigmatic forms of disrespect negatively corresponding to recognition through love. The basic insight here is that such extreme violations of physical integrity, where another forcibly assumes control over one's own body, are in fact the kinds of intersubjective experiences that are able to disrupt that basic, foundational self-confidence gained in early childhood. When the ordinary, taken-for-granted experience of being in control of one's body is taken away by another through torture and rape, one's basic confidence in oneself is attacked from the outside, and the trust in oneself that was carefully built up through early experiences of love easily breaks down. Such physical abuse, in depriving one of the feeling of autonomous physical control of oneself and in threatening one's trust in oneself, can leave one feeling deprived of a stable reality. And from the point of view of social theory, this kind of loss of self-confidence "affects all practical dealings with other subjects, even at the physical level" (SfR: 133). Hence, torture and rape are the paradigmatic forms of intersubjective disrespect that threaten the self-confidence component of personal identity.

From a moral point of view, the connection between physical abuse and the disruption of self-confidence speaks to a specific form of individual vulnerability. Because the personal integrity of each person is in fact dependent upon specific forms of recognition from others, each individual is *intersubjectively* vulnerable. Honneth proposes the over-arching concept of "disrespect" to refer to all of those negative experiences of a denial of appropriate recognition. Then, within that broad category, he distinguishes three specific forms of disrespect corresponding, as negatives, to the three main forms of recognition. In this case, the vulnerability concerns the impact upon basic self-confidence of the disorienting disruption of targeted violence. As we will see below, the arbitrary denial of rights is the paradigmatic form of disrespect negatively corresponding to self-respect, while systematic insult and denigration negatively correspond to self-esteem. But in all cases, the crucial claim for moral philosophy is that disrespect represents not only a form of harm to a person – insofar as disrespect impairs the person's psychological integrity – but also a form of wrong, a disruption of the appropriate social relations we owe to other persons. And it is precisely the connection between individuals' practical relation-to-self and specific forms of intersubjectivity that allows one to understand recognitional harms to persons as, at the same time, violations of what is owed to them, as injustices. Honneth aptly captures these points in a crucial few sentences about our everyday, moral use of concepts such as "insult" and "denigration":

> Negative concepts of this kind are used to designate behaviour that represents an injustice not simply because it harms subjects or restricts their freedom to act, but because it injures them with regard to the positive understanding of themselves that they have acquired intersubjectively. Without the implicit reference to the claims of recognition that one makes to one's fellow human beings, there is no way of using these

concepts of "disrespect" and "insult" meaningfully....What the term "disrespect" [*Mißachtung*] refers to is the specific vulnerability of humans resulting from the internal interdependence of individualization and recognition. (SfR: 131)

The consequences of violations of physical integrity are not only matters relevant to individual well-being, but also point to a basic moral infrastructure built into relations of intersubjective recognition. Because our practical identities – our understanding of ourselves as moral beings – are systematically tied to the quality and structure of intersubjective relations, an account of recognition can lay bare the normative character of our social lives together. Recognition is a vital need of each and every person, not just a nice benefit that one might happen to gain in a charmed life. Because our own personal integrity and identity is constitutively dependent upon due regard from others, recognition provides the key to a moral analysis of our social lives.

2.3   Self-Respect and Rights

The second major form of intersubjective recognition is found paradigmatically in legal relations. Honneth's central claim here is that individuals gain a sense of self-respect only in and through the individual rights that are granted to members of a legal community. In virtue of having a status under a given legal system, an individual is granted or afforded certain legal protections. Those legal protections, in turn, allow her to understand herself as a full and equal member of that community, capable of and responsible for her own decisions. When acknowledged as bearers of legal rights by the other members of their community through their legal status, individuals are able to gain a sense of self-respect, a sense of their inherent dignity as free and equal among others. In order to explain Honneth's idea of self-respect, it will help to examine (2.3.1) the relationship between legal rights and respect for moral autonomy, (2.3.2) the relationship between rights and the development of self-respect, and (2.3.3) disrespect as the denial of rights.

2.3.1   Rights and moral autonomy

Whereas self-confidence is gained through the medium of close intimate relationships of love and friendship, the practical relation-to-self Honneth identifies as "self-respect" is achieved through the medium of distant and anonymous relationships between members of a legal community. In virtue of having a generic legal status in a given community, an individual is afforded certain legal rights. Legal rights are predicated on two basic assumptions: individuals are capable of controlling their conduct toward others to a sufficient extent that they can be held responsible for that conduct, and individuals have basic normative obligations toward others that can be legitimately enforced by legal institutions. These two assumptions can be summarized in the notion that the law treats individuals as morally autonomous agents: capable of freely willing and acting in the light of their own rational considerations and legitimately held to account as such when their actions affect others.

Honneth employs Hegel's and Mead's analyses of how legal rights express a form of respect for the moral autonomy of each individual, but it should be clear that all three are essentially developing themes from Immanuel Kant's foundational work on morality and law. Kant in particular stressed the internal conceptual relationships between the ways in which the law holds individuals responsible, the individual rights the law affords to individuals, and the ideals of moral autonomy. Modern legal rights on this general conception are a way of institutionalizing the due regard individuals owe to one another as free and equal moral agents, a way of respecting the moral autonomy of each. Of particular importance, the respect involved here is *not* differential or graduated: it is not based upon a comparative evaluation of a person's traits, capabilities, or achievements. Respect, rather, is for a person as an end-in-herself, as an irreplaceable source of intrinsic worth, just insofar as and because she is a moral agent. The object of the respect, then, is not what differentiates her from others but more accurately the personhood she shares equally with all others on account of her moral autonomy: as a freely willing being, capable of reasoned insight into the moral requirements of social life (including the demands of law), and responsible for the choices and actions she makes in the light of that insight. Rights, in short, can be understood as "depersonalized symbols of social respect" (SfR: 118). This explains, for example, how we can hold a convicted criminal in low regard, thinking him unworthy of esteem, and yet still insist on his deservingness of respect and dignified treatment. While we disapprove of his willful actions and may judge his character as contemptible, the law rightly acknowledges the criminal's moral personhood precisely by granting him rights to due process and dignified treatment. The law is a medium for insuring the enforcement of the generic obligations we have to persons *as* morally autonomous agents, and through such enforcement the law simultaneously expresses a specific kind of respect to all legal subjects.

A few contrasts between love and legal respect can help show how they are different forms of intersubjective recognition. First, while love is expressed through emotional support, respect is expressed cognitively; while love involves having the appropriate affective dispositions toward others, respect is largely a matter of correctly comprehending the rational claims of both oneself and others. Although both are forms of regard for others, the one registers in and through affect, the other in and through rational understanding. Second, the potential scope of love is restricted to a small group of particular others in concrete and ongoing relationships with one. By contrast, rights are in principle unlimited in scope: while legal rights can usually extend to all of the legal citizens or subjects of a large contemporary nation-state, persons the world over can be regarded as having human rights. Thus, while there are severe limits to the number of persons I can have primary affective relationships with, there are few limits to the number of persons I could recognize as having co-equal legal rights. And these different limits are partially due to the different modes of recognition: the emotional support at the heart of love requires particularized attunement to the concrete needs and desires of others, whereas the cognitive respect expressed through legal rights requires only the proper comprehension and rational adjustment of behavior to the generic claims of anonymous others. That is to say, finally, that love is particularistic – directed at the specific and unique emotions of particular persons – while respect is universalistic – directed at the generic characteristics that all persons with rights share.

An important caveat here is that this analysis is most fully applicable only to modern legal systems, where the law is expected to give equal respect to each and every person, and do so in the same way for each. In pre-modern legal systems, different kinds of people were granted different degrees and kinds of legal rights based upon their different social statuses. In modern systems, the fundamental norm is equal treatment for all before the law. This is most clearly captured in Kant's universalization test: one is bound only to those norms that could be universally willed from the standpoint of a moral agent. This categorical imperative is then partly realized in the universality of legal rights. Both Hegel and Mead take up this theme and give it an intersubjectivist interpretation, pointing to the ways in which the law recognizes individuals from the point of view of expectations and responsibilities that are generically applicable to all. In this way, individuals gain the respect of being treated in the same manner as all other members of the legal community, at the same time as each recognizes all the others as deserving of the same legal rights.

2.3.2 Rights and self-respect

How exactly then do legal rights relate to an individual's development of self-respect? Honneth's central claim here is that a person can fully develop healthy self-respect only when he or she is granted the appropriate social recognition expressed through the full legal rights granted to other members of his or her community. I can only realize my dignity as an irreplaceable, unique source of moral worth when I can understand myself as a morally autonomous agent, freely choosing in the light of my own rational capacities. But in order to understand myself as morally autonomous, I must be able to regard myself as having normative obligations to others, and obligations of a specific kind. In particular, I must be able to grasp those generalized normative expectations that adhere to all legal subjects universally, within a generalized system of reciprocal normative expectations. And I can only grasp those moral expectations from the point of view of the generalized other where I can see myself as one bound reciprocally by the same obligations as others. From this perspective, of course, I can also see myself – just as I see others – as deserving of the legal protections that concretely and publicly realize the moral expectations. In other words, in grasping the system of obligations, I also grasp the system of legal rights that each is due. But from that generalized perspective I can now understand myself as *deserving* of legal rights, as a morally responsible subject of law, and so as deserving of self-respect. Thus the development of self-respect is tied to the social form of regard institutionalized in legal rights. One is able to respect oneself as a moral agent because one deserves – and is publicly recognized as deserving – the legal respect of others as a moral agent.

The point can perhaps more clearly be grasped by considering what would happen in a world without legal rights. Joel Feinberg's thought experiment of "Nowheresville" is apropos: consider a prosperous society where all individuals live comfortable lives, supported in part by the large degree of altruistic goodwill each displays toward compatriots, but where there are no legal rights granted to individuals (Feinberg 1970). In Nowheresville, persons could not stand up and demand their rights, could not insist on their own fundamental dignity. Each would only be at the disposal of the goodwill of others to right what might go wrong; one could only hope for a successful appeal to the good graces of others to rectify violations or make one whole after culpable losses. In other words, in Nowheresville, persons do not owe others unconditional consideration because of their generic moral autonomy, but only treat each other well when they are positively inclined to do so through altruism or some other accident of pleasant feelings toward others. In that case, one could not stand on one's rights and demand to be treated well. One could not then develop full and healthy self-respect as a dignified member of the community, equally deserving of the same treatment as all others in that community. And this inability to develop full self-respect would be directly tied to the lack of the generalized social regard appropriate to moral agents: namely, legal rights.

In contrast, when one can publicly insist on one's rights, one has the socially recognized ability to raise claims to proper treatment that others must acknowledge since they already acknowledge those claims as generically appropriate for all moral agents. One is able to stand up in public and demand acknowledgment as a co-equal member, as a moral person with valid social claims to proper treatment. Finally, this public acknowledgment is then the basis for one's own self-respect as a free moral agent, equal in legal status to all other free moral agents. Because rights are public and socially effective, I always have the option of raising a rights claim that must be acknowledged as such by others. And that possibility is constitutive of being able to see myself as an autonomous actor, worthy of self-respect because of the respect I am afforded as an equal bearer of legal rights with others. My own perception of myself as having moral rights is insufficient for full self-respect. I need also to be "able to raise claims whose social redemption is considered justified" (SfR: 119), and legal rights afford precisely that ability.

2.3.3   The denial of rights

Honneth identifies two paradigmatic forms of legal disrespect: the denial to a person of some or all of the legal rights granted to others; or, outright exclusion from any legal standing whatsoever, that is, legal ostracism. When one is disrespected in these ways, one is not able to regard oneself as a morally autonomous agent, as a free and equal person among other free and equal persons. The harm here goes beyond the substantive restriction involved with the loss of the rights protections, although this itself is a serious wrong. It is also a fundamental injustice because it involves the denigration of one's ability to act for oneself and be answerable for the foreseeable consequences of action: it is a violation of one's social integrity, a social integrity owed to all members simply on account of their equal status. The denial of rights or legal ostracism impedes one's capacity for a practical understanding of oneself as an equal subject of law, deserving of the dignity of free and equal persons.

Consider, for example, the legal doctrine of coverture whereby women, upon marriage, lost all independent legal personality and were legally subordinated to their husbands.[7] One legal consequence of coverture was that, directly upon a woman's betrothal to a man, she was barred from holding personal property in her name alone and from independently concluding contracts with others. With respect to rights to property and contract, she was entirely dependent upon and at the mercy of her husband's contingent will. So, under coverture, the wife is recognized – in no uncertain terms – as incapable of acting as an autonomous actor in that society, a capitalist society structured fundamentally around property, markets, and contracts. This form of disrespect thereby makes it impossible for her to understand herself as a free and equal moral agent in her community and so deprives her of the ability to develop a full and appropriate sense of self-respect, of equal dignity with fellow legal subjects. Upon becoming a wife under coverture, a woman suffered a kind of social death.

Because disrespect is not just a harm but a moral injury, the emotions of outrage and indignation that may accompany the denial of rights (especially if it is an unusual case for that society) are not simply indeterminate negative feelings on the part of the sufferer. They are moral emotions with cognitive content: they indicate a specific violation of the normative regard or treatment that one has good reason to expect as one's due. In this case, the expectation is that one will be treated as a free and equal legal subject. The outrage, the feelings of unfairness and injustice, then, provides a kind of clue which points to the moral infrastructure of intersubjective relations of rights. Insofar as a society employs the medium of legal rights in order to express a kind of cognitive respect for the inherent dignity of free and equal moral subjects, it commits itself to generalizable patterns of intersubjective recognition. The moral emotions experienced when legal rights are denied are sensitive to that pattern of normative expectations and highlight its contours precisely through the withholding of the recognition that would otherwise be due to a person.

We should keep in mind that this analysis is largely directed at modern legal systems where legal rights are granted to individual persons based on generalizable, even universalistic, characteristics, rather than their membership of limited groups with high status like aristocrats, males, property owners, racial and ethnic majorities, and so on. As the discussion of coverture makes clear, there is a great deal of variety across different societies and time periods concerning who is granted rights and which rights persons actually have. Significantly, then, the social conditions necessary for the development of healthy self-respect are socially and historically indexed in a way that the social conditions necessary for self-confidence – namely, the existence of close primary relationships of love and friendship – do not appear to be. As we will see shortly, the social conditions for the development of self-esteem are also context-dependent, changing across different societies and times. We will return to the historical nature of recognition in the discussion of social learning and progress in chapter 3.

2.4   Self-Esteem and Solidarity

Persons are positively recognized through the emotional support of love and positively recognized through the cognitive respect expressed through legal rights. But they are also positively recognized through the social esteem expressed in solidaristic relations with others. For

Honneth, this third major form of intersubjective recognition is what enables individuals to realize a third form of practical relation-to-self: self-esteem. Before turning to a more detailed treatment, it may help to simply summarize some of the main contrasts between the three forms of recognition. First, while love is concerned with the particular needs and emotions of persons, and legal rights are focused on persons' moral autonomy, the objects of social esteem are individual's distinctive traits, abilities, and achievements. To put this in terms of Hegel's language, emotional support is directed at persons' particularity, specifically their naturally given and concrete makeup as desiring and affectively vulnerable creatures; cognitive respect at persons' universality, specifically that capacity for autonomous and responsible agency they share with other humans; social esteem at persons' individuality, specifically their distinctive form of self-realization. These three different types of recognition enable three different ways in which individuals can develop a practical conception of themselves as moral beings, rightly expecting certain kinds of treatment according to socially shared understandings of normatively appropriate regard: self-confidence, self-respect, and self-esteem. The relevant communities from which individuals can expect the form of recognition also differ: love and friendship are developed in small groups of intimates; legal rights can be potentially extended to the entire human race; and, esteem relationships extend as far as those who share the same substantive ethical values concerning what is socially worthy and in what way (what Honneth calls "communities of value"). Finally, three paradigmatic forms of disrespect are encountered when the appropriate form of positive recognition is withheld, distorted, or violated: rape and other forms of physical and emotional abuse; the denial of rights and social exclusion; and, cultural denigration and insult to ways of life. To put a bit more flesh on these bones, I look next at Honneth's substantive analysis of esteem recognition and its relation to the development of self-esteem (2.4.1), and his claim that cultural denigration is the paradigmatic form of disrespect corresponding to social esteem (2.4.2).

2.4.1   Esteem

The logic of social esteem is essentially different from that of legal rights and of love. Whereas rights respect persons for the universal qualities of moral autonomy they are presumed to share equally with all others and love provides unconditional support that enables individuals to be at home with their own needs and emotions, esteem is a form of social valuing that is differential across persons precisely because it involves scalar judgments of worth of the specific traits, abilities, and achievements of particular persons. When I esteem you for, say, your tolerant disposition or your diligent completion of a difficult project at work, I am making graduated positive assessments of your character and achievements according to a (perhaps implicit) scale of values. By contrast, when considering your right to, say, enter into a contract, this is a binary matter: I either respect your rights to do so or I do not, according to a cognitive assessment of whether you have fulfilled the relevant criteria for being a bearer of contracting rights. Finally, while love, like esteem, is particularized to individuals, love properly promises unconditional support. If, however, esteem were unconditional positive recognition of an individual, regardless of their character or accomplishments, it could hardly be of much worth to individuals. Esteem then is a proportional assessment that is particularized to individual persons and takes as its object the person's own traits, abilities and achievements.[8]

Honneth's crucial claim, once again, is that gaining social recognition is constitutively tied to developing a healthy sense-of-self. In this case, individuals can only gain a healthy sense of self-esteem – where they are able to positively and appropriately value their own talents and accomplishments – to the extent to which they have received esteem from others for those very traits and accomplishments. The connection between healthy and appropriate self-regard and normatively appropriate regard from others is almost self-evident. While there are innumerable ways that each person is unique – from number of hairs to choices of headwear to accomplishments of the highest values – only some of these unique characteristics and achievements deserve positive evaluation, both from others and in one's own eyes. In order to understand and properly value what is of value (and to disregard those unique aspects of oneself that are normatively indifferent), and so to grasp one's own worth from a practical point of view, one must be able to understand the set of socially current expectations and aspirations. With a grasp of that social schema of evaluation, one is able to look back at oneself, as it were, from the perspective of one's interaction partners and interlocutors. And that perspective is expressed by the attitudes and actions of esteem-based recognition (and disrespect) that one receives from others on account of one's specific traits, abilities, and achievements. Thus, once again, the thesis is that a particular form of practical relation-to-self is dependent upon a specific form of social recognition – one can only realize oneself fully in a social context, in particular, a social context affording one adequate and appropriate forms of intersubjective recognition.

As already intimated, the specific objects and scope of social esteem are context-dependent. That is because which specific personal characteristics and achievements are proper objects of esteem, and to what extent they are to be valued, and who has the legitimate authority to make such evaluations for which others are all determined by socially specific schemas of social value. For two persons can only sensibly esteem each other if they share some of the same values and goals that serve to define what is and isn't to be esteemed, to what degree, and who is permitted to make such reciprocal assessments. Esteem then has an internal relation to a society's complex set of meanings, values, goals, and their interrelations: its "esteem order." Honneth focuses in particular on a culture's understanding of the goals of society and their relationship to cooperative social activity as crucial for setting the standards for esteem relations.[9] In such a "community of value," differential evaluations of individuals' concrete traits and achievements are made according to the contributions they make to the realization of broadly shared societal goals. Thus it makes sense to say that self-esteem is made possible in the specific relations of *solidarity* that hold between persons who participate in a community of value and further its shared goals. Social esteem, then, is not only crucial to integrating individuals into mutually supportive social relations – solidarity – but also to individuals' practical understanding of themselves as worthy members of that solidaristic community. Apparently the scope of "communities of value" can be quite different for Honneth, ranging from relatively insular subcultures that have a significantly different esteem order from mainstream society to the broad community of value that might be shared across contemporary western capitalist democracies. At any rate, it is clear that the various conceptions of societal goals and of the personality traits and achievements that are to be esteemed will be different both across societies and within them. And, as we will see in chapter 3, esteem orders and communities of value are themselves regularly challenged and changed through the interpretive politics of social struggles for recognition.

2.4.2   Denigrating ways of life

The fundamental form of disrespect corresponding to esteem recognition is cultural denigration: insulting or degrading particular ways of life that are the vehicles for self-realization of individuals. Particularly when a given society's cultural norms systematically denigrate and downgrade certain ways of life, the social conditions for the development of healthy self-esteem are blocked for members of those disrespected communities of value. That is because those individuals can no longer relate to those patterns of self-realization as having value within their society and cannot thereby receive positive recognition for their own traits and accomplishments that are oriented by that way of life. Under conditions of society-wide denigration of a minority way of life, positive esteem from others within one's own group may be the best one can hope for. While such in-group solidaristic esteem may compensate somewhat, members of denigrated groups still will not have the full and equal opportunities to develop healthy self-esteem that others in the wider society do. Thus, for example, slurs against an ethnic group for their practices constitute not just insulting harms but may block or destroy the ability of group members to develop a healthy practical relation-to-self insofar as they make it impossible for group members to understand their own characteristics and accomplishments as worthy in the light of society-wide shared conceptions of societal goals and values. In such a situation, there is not yet the possibility for the kind of society-wide solidarity that is expressed through fully reciprocal practices of mutual recognition amongst all members of society. And, as was the case with violations of physical integrity and with the denial of rights, the negative emotions associated with cultural denigration – moral outrage, indignation, resentment, shame – signify not just negative feelings spurred by the slings and arrows of others. Because such emotions are sensitive to deformations in appropriate intersubjective relations between persons, they highlight violations of normative expectations and thereby help map the moral infrastructure of our ways of regarding and acting toward others. Indignation and shame caused by cultural denigration signal, then, that something has gone profoundly wrong in our society-wide practices of mutual regard.

2.5 Antecedent Recognition

The topic of a form of recognition that is developmentally and conceptually prior to the other three forms of recognition – called alternatively antecedent recognition, antecedent identification, primordial acknowledgment, affective sympathy, or sympathetic engagement – first clearly arises in a 2001 article on social invisibility (Honneth 2001a), then gets an extended treatment in *Reification*, first delivered as Tanner Lectures in 2005. Honneth develops this idea out of a complex of converging research, ranging from the author Ralph Ellison's insights into a peculiar form of invisibility suffered by blacks in the United States to the conceptual and phenomenological analyses of philosophers as diverse as Martin Heidegger, John Dewey, Stanley Cavell, and Theodor Adorno to the research of developmental psychologists like Peter Hobson, Daniel Stern, and Michael Tomasello. For simplicity's sake, I present the idea mainly through the lens of the developing child. The fundamental idea here is that, before any normatively substantive form of interaction with others can occur, interaction partners must become aware that they are dealing with persons – and not, say, insects or things or machines. Honneth conceives of such antecedent recognition as the "spontaneous, nonrational recognition of others as fellow human beings" (R: 152).

The achievement of antecedent recognition can be seen developmentally in pre-linguistic children. Around the age of nine months, an infant's meaningful gestural exchanges with parents, especially facial expressions, begin to take on a new quality and enable important new stages in learning. Because these exchanges of expressions involve the communication of the parents' willingness to interact in and through emotional engagement – through sympathy, love, hurt, surprise, etc. – the infant begins to be able to see how the parent meaningfully reacts to the world, and so begins to be able to take up a second-person perspective on the world.[10] The key claim here is that a host of developments related to the ability to adopt the perspective of another is made possible only if the infant has "already developed a feeling of emotional attachment to a psychological parent, for it is only by way of this antecedent identification that the child is able to be moved, motivated, and swept along by the presence of a concrete second person in such a way as to comprehend the person's changes of attitude in an interested way" (R: 43–4). Following developmental psychology research, Honneth stresses the contrast with autistic children who, because they are blocked from developing emotional attachments to others, are unable to adopt the perspective of others on the world and are thus, in a significant sense, socially blind.

The ability to take up the second-person perspective, to be able to anticipate the reactions of an interaction partner to the world of things and humans, is a foundational skill for the later development of symbolic communication, language, and a range of other cognitive skills. However, importantly for Honneth, these exchanges are not achieved in a cognitive manner: it is not a matter of the infant *understanding* and rationally processing the second-person standpoint. Rather, it concerns a kind of *sympathetic engagement* with the interaction partner, where the other is encountered as an emotional and intentional creature with his or her own desires, goals, and projects. Such engagement differs fundamentally from interactions with the world of things which cannot have their own desires and goals, their own emotional responsiveness, and their own perspectives which can be taken up by others. In short, this form of primordial sympathetic engagement with an interacting *alter* involves the recognition of the other's existence as a human being. Hence the object of antecedent recognition is precisely those characteristics of the other that identify it as a living human, a person with her or his own emotional and intentional life.

With the beginning achievements of the ability to take over the perspective of another, the infant must also be able to distinguish objects in the world from that second-person perspective: differentiating, for instance between things and persons, including the personhood of the infant her- or himself. As with the other forms of recognition, spontaneous nonrational engagement with another as a human enables the infant to encounter *her- or himself* as an entity with the characteristics of personhood. Hence antecedent recognition enables a basic form of antecedent self-affirmation. While this has clear connections to the kind of basic self-confidence we encountered above, here the self-relation is not really a fully practical one: it does not concern the set of legitimate normative expectations an individual can have of another's treatment toward one, at least any farther than treatment as a living human person. Again, the issue with antecedent self-affirmation, as with antecedent recognition of another, is simply the existential awareness that one is dealing here with a person, possessed of his or her own drives, desires, and independent existence. It does not concern, for instance, the kind of claim to legitimacy of one's own needs and desires, nor the normative expectations that others should be appropriately receptive to those needs and desires.

This mode of recognition – primordial acknowledgment of the existence of another human – is a necessary precondition for all human communication and indeed for human cognition of the objective word generally. In short, (antecedent) recognition precedes cognition. It is also a clear precondition for the forms of intersubjective recognition that enable the development of self-confidence, self-respect, and self-esteem. However, this form of recognition itself is not taken to have any further normative implications for the moral infrastructure of human life. One clue to this is the fact that one can acknowledge the existence of another in this way without any positive feelings toward the other or any further normative expectations concerning the other's behavior. In fact, one can engage in antecedent recognition through purely negative emotions toward another – say in a traffic jam. The question is simply whether one encounters another as a human person. For Honneth, it is the other three forms of recognition that evince an intrinsic normative patterning and call upon us to take up certain forms of positive stances toward others, according to our relationships to them and the background schemas of evaluation in our society. Antecedent recognition, then, is a necessary precondition of love, rights, and solidarity – each presupposes that we are involved with other humans rather than things – but is not itself normatively imbued.[11]

Honneth's main interest with antecedent recognition is not primarily spurred by systematic or theoretical concerns. It springs more from his interest in understanding certain social pathologies that can only be understood if a distinction is made between moral recognition and a non-moralized form of existential recognition. One such pathology, explored further in 4.2.3, concerns the type of social invisibility experienced by racial minorities in many societies. In such cases, even though antecedent recognition is afforded to minority members, they are nevertheless actively disregarded, "looked through," and thereby subjected to disrespectful misrecognition.

For an even more extreme pathology, consider reification: the complete and thorough dehumanization of others involved in treating them as things, as objects in the natural world to be manipulated or destroyed as one's own prudential calculations determine. As we will see in 4.2.5, reification on Honneth's analysis requires individuals to systematically forget antecedent recognition, to forget the primordial grasp of others as humans. Given the depth of antecedent recognition, sustained reification could only be achieved through extensive social practices that de-habituate persons from the existential acknowledgment they ordinarily and automatically afford to all persons. Therefore, the social pathologies of invisibilization and reification require us to consider a fourth form of antecedent, non-moralized recognition of others that forms a necessary precondition for the other three forms of normative recognition.

We can now summarize the results of the four forms of recognition in the following table.[12]

	Antecedent recognition	Love recognition	Respect recognition	Esteem recognition
Practical relation-to-self	Antecedent Self-affirmation	Self-confidence	Self-respect	Self-esteem
Type of relationship	Social interaction	Love and friendship	Legal relations and rights	Solidarity
Mode of regard	Primordial engagement	Emotional	Cognitive	Esteem
Object of recognition	Human personhood	Needs and emotions	Moral autonomy	Traits, abilities, and achievements
Aspect of personhood acknowledged	Human existence	Particularity	Universality	Individuality
Community of recognizers	Interaction partners	Intimates	Fellow legal subjects	Members of communities of value
Paradigms of disrespect	[Reification]	Abuse and rape	Denial of rights; legal exclusion	Cultural denigration

2.6   Critical Perspectives

I now turn to some critical questions and objections that might be, and have been, raised to Honneth's recognition-based account of the development of individuals' practical relations-to-self. Understanding how Honneth has responded (and might respond) to various challenges should help further clarify the central theses of his theory. Amongst the many interesting objections raised, the following focuses on three central issues. Is Honneth's account of personhood overly optimistic about the prevalence of pro-social attitudes – does it thereby ignore too much of the dark, antisocial side of human nature (2.6.1)? Second, wouldn't a defender of rugged, self-reliant individualism balk at recognition theory's focus on what others think about persons (2.6.2)? And, third, how should the philosophical analysis of recognition negotiate the shoals between objectivism and constructivism (2.6.3)?

2.6.1 Anthropological optimism

Consider first the charge that Honneth's philosophical anthropology is altogether too optimistic, too focused on the positive and affirmative pro-social attitudes that motivate individuals to recognize others in an affirmative manner, and too inattentive to the negative, aggressive and destructive antisocial attitudes that drive individuals to denigrate and hurt others. All three of the commentators on Honneth's Tanner Lectures on reification raise this kind of concern with respect to Honneth's account of antecedent recognition (Butler 2008; Geuss 2008; Lear 2008). In that context, Honneth's response is to clarify his account of antecedent recognition, insisting that it does not necessarily involve positive emotions toward the other who is acknowledged as an existing, living human being (R: 147–59).[13] Even if that response is adequate with respect to antecedent recognition, it clearly is not available to Honneth with respect to the three forms of moral recognition: love, respect, and esteem. For each of them essentially involves a particular kind of other-regarding attitude that seeks at the least to positively evaluate, and at most to protect and promote, those characteristics of the other which are recognized: their needs and emotions, their moral autonomy, and their distinctive contributions to collective endeavors.

One powerful way to make this charge is to contrast Honneth's moral psychology with the later work of Sigmund Freud (Freud 1961). Claiming that there are two fundamentally different drives motivating all persons – a drive toward love and unification with others and a drive toward aggression, death, and the destruction of others – Freud would criticize Honneth's theory for downplaying or simply ignoring the manifold of prevalent phenomena related to aggressive antisocial forms of intersubjectivity. This failure would then be traced to Honneth's naively optimistic psychology. Joel Whitebook forcefully updates the psychoanalytic critique of Honneth's theory for ignoring intrapsychic sources of negative and aggressive affect – especially primary narcissism – and argues that this problem is connected to Honneth's mistaken claim that the self is social all the way down (Whitebook 2001).

Honneth's first response to these charges is to acknowledge that negative and aggressive affects exist and are central to human emotional life. Consider his endorsement of Winnicott's account of destructive energies as manifested in infant behaviors such as biting, hitting, or kicking significant others: such aggressive behaviors are in fact crucial elements in the dynamic negotiation between fusion and individuation. In a similar vein, consider his endorsement of Benjamin's account of the infant's attempt to destroy the parent as part and parcel of the infant's struggle for recognition as an independent entity. Thus he does not deny negative affect.

More technically, Honneth's response to the Freudian drive theory is to deny that it is true. He argues that, in contrast to the idea that emotions and needs well up solipsistically from within a person's biological organism and are simply projected onto the world, object relations psychoanalysis, as well as a host of other approaches in psychology, has shown the crucial importance of interactions between persons for the character and dynamics of emotions. Freud's theory of the intrapsychic unfolding of drives is no longer believable, given the wealth of studies that have shown that the *interaction* between parent and child is decisive for emotional development, and hence for the development of an individual's moral identity (SfR: 95–107 and (Honneth 2009a, 2012d, 2012l)). He argues further against Whitebook that aggression isn't best characterized in terms of a given, innate drive or some other biologically determined unalterable fact of nature. It is better interpreted in terms of reactions to failures experienced in coping with the world, especially the social world, where feelings of pain and suffering result from the end of temporary feelings of emotional union with significant others, and the infant (or the adult) experiences anger at the independence and uncontrollability of the other. Thus antisocial affect arises in the development of individuals, paradoxically, from the basic *intersubjectivity* expressed through love and care (Honneth 2012d).

Honneth thus argues that his psychological theory is better equipped to account for negative psychic phenomena, both theoretically and empirically, than competing psychologies. However, it is worth considering another approach that Honneth might usefully adopt. Acknowledging that theory's psychological theses must be accurate, he might nevertheless decline to get drawn into an attempt to articulate a comprehensive psychology of the self. After all, the empirical psychology is employed not in the service of a complete picture of human nature, but for a philosophical theory of moral identity, one that can be used productively to articulate the moral logic of social relations of intersubjective recognition. He might claim, that is, that he is articulating only a *limited* moral anthropology, not a full-scale philosophical anthropology. Of course, such a moral anthropology needs to acknowledge realistically negative psychic phenomena, but it need not provide its own account of their origins, character, and pathological tendencies. As an analog, consider Kant's moral theory. It need not deny the crooked timber of humanity in order to point to the possibility of doing one's duty. Kant's moral psychology does need to establish that it is possible for persons to overcome their antisocial impulses, but it need not develop a comprehensive explanatory theory of all of those impulses in order to do so. In a similar way, Honneth might acknowledge the affective negativity that psychologists study, while insisting that the pro-social emotions central to positive recognition of others are also real and effective elements of our psychological makeup, crucial to the psychological anchoring of morally valid treatment of others. This more limited appropriation of empirical psychology would, it seems to me, have a real advantage in insulating the philosophical theory from some of the more complicated and technical disputes between different schools of psychology, especially where there is reason to think that the large degree of disagreement between researchers indicates the unsettled state of empirical research on such issues. It is important to note, however, that Honneth's most recent sustained engagements with psychoanalysis show that he has not adopted this more modest approach (Honneth 2009a, 2012b, 2012d, 2012f, 2012l).

2.6.2 Rugged individualism

We can imagine another challenge to Honneth's theory coming from a person who espouses a rugged, self-reliant individualism. He might ask: "Why should I care what others think?" Perhaps spurred on by thinkers as diverse as Diogenes of Sinope, Sade and Wilde, Thoreau and Emerson, Nietzsche and Sartre, our objector might find the very idea of a struggle for recognition from others to be not only a belittling requirement to submit his own personality to the inferior judgment of others, but also to falsely assume that judgment as the very source his unique individuality. The broad sense of the objection is quite familiar in our everyday culture, with the predominance it gives to individual choice and personal authenticity. There are at least two different interpretations of the objection from self-reliant individualism: as a moral objection to intersubjective recognition, and as an objection to the intersubjectivist explanation of the self.

Taking the latter, explanatory, interpretation first, the objection claims that the radical intersubjectivist thesis is empirically false: it is wrong to say that the development of individual identity is fundamentally and constitutively dependent on the recognition of others. Rather, there exists a kind of pre-social self, one not constituted through intersubjective interactions, perhaps arising out of pre-social drives (*à la* Freud) or in some other way a result of the biological makeup of the human organism.[14] I think that recognition theory's general response to the explanatory question "Why should I care what others think?" would be empirical. According to Honneth, you have no choice but to pay attention to what others think since, as a matter of fact, intersubjective recognition is constitutive of one's practical relation-to-self. Honneth draws on an imposingly broad set of empirical sources and theoretical arguments to back up this claim, beyond those already referred to in the previous sections of this chapter. At the end of the day, adjudicating the strength of his response would involve an overall assessment of the cogency of the relevant psychological and social scientific evidence, in comparison with countervailing empirical considerations that an objector might bring up.

With regard to the second interpretation of the rugged individualist's objection, the "Why care?" question asks whether we ought, as a moral or ethical matter, to pay attention to the opinions of others. Even if we are socially constituted, even if we can only come to have a practical identity through the internalization of social norms and through socialization into intersubjective relations of recognition, why should we seek out and continue to strive for their recognition? Isn't it better to think, as Ralph Waldo Emerson memorably argued, that "society everywhere is in conspiracy against the manhood of every one of its members.... Whoso would be a man must be a nonconformist" (Emerson 1979)? Doesn't the moral theory of recognition precisely demand of us that we conform to the opinions of others? And for what reasons, and with what losses?

In a broad sense, it seems clear what Honneth's answer here would be. We should care about how others regard us because, as an anthropological fact, we are intersubjectively vulnerable. Misrecognition or nonrecognition is a threat to the personal integrity of individuals since it can harm them in their capacity to achieve an undistorted practical relation-to-self. Further, such undistorted personal integrity is a vital part of human well-being, a central component of the good life for humans. And in line with other teleological moral theories, we have moral responsibilities to others in the light of what constitutes their good. Thus, since personal integrity is a vital aspect of the good life, and since appropriate social recognition is a necessary condition for the achievement of personal integrity, we have obligations to promote, or at least not violate, the recognitional conditions necessary for personal integrity. Because we are all vulnerable to distorting and harmful expressions of disrespect from others, we have obligations to regard people with the appropriate kinds of moral attitudes in relevant interactions with them (Anderson and Honneth 2005; Honneth 1995e, 2007a). As Honneth summarizes the basic insight of his moral theory, "the 'moral point of view' refers to the network of attitudes that we have to adopt in order to protect human beings from injustices arising from the communicative presuppositions of their self-relation. Shorn of all negative determinations, the appropriate formulation now runs: morality is the quintessence of the attitudes we are mutually obligated to adopt in order to secure jointly the conditions of our personal integrity." Morality is "a collective institution for securing our personal integrity" (Honneth 2007a: 138). In objecting to the relevance of social recognition, the rugged self-reliant individualist not only falsely denies the constitutive intersubjectivity of his own practical selfhood, he also wrongly ignores his obligations to appropriately recognize others.

2.6.3   Conceptual issues

The talk of the constitutive nature of intersubjective recognition in the previous sections raises a third set of worries about conceptual fundamentals. For instance, what exactly is an act of recognition? Further, when I successfully recognize something about you, am I merely projecting that quality onto you, or do I perceive something true about you? Relatedly, do you contribute to my act of recognition, or can I successfully recognize you without your participation? Honneth has clarified how he intends to negotiate the shoals between objectivism and constructivism in response to critical engagements with his work. The following gives a flavor of the interesting issues at play here.

To answer the first question about what recognition is, begin by recalling Honneth's basic schema: depending on the kind of relationship involved, individuals express to one another four different forms of recognition – antecedent, love, respect, and esteem – recognition that is directed at four different kinds of characteristics of the persons – human personhood, needs and emotions, moral autonomy, and valued contributions – where the different forms of recognition enable the development of four different forms of practical relation-to-self – antecedent self-affirmation, self-confidence, self-respect, and self-esteem. For example, by acknowledging Sally's right to choose her own career, her father Bob expresses respect for her moral autonomy, and when Sally is able to internalize that recognition from the generalized perspective of free and equal rights bearers, she is also able to develop respect for herself as a moral agent with a distinctive dignity. Alternatively, in esteeming her co-worker Tom's contribution to a departmental report, Mia expresses recognition of the worth of Tom's hard work and achievement, thereby making it possible for him to realize self-esteem when he internalizes Mia's perspective on his work.

There seems to be widespread agreement on a basic analysis of such acts of recognition.[15] Accordingly, an instance of recognition between two persons, at its core, involves *attitudes* that one individual takes up toward one another, a set of dispositions to regard the other in a certain way, and where those dispositions are *responsive* to and *evaluative* of the recipient's particular characteristics or actions. When we are considering the three moral forms of recognition, these attitudes are positive toward or affirmative of the recipient; as we have seen, they need not be positive for antecedent recognition. In order to be an instance of recognition, these attitudes must be *expressed* by the recognizer – for instance in words, nonverbal gestures, actions, practices, institutional treatment, and so on – in a way in which the recipient can *identify* the expression as an instance of responsive regard toward the characteristics responded to, thereby contributing to the development of the recipient's practical relation-to-self. So, Bob expresses his positive attitude – moral respect – toward Sally through the action of allowing her to exercise her right to choose her own career; that respect is in response to her autonomy, her capacity to choose for herself in the light of her own convictions; and, Sally can comprehend that action as a positive attitude from her father in a way that contributes to the development of her own self-respect.

We can now take up a first issue of ambiguity; whether we should understand acts of recognition as *attributing* or as *responding* to the relevant characteristic. On the one hand, if recognition is supposed to have a constitutive role in the recipient's development of self, then it would appear that the recognizer takes the lead here, in some way or another constituting or constructing or determining the positive quality given positive regard. If this *attributive* model is correct, then when Mia esteems Tom, she is in some sense ascribing to Tom those positive characteristics of hard work and achievement, and thereby constituting those characteristics in the first place as characteristics of positive value, as being worthy of appropriate acknowledgment. On the other hand, it would seem that Tom would actually have to display real hard work and achievement in order for the act of recognition to be appropriate. For instance, Mia's expression of esteem would simply be misplaced if Tom is lazy and has not contributed to the departmental report – she would have misperceived Tom's actual characteristics. Thus, if this *responsive* model is correct, successful acts of recognition need to be something like perceptions of the objective characteristics in the recipient that are evaluated. Honneth clearly endorses this second perceptual model, in large part because it is required in order to explain how we can often distinguish successful (true, right, appropriate, adequate) from unsuccessful (false, wrong, inappropriate, inadequate) recognition in terms of whether it is properly responsive to the actual characteristics possessed by persons. This is easily seen in everyday interactions where one person is unjustly disrespected by another: the injustice lies precisely in the fact that the former's actual characteristics have not been given adequate regard by the latter. In the same vein, social struggles over recognition presuppose that there is truth of the matter about an instance misrecognition: some persons are collectively being disrespected because the broader society is not giving due or appropriate regard to some morally significant characteristics or achievements that the disrespected persons objectively possess or have achieved (Ikäheimo and Laitinen 2007: 53ff).

Given this position, however, we are confronted by new puzzles. In endorsing the perceptual model, doesn't Honneth also have to endorse the idea that there are objective values written into the structure of the world just waiting to be perceived, in the same way that, say, there are objective qualities of a robin's feathers that are just waiting to be perceived as red? Is Sally's moral autonomy an objective fact about her that can be correctly or incorrectly perceived in the same way as the size of her feet? The problem is that such an idea of value realism appears to require a peculiar ontology, one no longer credible for a philosophy that sees itself as "post-metaphysical." Honneth's response here is to endorse what he calls "moderate value realism" (Honneth 2002a: 508ff). On the value realism side, there is a sense of the objective correctness of a morally relevant perception of the qualities of another: Sally really is capable of making rational choices for herself, while Sally's four-year-old son really is not. But that realism must be moderated by awareness that moral autonomy is not a natural feature of the world, but a product of our society's particular moral concepts, practices, and institutions. One need only consider that Sally's moral autonomy would not be a positively regarded moral feature of personhood in a medieval nunnery, but would likely be seen as a form of sinful willfulness and self-assertion, especially for women who were categorically not seen as free and equal rights bearers. Therefore, the evaluative properties of persons that recognition responds to are socially constructed. However, in our everyday lives we easily make judgments concerning such properties that have a sense of objectivity because we have been thoroughly socialized into our society's particular lifeworld, its specific constellation of moral values, norms, practices, and institutions. This moral horizon of the lifeworld forms, as Honneth puts its, a kind of second nature for us. The realism of moderate value realism, then, is sociological, not ontological.[16]

Consider another puzzle generated by the perceptual model of recognition. On the analogy with perception, the recipient of recognition must fully possess the relevant characteristics in order for them to be perceived. But if the recipient already has the characteristics, then why does she need the reassurance of another person in order to develop a healthy relation-to-self with respect to that characteristic, as the general theory of recognition claims? If Tom is a hard worker and has achieved, why does he need Mia's esteem in order to develop self-esteem? And if Tom does need Mia's esteem to develop self-esteem, then it seems we have returned to the attributive model of recognition, where Mia's ascription of the qualities to Tom is what is constituting

Tom's esteem-worthy traits and achievements in the first place.[17] Here, Honneth in a sense splits the difference between the perceptual and the attributive models, agreeing with the perceptual that Tom must possess the characteristics in order for them to be esteemed by Mia, and agreeing with the attributive that Tom can only fully and positively identify himself with those characteristics when Mia (or someone else) actually esteems him on account of them.

> With regard to the capabilities to which, in virtue of my culture's normative presuppositions, I am entitled as a subject, I can really affirm only those capabilities that are reinforced as valuable through the recognitional behaviour of those with whom I interact. To this extent, an explanatory model of this sort actually represents a middle position between pure constructivism [the attributive model] and mere representationalism [the perceptual model]: although we make manifest, in our acts of recognition, only those evaluative qualities that are already present in the relevant individual, it is only as a result of our reactions that he comes to be in a position to be truly autonomous, because he is then able to identify with his capabilities. (Honneth 2002a: 510)

To put the point in the terms developed by Arto Laitinen, recognition theory must account for two correct insights at once: the *adequacy* insight (e.g., that Mia's esteem of Tom is successful only if that esteem responds truthfully to his hard work) and the *mutuality* insight (e.g., that success also requires that Tom acknowledges and internalizes Mia's positive attitudes toward him) (Laitinen 2010).

To summarize a complex of issues, we can say that Honneth attempts to steer carefully between perceptualism and attributivism by endorsing aspects of both positions, while avoiding pitfalls of absolutizing either position. The key to this delicate maneuvering is to acknowledge that both the recognizer and the recognized have crucial roles in successful acts of recognition. On the recognizer side, successful regard of others involves the expression of evaluative attitudes that are truthfully responsive to the normative characteristics objectively possessed by the recognized (and picked out by one's society as morally relevant). On the recognized side, successful recognition requires a positive grasp of the act as an expression of normatively positive attitudes in such a way that those attitudes can be identified with and thereby contribute to the development of a healthy practical relation-to-self. Both recognizer and recognized are in the driver's seat, as it were, for successful recognition: both have a constitutive role in the dialectic between other-regarding attitudes and practical relation-to-self.

3

Social Struggles for Recognition

3.1 Conflicts of Interest vs Moral Conflicts

When we ask the question, "What are the root causes of social conflicts?," one dominant type of answer is that individuals struggle against one another in order to secure their own share of scarce resources that will serve their own personal interests. This idea is at the heart of a whole tradition of analyzing social conflicts in terms of conflicts of interest, a tradition Honneth traces back to Machiavelli and sees coming to fruition in the social contract theory of Thomas Hobbes.

Recall Hobbes's basic picture of the state of nature, that situation where there is no overarching political power that can coerce individuals into acting according to legal rules. In the state of nature, there is a diversity of individuals, each of whom has a set of desires particular to them: some like good food, some like adventure, some are social, some prefer solitude, and so on. As adult humans with some experience of trying to secure their desires, all are equipped with basically equivalent powers of reason. Rationality here has a specific meaning for Hobbes: the ability to calculate the most likely and efficient way to achieve one's given goals. So if one desires good food (or adventure, or...), there are a number of possible avenues to getting it (foraging, harvesting, stealing), and reason's job is to figure out which of those ways is the best. There is, however, not enough stuff to satisfy everyone's desires. Thus rationality will soon reveal to each that he is in competition with other for those scarce resources, and that each is vulnerable to the attacks of others. Given these basic premises – the diversity of desires, instrumental rationality, scarcity of resources, and competitive vulnerability – Hobbes deduces that the state of nature will inevitably devolve into a state of war, in particular, a state of war where each individual is perpetually pitted against every single other individual. Some will invade to gain others' stuff, some to preempt others from pillaging, and a few to gain glory over others.[1] The conflict is, in short, a conflict of interests, one over scarce resources necessary to secure individuals' own self-preservation.

If we transfer this basic Hobbesian model to existing society, where there are established political states with coercive powers and economic institutions that distribute the burdens and benefits of social cooperation, then we quickly arrive at the dominant type of explanation for conflicts between different groups within society. Individuals are still in strategic competition with others in a zero-sum game for scarce resources necessary for self-preservation, even if everyday life does not involve the perpetual threat of physical violence, is not "solitary, poor, nasty, brutish, and short." Further, the institutionalized mechanisms of both the state and the economy distribute power and money, that is, all-purpose means to fulfilling whatever particular desires one has. Individuals seeking to gain power and money will tend to get more when they organize into groups with similar interests. Thus conflicts in society will be between major interest groups strategically competing in the zero-sum game for scarce resources. According to Honneth, this conflict-of-interest model of social struggles is the dominant model in twentieth-century social science, whether one is considering the materialism of "scientific" Marxism, the perpetually renewed varieties of social Darwinism, the moralization of the model in utilitarianism, Weber's model of modernity centered on purposive-rational action, or, neoclassical economics and its rational choice epigones.

Honneth also detects, however, what he calls "traces" of an alternative theory of social conflict, one that focuses to a greater extent on moral conflicts between groups. This alternative model, at its core, sees social struggles as arising where the ideals implicit in the moral grammar of society are not matched in the reality of actual social relations. Conflicts then arise in reaction to moral feelings of violated expectations, where those violations are seen as resulting from distorted relations of recognition anchored in certain social practices, understandings, and institutions, and where individuals and groups struggle to overcome misrecognition or nonrecognition by reworking the recognition order of the present society. Consider, for instance, historical struggles by American blacks for equal civil rights or conflicts over racial apartheid in South Africa. While in both cases people of color surely suffered deprivations of material resources of money and power because of the racialized social structures – as the conflict-of-interest model would highlight – there is nevertheless something wrong with a picture that focuses only on fights in a zero-sum game over scarce resources. More importantly, the core of the justifiable outrage at both systems centered on the evident disrespect, denigration, and contempt that American and South African practices, understandings, and institutions expressed toward nonwhites. The heart of the problem was a moral problem – a disconnect between egalitarian ideals and the actual recognition orders of the two societies – and the motives for struggle centered more on the violation of legitimate expectations than the acquisitive desire for more resources.

Honneth finds elements of such a moral theory of social struggle in a variety of places. The early writings of Marx, especially those concerned with alienated labor, indicate how a society's specific division of labor can be a medium for intersubjective relations of recognition or misrecognition. The writings of Georges Sorel highlight the way in which negative moral emotions, feelings that arise in response to violations of normative expectations, can serve as a motor or catalyst for the formation of groups committed to social struggle to transform the present. Sartre's political writings (as opposed to his formal philosophical work) analyze anti-Semitic and colonial relations of domination and oppression in terms of distorted, asymmetric relations of reciprocal recognition, and intriguingly suggest that certain social pathologies arise from the necessity of simultaneous recognition and denial of recognition in such relations. E. P. Thompson and Barrington Moore, English social historians of the working class, eschew the standard conflict-of-interest model of class antagonisms to show how even economic struggles are shot through with moral motives for resistance, based in particular on a sense of what class members deserve but are not receiving. Despite these traces of an alternative theory of social struggle, however, Honneth argues that mainstream social science has generally ignored their key insight: that there is an internal connection between a sense of moral violation of legitimate expectations and the emergence of social movements. Focusing instead on "objective" material interests as the motor for social conflict, social science has missed the way in which many conflicts arise from moral reactions to disturbed intersubjective relations.

We can summarize the differences between the conflict of interests and the recognitional models of social struggles in a set of contrasts. Whereas conflicts over interests are at bottom about self-preservation, struggles for recognition are about normative self-identity: what is at stake in the former are one's objective interests which are threatened with material deprivations, in the latter moral expectations are at stake and their violation incites feelings of outrage. Interest-based conflicts then concern the objective conditions individuals need to survive, whereas recognition struggles concern the social conditions individuals need to secure their personal integrity. The object of interest conflicts is generally material resources, where those resources are both scarce – there is not enough to satisfy all desires – and rivalrous: if one person (or group) gets a given resource, then it is not available for others. The object of recognition struggles is a form of moral regard where there is a lack of or distortion in the due regard given to some – for instance, not all get equal civil rights – but due regard need not be rivalrous – for instance, according civil rights to one group does not exclude other groups from getting equal rights. Hence conflicts of interest concern the patterns of distribution of material goods whereas moral conflicts concern the recognition order of a society. In short, the former models social relations as essentially atomistic. Self-interested individuals encounter other persons in the same way they encounter other natural phenomena – as help or hindrance to the individual's private desires – and instrumental rationality is employed to calculate the most efficient way to manipulate the environment (whether natural or social) to secure self-serving benefits. The moral account of conflicts, by contrast, starts with an essentially intersubjective model of social relations. Interactions between agents are essentially different than interactions with tornados or cats, for only other recognizing agents can engage in the mutual interactions that involve normative behavioral expectations, expectations that form the basis for legitimate claims on one another, and only other moral agents can give one the kind of recognition that is necessary for securing one's own practical identity. The kind of reasoning involved in the two kinds of conflict also differs: instrumental, means–ends rationality for the one, moral judgments about appropriate relationships for the other. Finally, the political visions of the point of the state also differ: the interest model sees the state as the medium for an instrumentally rational establishment of power; the recognition model understands the state as a vehicle for establishing the social conditions of individual freedom and self-realization.

It is important to note a few caveats here. First, Honneth is not claiming that *all* social conflicts should be understood as moral conflicts. Many social conflicts do in fact revolve around material deprivation and competition over the allocation of scarce resources. For example, riots over the scarcity and price of food are a persistent feature of the modern social world, from the mid-seventeenth century riots in Moscow over high taxes on salt to the Algerian riots in 2011 over the rapid increase in the prices of staple foods. Such conflicts clearly follow the logic of conflicts over the material conditions for self-preservation. Second, Honneth is not claiming that all social conflicts *exclusively* fall into one category or the other. Many particular social conflicts have varying mixes of interest-based and recognition-based elements. For example, the famous sanitation workers strike in Memphis, Tennessee in 1968 involved both claims to safe working conditions sparked by recent job-related deaths – thus invoking the objective conditions necessary for self-preservation – and demands to end race-based discrimination by supervisors – thus invoking the social conditions necessary for equal self-respect. Third, Honneth argues that in any particular social conflict or struggle being studied, it is an open question whether material interests or moral expectations or some combination of both are doing the real work. In the end, social analysis cannot settle such questions theoretically, but must look at the empirical evidence. Nevertheless, he does want to claim that important social struggles cannot all be reduced to the logic of atomistic conflict between strategic individuals, and so social analysis must remain open to a different kind of social conflict, one in which the recognition order of a society and the practical identities of socialized individuals are at stake.

3.2 Social Struggles for Recognition

In order to appreciate the breadth and diversity of struggles for recognition, it will help to see further examples before turning to Honneth's schema for explaining them. There are three different types of social struggles recognition that correspond to the three different forms of practical identity: struggles for the social conditions necessary for self-confidence, for self-respect, and for self-esteem.[2] Although any particular social movement often does press claims along more than one axis of recognition at once, while often also including claims to the satisfaction of bare interests, it may be helpful to abstract from the messier realities of actual social conflicts. We can then categorize in a rough and ready way – aware of oversimplifications and potential distortions – many particular social recognition conflicts into one of the three forms.[3] Such an overview of the breadth and variety of social struggles that can be productively analyzed by Honneth's recognition theory should also help to dispel the exclusive association of the politics of recognition with multiculturalism. While Honneth agrees with theorists like Charles Taylor and Iris Young that multiculturalism and the politics of identity are indeed important forms of recognition struggle, Honneth's broader model encompasses a much wider scope, ranging across anti-violence, civil rights, and economic redistribution struggles, and beyond.

3.2.1 Three examples

Consider first struggles over the social conditions necessary for basic self-confidence. Here social struggles have been waged to redefine and delegitimize forms of violence and abuse that had been accepted as part of normal everyday practices and institutions. The moral claim in each case is that the particular form of violence or abuse targeted is so destabilizing to an individual's trust in the stability of the social world and confidence in oneself that it leads to a particularly cruel attack on the personal integrity of the individual. The harm is not simply the physical pain involved – though this may be severe and of real moral seriousness – but also that the abuse serves to undermine the individual's very ability to maintain an intact ego identity over time. A paradigm form of this disrespect is rape. While we might recognize rape in particular cases as cruel and damaging, some degree of collective interpretation and collective social struggle will be required to transform an individual crime into a social struggle. For example, for hundreds of years, there was an exception to criminal rape laws in common-law jurisdictions whereby husbands could not be convicted of raping their wives. Through determined feminist struggle and focused legal activism, the marital exception to rape laws has finally been overcome within the last forty years.[4] Think also of the recent focus in the last two decades on defining, highlighting, condemning, and prosecuting the use of systematic rape of civilian populations as a weapon of war. Of course, such struggles are not waged only through the law, nor only aimed at securing legal protections. The cultural conditions that contribute to the acceptance or minimization of the rape of women, sexual minorities, and subalterns are also crucial. For more than thirty years, feminists around the world have sought to heighten awareness of rape culture through events like "Take Back the Night" or "Reclaim the Night" marches,[5] through passionate and persistent advocacy for rape victims, and through the new concept of "date rape" which redefined rape to include rapes committed by acquaintances, not just strangers. The redefinition and reconceptualization of "wife beating" as "domestic violence" – along with pointed social activism – has also had a profound effect on the set of normative expectations concerning legitimate behavior between intimate partners.

Similar developments in social struggles concerned with forms of torture, violence, and targeted abuse are evident. In the United States, high-profile mob violence by whites against blacks extends from before the outbreak of the Civil War in the nineteenth century, through the Reconstruction and Jim Crow eras of the late nineteenth and early twentieth centuries of targeted violence and lynchings, and on through the coordinated violence of reactionaries against the civil rights movement of the 1950s and 1960s. In each of these cases, the violence had crucial social and expressive components that distinguished it from routine interpersonal aggression: it was organized by one social group against a distinct social group and it was intended to express misrecognition in its rawest form. Aiming to terrorize and subjugate blacks (and other nonwhites), the violence had a specific moral meaning: it expressed the idea that nonwhites were not worthy of the most basic consideration given to humans as humans, not deserving of the basic bodily and emotional integrity required for the maintenance of basic self-confidence. The manifold of social struggles against racialized violence across the years, waged simultaneously through cultural, legal, and institutional means, sought to reconstruct a seriously distorted recognition order so that social practices and institutions would come more into line with implicit ideals of reciprocal recognition. More recently, social struggles against violence targeted at sexual minorities ("gay bashing") have followed the same moral logic. At the international level, successful social struggles have changed international norms of state behavior such that torture by states against persons has gone from behavior routinely expected of states to action prohibited by international treaty adopted and ratified in the 1980s.[6] A crucial component of these struggles is the move to broaden the legal definitions and cultural understandings of state-sanctioned and state-inflicted torture to include forms of emotional and psychological abuse, thereby acknowledging that the moral problem at the heart of torture is not so much the physical harm but the threat to personal integrity. Finally, a similar expansion of the understanding of illegitimate violence is evident in disparate social movements against various forms of child abuse – from nineteenth-century movements against child labor to more recent movements against corporal punishment in the home and at school – as well as peer-on-peer abuse such as bullying. All of these examples and more, I would submit, presuppose an acknowledgment of the internal connection between individuals' personal integrity and social practices of intersubjective regard (and disregard), an internal connection that is at the heart of Honneth's theories of both individual and social struggles for recognition.

Social struggles for the conditions necessary for self-respect are perhaps more familiar as moral claims for equal human freedom since the story of the expansion of universal legal rights is a central part of our everyday narratives of social progress. I mention only a few episodes in a long history. There is a traditional scholarly history of the expansion of rights powerfully captured by T. H. Marshall and relied upon by Honneth that highlights the eighteenth-century expansion of civil rights, the nineteenth-century expansion of political rights, and the twentieth-century expansion of social rights (Marshall 1950). Through social struggle, legal rights became increasingly attached to individuals, and their content began to expand beyond basic rule-of-law rights concerning fair trial and treatment by authorities. Crucial here was the establishment of individual rights to private property, a development absolutely essential to the emergence of early mercantilist forms of proto-capitalism in the sixteenth century (Heins 2009). By the end of the eighteenth century, Enlightenment ideas had progressed to the point that the promise of universal human rights was not only an idealistic aspiration, but had taken on some institutional heft in the new states resulting from the French and American revolutions. If the eighteenth century witnessed struggles for the establishment of universal civil rights – at least for males of the correct religion, ethnicity, nationality, and wealth – the nineteenth century witnessed manifold struggles for the establishment of equal political rights for individuals. Not only did persons deserve legal protection of their basic freedoms, but they also demanded an equal say in the forms of government over them as a requirement of their equal autonomy. And, as time progressed, the scope of the persons deserving of equal suffrage and other political participation rights also expanded: from property-owning males to all adult males, to women, and on to ethnic, racial, national, and religious minorities. Along with the expansion of the scope of rights bearers of civil and political rights, the twentieth century witnessed struggles for a new form of rights: social rights. The underlying idea is that society does not fully recognize the equal autonomy of each if some are arbitrarily subjected to the risks created by persistent boom–bust cycles of the capitalist economy. As the US President Franklin Roosevelt insisted, freedom cannot be realized if one is not free from want and free from fear. Finally, the end of the last century and the beginning of the present have been witness to the rising doctrines of universal human rights owed to all persons, regardless of their citizenship or place of residence, and correlative responsibilities to protect those rights incumbent on states and the international community. Thus states have obligations – at least in theory, if not yet in practice – not only toward their own citizens but also toward those they are capable of protecting from human rights abuses.

This general historical view of the expansion of rights categories, from civil to political to social to human, might seem at first glance to be simply a case of ideals being worked out in practice. But this general view hides the actual social struggles and serious conflicts involved in realizing such ideals of expanded recognition in the actual legal orders of societies. More of the flavor of these social struggles comes from thinking about, say, feminist fights over a hundred and fifty years to undo the different legal doctrines of coverture, to achieve the rights to hold private property, to divorce abusive husbands, to vote and hold public office, to control one's reproductive capacities, and so on.[7] In a similar vein, think about the degree of conflict and resistance to establishing equal legal rights for whites and nonwhites in various countries throughout the twentieth century. Overcoming the diverse forms of legal apartheid in these countries involved not only moral appeals to the equal dignity of each person, regardless of race or ethnicity, but also persistent, coordinated social movements acting collectively to overcome discriminatory law. Consider finally the relatively recent struggles for equal legal recognition of gays, lesbians, and bisexuals. From nondiscrimination to marital equality to family freedom, struggles by sexual minorities have taken center stage in the expansion of the scope of equal legal treatment, even as they still have to overcome fierce social reactions against their claims to symmetrical recognition. According to

Honneth, all of these diverse rights struggles can be understood as struggles for adequate recognition, specifically for the social conditions necessary for the development of self-respect through the legal regard of the inherent autonomy of persons as free and equal.

Turning now to the third form of social struggle – movements to establish the social conditions for healthy self-esteem – it becomes more difficult to discern general patterns across different societies. This is because, as Honneth stresses, individuals gain a sense of self-esteem for socially recognized traits, abilities, and achievements, and this esteem-based social recognition is itself tied to the specific horizon of values within a society or social group, a horizon that defines which traits, abilities, and achievements are to be esteemed and to what degree. Given the value pluralism of the modern world, where there are many competing and only partially overlapping horizons of values, esteem struggles will be more varied and often incomparable across these differences. This pluralism also means that social struggles concerning the bases of self-esteem will likely be more unsettled and more contested over time than confidence- and respect-based struggles. Nevertheless, an examination of forms of esteem disrespect – paradigmatically insult and cultural denigration – can reveal a few clear examples of recent social struggles on esteem's terrain.

Consider struggles for multicultural and multinational policies that seek to accommodate ethnic and national differences within a diverse, pluralistic national polity. Using the example of political conflicts over bilingual and bicultural education policies in Canada, Taylor has famously analyzed such recent identity-based forms of conflict as recognition struggles. His key insight, consistent with Honneth's theory, is that the denigration of a culture or way of life is not just an arbitrary verbal barb but can represent a threat to one's personal integrity because one's practical sense-of-self is constitutively tied to intersubjective recognition, and such social recognition is itself tied to the evaluative frameworks of one's culture. Cultural denigration of one's way of life, then, threatens one's identity: "Nonrecognition or misrecognition can inflict harm, can be a form of oppression, imprisoning someone in a false, distorted, and reduced mode of being" (Taylor 1994: 25). Struggles for the political accommodation of cultural, ethnic, religious, and national diversity within a polity, then, can be interpreted both as ways of combating harmful forms of insult and denigration, and as ways of providing the space for the existence of alternative or minority frameworks of value within which individuals may have an equal chance of realizing self-esteem.

Iris Marion Young's powerful indictment of cultural imperialism also evinces the language and logic of esteem-based recognition. For cultural imperialism – where a dominant group's culture and experiences are projected as representative for all members of society

– impairs individuals' ability to establish self-esteem by either marking as deviant or even effacing their social group's own ethical self-understanding. Young's call for a politics of difference where social policies are adopted in order to enable "despised groups [to] seize the means of cultural expression to redefine a positive image of themselves" (Young 1990b: 11) is precisely a call for establishing the socially necessary bases of self-esteem in solidaristically shared forms of ethical life. She connects the need for self-esteem to the intersubjective recognition of both an individual's and an "affinity" group's specificity, precisely because here esteem can only be generated through the solidarity of a group which defines itself through its relationships to and differences from other groups.[8]

Another example of self-esteem politics is the fight by sexual minorities for a space within which gay, lesbian, bisexual, transgender, and transsexual persons can realize alternative forms of intimacy, sexuality, and intersubjectivity, free from hateful insults and degradation. Such self-consciously "queer" politics is not aimed at achieving equal legal rights for sexual minorities – even though this is acknowledged as an important achievement in its own right – nor is it aimed at normalizing sexual minorities by recommending their assimilation into the ethics, expectations, and practices of mainstream "straight" heterosexuality (e.g., Sullivan 1996). The idea is rather more akin to John Stuart Mill's passionate advocacy of diversity in forms of living (Mill 1978): potentials for full individual self-realization are increased where societies do not habitually denigrate and disparage forms of intimacy and intersubjectivity that are out of the mainstream. Michael Warner has made a similar point in arguing explicitly in favor of queer social struggles against the normalizing stigmatization of nonstandard sexual practices and identities (Warner 2000). Queer politics is then based in a claim about the social conditions necessary for individuals to have an equal opportunity to achieve undistorted self-esteem vis-à-vis their sexual practices and identities.

One final set of examples of esteem-based recognition struggles centers around the definition and evaluation of labor. Social conflicts over the definition of productive labor, the cultural valuation of different tasks within the division of labor, and even the differential remuneration of labor are all analyzed by Honneth as struggles over the social bases of self-esteem. So, for instance, attempting to redress the typical gendered division of labor – the division by which work outside the home in the official economy is remunerated, while necessary reproductive labor within the household is unpaid – counts as an esteem-based struggle for Honneth. Feminist struggles over care and housework, typically coded as feminine and overwhelmingly performed by women in a "second shift" (Hochschild and Machung 2003), are clear paradigms of recognition struggles. Likewise, movements attempting to establish equal pay for equal work for both women and men are esteem-based struggles. In fact, many of the demands of the labor movement could be construed as struggles over the social bases of self-esteem.

In one respect, this recognition-based analysis of economic conflicts is not surprising since, according to Honneth, esteem is a form of social recognition that responds to the particular traits, abilities, and achievements of individuals where those individual characteristics are evaluated in the light of their overall contributions to collective projects and forms of life. Labor, whether in the official paid economy or unpaid reproductive labor, is then a fundamental site for the development of self-esteem, the sense that one has made valuable contributions to collectively valued social projects. In another respect, however, it is quite unusual to analyze broad conflicts over labor in terms of the struggle for recognition since the dominant conflict model employed in the social sciences comprehends (paid) labor in terms of competition for scarce resources necessary for self-preservation between atomistic individuals in a zero-sum game. The idea that labor conflicts are about struggles for appropriate interpersonal treatment and symmetrical social regard is simply quite different than the picture painted by the dominant conflict-of-interest model. A fuller treatment of Honneth's analysis of economic struggles is in chapters 5 and 6. In the meantime, we should not lose sight of the fact that labor conflicts, broadly construed, function as one of Honneth's central paradigms of esteem struggles.

3.2.2 The explanatory model

With these examples in hand, we can now turn to Honneth's general explanation of struggles for recognition, keeping in mind contrasts with the typical explanations of conflicts of interest. As a general pattern, recognition struggles start from feelings of disrespect, where individuals' expectations of intersubjective treatment are violated by negative attitudes expressed in social practices and institutions. As we've seen, these violations can be sorted into the three large groups: forms of abuse, torture, and rape; legal exclusion and denial of rights; and insult or denigration of ways of life. Therefore, recognition struggles are motivated by negative moral feelings generated by specific social relations, as opposed to interest-based conflicts which are motivated by a lack of objective resources needed for self-preservation.

These moral feelings must, according to Honneth, point to an "untapped normative surplus" in current relations. To understand this idea, consider that current social relations may well be structured by a particular recognition order – for instance, one that systematically codes minorities as undeserving of equal rights – such that those who feel violated are in fact being given due recognition according to prevailing standards. But, on the other hand, that society's recognition order is deficient by the implicit moral standards built into the logic of recognition relations – in our example, the logic of respect. Thus members of the minority are being duly respected in one sense by being denied equal rights – the sense according to the prevailing recognition order – and they are being disrespected in another sense by being denied equal rights – the sense according to the normative potential of legal recognition relations that has not yet been actualized in law. A social struggle can then make manifest the difference between the extant practices expressing an unequal recognition order and the untapped normative surplus of symmetrical respect-based recognition. Incidentally, this notion of an untapped normative potential also explains an otherwise puzzling phenomenon: namely, that individuals can develop a degree of relevant practical relation-to-self even in the absence of full social recognition. To continue the example, while the broad society is denying minorities the full legal respect that is required for the full development of self-respect, it is the anticipation of full legal respect from the community – an anticipation connected to the untapped normative potential of symmetrical and egalitarian legal relations – that allows individuals to develop some degree of self-respect, even in the face of rights denials from the broader society. In fact, collective political or social activism can itself furnish a secondary motivation for social struggle, beyond the primary one of moral outrage, since participating with others itself has positive effects for one's own self-regard, a self-regard negatively impacted by the broader society's misrecognition. For example, consciousness raising groups function not only to highlight the difference between current moral disrespect and an untapped normative potential, but also to begin to overcome the debilitating effects on participants' personal integrity of that form of social disrespect.

Mere episodic feelings of outrage by a few individuals are of course not enough to spark a collective struggle for recognition. In addition, a number of *social* dimensions must be involved. Different individuals must be able to realize that their own sense of violated moral expectations is relevantly similar to experiences of others and caused by the same factors. For when individual experiences of disrespect are understood as the norm for all members of a certain group and for the same reasons – when disrespect is experienced epidemically – the potential motivation exists for collective political resistance to the structures of society which systematically deny the members of that group the recognition they need for full self-realization. In such a case, then, three different social dimensions of the situation must be brought to light: the group-typical or group-directed nature of the disrespect; the social causes of violated expectations in distorted recognition relations; and a moral interpretation of the situation condemning the violation as a distortion of appropriate social relations.

There is, therefore, a crucial role for innovative semantics in social movements, one that can provide a language of interpretation that transforms what was experienced as private, episodic, individual outrage into public, systematic, and collective moral violations. Consider, for example, the sheer social power unleashed by symbolic interpretive changes. The concept of "racial profiling" is barely more than a decade old in the United States, but, by introducing a moral grammar highlighting group-based disrespect, it transformed routine, episodic, and individual police practices of using the race of persons in making enforcement decisions into morally wrong practices whose institutionalization within policing needed to be rooted out through regulation. An interpretive semantics, carried forward by targeted social activism, helped transform individual moral outrage into a social struggle for recognition. Many examples of successful interpretive reframing are furnished by feminist semantics. Consider the influence of newly introduced conceptual languages when combined with movement activism: sexism, domestic violence, date rape, the second shift, care work, sexual harassment, reproductive freedom, and so on. According to Honneth, there is not nearly such an important role for interpretive semantics in conflicts of interests. While it is true that movements oriented toward increasing their members' share of the material pie must enable those members to see the similarity of their individual situations in order to generate and maintain necessary solidarity, there are not similar requirements for locating the cause of the problem in society's moral order, nor for comprehending the deprivation as a moral injury. It is enough simply to point out the various competing groups in the zero-sum game, and to encourage one's own group to get a bigger share.

Although the main foil of Honneth's theory of social conflict is the Hobbesian model of conflicts of interest, we should not forget that it has important advantages over competing purely philosophical theories of moral conflict as well, such as those implied by Kantianism or utilitarianism. First, recognition theory provides a clear account of the motivational wellsprings that are essential to actually engaging in collective social action intended to improve society. While both Kantianism and utilitarianism tell us that we ought to right social wrongs – by aiming for a kingdom of ends or promoting the general welfare – neither can clearly explain how these abstract "oughts" are anything more than impotent demands. Beyond the demand of abstract morality, why do individuals make sacrifices of their personal interests in order to promote the kingdom of ends or the general welfare? The theory of recognition clearly explains why individuals do so: precisely because of the internal connection between social structures of moral regard and individuals' practical sense-of-self. Thus the connections between moral feelings of violation, the conditions of personal integrity, and social misrecognition serve to anchor the theory's normative aspirations in actual social processes. Recognition theory thereby overcomes the problem of Kantian morality that Hegel astutely critiqued: the problem of theoretical idealism, of the impotent mere "ought." Second, unlike abstract philosophical moralities, recognition theory arises out of, and so significantly mirrors, the everyday moral vocabulary of disrespect that is so crucial to actual social protests and movements. It does not attempt to analyze social conflicts according to a foreign philosophical language. Third, it holds out the prospect of a distinct kind of role for theory as a helpmate to social movements. Because interpretive semantics are so crucial to the formation and maintenance of social movements – in identifying hurt feelings as violated social expectations, in locating the social causes of some violations, and in teasing out the moral logic of the particular kind of recognition violation – theory can contribute to the morally powerful language that movements employ in making claims for change to the broader society.

These various advantages all come from anchoring theory immanently in social reality. As we have seen in 1.3.3, bringing theory and practice together was crucial to the first generation of critical theory, and Honneth believes that his theory of intersubjective recognition carries on this central tradition more successfully than other alternative social and political theories – including Habermas's alternative critical theory based in linguistic pragmatics. As we will see in chapter 6, it also forms a central motivation for steering critical theory more toward its roots in Hegel rather than its roots in Kant.[9]

3.2.3   Three moral logics

We've seen how Honneth provides a social theory explaining many signal social conflicts, but more needs to be said about the moral logic that forms the backbone of a social movement's claims to the larger society. At the most general level, social struggles are potentially normatively justifiable on the grounds that systematic forms of disrespect impede the mutual recognition required for the maintenance and reproduction of personal integrity. Hence recognition struggles make claims to social conditions adequate for healthy self-realization across the different forms of practical self-relation. But there are quite different kinds of social conditions that are relevant to self-realization, and the provision of them must be justified in different terms. Here again, the three-part analysis of recognition points the way to one of Honneth's most useful insights: that although all of these different conflicts can be understood in terms of moral relations of recognition, the three different types of struggle make different kinds of moral claims, with different scopes, context sensitivity, and burdens of justification. Once we see these differences, many of the apparent tensions and dilemmas within social movements for expanded justice might be resolved or at least ameliorated.

Take first claims for the social conditions necessary for the development of basic self-confidence. The key claim of struggles against the culture and practices of torture, abuse, or rape is that individuals' basic self-confidence is vulnerable to violation by others through extreme physical and emotional degradation. Insofar as one's basic trust in the constancy of the intersubjectively shared world is shattered, one is fundamentally unable to maintain trust in oneself, establish a stable identity, or participate adequately in social relations, let alone fully realize oneself. Precisely because the degradation of one's own body involves the destruction, from the outside, of one's basic form of relation-to-self and because, without this basic self-confidence, individuals cannot maintain a stable identity, everyone deserves an environment free from abuse and violence simply on account of their personhood. Hence the claims of struggles for the social conditions of self-confidence are quite strong. It doesn't matter what society or legal system one is in, what the particular values of that society are, how old or young one is, whether one has developed particular traits or made distinctive social contributions or even has the capacity for autonomous action – torture, rape, and abuse are wrong. To put the claim in schematic form: x is a person; self-confidence is a necessary precondition for any chance of self-realization; x's basic self-confidence is vulnerable to abuse; therefore, x deserves protection from social conditions undermining the development of basic self-confidence.

Struggles for the social bases of self-respect, by contrast, make a different kind of moral claim. When some individuals are denied legal rights that others have been granted, it impairs those individuals' ability to develop a full sense of self-respect as autonomous persons equal to others in society. That means, of course, that such claims are tied to particular legal contexts. For instance, claims to equal social rights such as retirement insurance have traction only where the government already grants retirement insurance rights to some members; women's claim to equal voting rights only have traction where some men have voting rights. On the other hand, claims to equal legal rights do have a universalist core: where some members are granted rights, all who are in the relevantly same social situation must be granted equal rights. Morally arbitrary legal discrimination undermines members' ability to regard themselves as having equal dignity with others, as deserving of full self-respect on a par with others. Therefore, while claims for the expansion of legally just relations are universalist in abstracting from arbitrary individual particularities like race, sex, nationality, and so on, they are context-specific insofar as the

determinate set of rights enacted in any given society is tied to the
history of legal struggles in that society. Recall also that there are two
different ways in which rights become expanded over time: through
greater inclusion of persons in existing rights and through expansion
of the catalog of rights. Existing rights become more inclusive as previously excluded groups struggle to be granted rights that others already
have. New rights are granted as claims that they are indeed necessary
social conditions for full and equal autonomy become accepted and
institutionalized in a society. We can summarize the schema of such
moral claims as follows: x is a member of a given legal community; x
has the relevant rights-bearing characteristics; x is denied rights necessary for the full development of self-respect (either through arbitrary
discrimination or insufficient rights); the denial of rights to x undermines the ability to achieve full self-respect; therefore, x must be
granted the rights currently denied. Note that much more needs to be
said in any particular case to justify such claims. For example, some
particular account of why the denial is arbitrary will need to be given,
or some detailed analysis of how a proposed right is necessary to full
and equal autonomy will have to be provided.

Struggles for the social conditions necessary for the development of
self-esteem raise even more complex moral claims. Since self-esteem is
realized through the intersubjective recognition of one's unique traits,
abilities, and contributions by those who share one's horizon of values,
the claim to be esteemed is inextricably bound up with the interpretive
understanding of a specific ethical community. Just as an extreme contrast, consider the different esteem given to self-abnegation versus
ostentation in ascetic religious communities versus thespian communities. This makes it clear that esteem for individuals is constitutively
connected to a specific ethical community. But in modern, diverse, and
pluralistic societies, there are many different acceptable ethical ways of
life, with different comprehensive doctrines and quite distinct constellations of values against which evaluative assessments of esteem or
disesteem are made. That means that it is simply structurally impossible for an individual to expect to be regarded with equal esteem by
all of society's members: monks are not going to value the dandy, and
actors will not esteem self-effacing humility. Furthermore, esteem is
essentially differential and responsive to individual particularity: not
everyone deserves esteem in the same way or in the same degree.
Those with remarkable virtue and notable achievements merit positive
evaluation that is greater than those without either virtue or achievements. Thus one cannot categorically demand esteem; one can, however,
demand an equal opportunity to be esteemed and so an equal opportunity to develop self-esteem if in fact one's traits, abilities, and achievements warrant such. By the same token, merely having the feeling that

one has been disesteemed does not by itself warrant a justified claim to recognition relations that would make one feel better.

For these reasons, social struggles for the conditions of esteem cannot be universal claims made to the society as a whole that each individual deserves unconditional esteem simply by virtue of being a person or a member of a legal community. Here we can take our clue from the negative forms of esteem-based recognition: the forms of disrespect here are typically denigration of particular ways of life, insult of specific comprehensive doctrines, or cultural imperialism that claims one way of life as superior to all others. When groups struggle against such disrespect, they are not demanding that others share their particular values or ways of life – they are not demanding that everyone adopt their own scale of estimable traits and achievements. Rather, they are demanding that their community's ethical way of life be accepted by other groups as one among many acceptable and potentially worthy ways of life.

The justification of claims for expanded esteem will involve, then, convincing others who do not share one's vision of the good life that there is something worthwhile and meaningful in one's way of life, and that one cannot fully realize oneself while this way of life is systematically denigrated in the broader culture. Note that the claim is *not* that other communities of value should recognize one's own horizon of value as worthy for *them*, but only that one's horizon of values is, in some sense, a viable form of life that creates conditions for reciprocal relations of esteem within it. Convincing a majority that a minority way of life should not be denigrated involves showing, first, that slurs on that way of life negatively impact the ability of individuals living within it to develop a healthy sense of self-esteem and, second, that the minority way of life provides the enabling conditions for the full self-realization for its members. Of course, as Honneth repeatedly insists, this latter claim will depend on the crucial proviso that the way of life under consideration does not negatively impact the ability of those who identify with it to develop both self-confidence and self-respect. So, for instance, a community of value cannot selectively deny physical protection or legal rights to some of its members – even if it provides the evaluative horizon for esteem – since this would impair their ability to realize self-confidence and self-respect.[10] Again, what the denigrated group needs to convince others of is *not* that their particular way of life is worthy, valuable, or "true" for all persons, but only that it is one viable form of life that articulates an evaluative horizon within which individuals can develop and realize their own self-esteem. Because everyone deserves an equal opportunity to develop self-esteem, everyone also deserves an environment free from the denigration of their legitimate way of life.

There are a few complexities here which warrant further attention. First, some groups do in fact proselytize for the supreme worthiness and indeed truth of their own way of life for all persons.[11] But this is then a claim about the universality of ethical values and the one proper understanding of the good life – a claim quite different from the more limited one for the cessation of group denigration and the institutionalization of pluralistic tolerance that it requires. This is no longer a claim about the necessary social conditions for the development of self-esteem, but instead a claim about which substantive values are ultimately best or most worthy. So there is an important difference between esteem-based social struggles for recognition and social struggles for the universal esteem of one form of ethical life – even as this distinction is not always honored in the heat and rhetoric of everyday social conflicts.

Second, it is crucial to see that the object of esteem claimed in social recognition struggles is the individual person, not the group one belongs to or one's way of life or comprehensive doctrine. Ethical communities of value provide the necessary social conditions for the development of an individual's self-esteem. Ethical communities are not themselves the proper object of esteem. Rather, they provide the background of shared interpretations and evaluations against which an individual's particular accomplishments and abilities can be judged as valuable. Thus the claim in esteem-based social struggles is not that one's own community and its values should be seen as equally worthy for all the members of the broader society, but that one's communities and its values should not be systematically denigrated because they provide a viable esteem-engendering structure for the individuals who identify themselves with that community and its values.

The complexity of these various distinctions, and the ineliminable contextual and hermeneutical aspects they involve, give rise to much of the highly contested nature of contemporary "cultural politics."[12] Nevertheless, we can summarize the claim of esteem-based social recognition in schematic form: x is a member of a community of shared values y; y is a legitimate and viable esteem-engendering community; the values of y are the yardstick against which assessments of esteem for x are made; insult and denigration of y blocks the equal opportunity of x to develop a healthy sense of self-esteem; all persons deserve an equal opportunity for developing self-esteem through social esteem; therefore x deserves an environment free from disrespect of y through denigration or cultural imperialism.

I claimed earlier that identifying these different logics can help sort out tensions and dilemmas in current social controversies. Perhaps an example will help also bring things down from the heights of abstraction. Consider first a diverse set of social struggles waged by gay, lesbian, transgender, and transsexual persons over the last forty years.

At a most basic level, sexual minorities have been subject to group-specific violence and horrific abuse, often not only condoned by police and other authorities but actually carried out by them. One central goal of lesbian, gay, bisexual, and transgender (LGBT) social movements has been simply to end such targeted violence and abuse, so that sexual minorities will not be impeded in the full development of healthy basic self-confidence. The moral claim to the straight world is forthright and clear – anyone's basic psychological integrity is vulnerable to destabilization through violence, abuse, or torture – and there has not been much difficulty achieving acceptance of the basic moral argument. The central focus of activism has instead been on making the broader community aware of the prevalence and variety of different kinds of "gay-bashing," trusting that the moral claim against such abuse is more or less obvious. This explains the importance in the United States, for instance, of public memorializations of violent events from the Stonewall riots of 1971, to the killing of Harvey Milk in 1978, to the killing of Matthew Shepherd in 1998.

The logic of rights struggles is different. While sexual minorities struggle for the same rights routinely granted to sexual majorities, which particular rights are involved is different in different legal systems. In the United States, the last forty years have witnessed remarkable successes for LGBT social movements in the domain of extending equal legal rights. Movements for equal rights with respect to employment, housing, military service, child rearing, marriage, immigration, and so on have all made remarkable forward progress in a short space of time. In each case, the basic moral claim is one already very familiar to the broader society: the dignity of each as a free and equal person is recognized through equal legal rights and each has a claim to the social conditions necessary for full self-respect. While it is clear that the battles are far from over and that many areas of arbitrary legal discrimination still exist, the direction and dynamics seem clear. In the end, despite the resistance and reaction of certain segments of the population, the moral logic of the extension of rights appears irresistible; it is a matter of time, politics, and effort.

The logic of esteem struggles is different yet again. What social movements have claimed here is that the persistent insults, slurs, and denigration of sexual minorities, coupled with a culture suffused with heteronormativity – cultural imperialism by the straight community – make it impossible for nonheterosexuals to have an equal opportunity to develop self-esteem. Despite ungrounded paranoia to the contrary, the claim of such anti-denigration struggles is not that everyone should become gay or that there is a set of homosexual values that everyone ought to accept. The claim is, rather, that a culture that systematically deprecates ethical ways of life associated with LGBT persons is a culture that destroys the equal opportunity for self-esteem by attacking viable and legitimate esteem-engendering communities. This is a different – and more complex – kind of claim to make than that concerning legal discrimination. It is no surprise, then, that such movements have a harder road in making the case, nor that success seems much less certain given persistent reactionary forces in societies that would rather stifle diversity in general. While there seems to be a general acceptance of the idea that insults and slurs against sexual minorities are problematic, it has been more challenging to get the broader society to understand the variety, depth, and harmfulness of particular insults and stereotypes, and perhaps more challenging still to make straight society aware of its heteronormativity.

So while all of these struggles involve the claims and social activism of LGBT persons, they are different kinds of recognition struggles, with different moral claims made on society, different justificatory burdens, targeting different social practices and structures, and aiming for different types of social change. Furthermore, such recognition struggles have a fundamentally different logic than that pictured by the conflict-of-interest model. This explains why, for instance, criticisms of struggles for the extension of marriage to gay and lesbian couples in vaguely economic terms fall so wide of the mark. Despite the rhetoric of "devaluing marriage," the gaining of equal rights by some is distinctly not at the expense of others since rights are not scarce, rivalrous goods necessary for self-preservation that are fought over by self-seeking individuals in a zero-sum game. Marriage is not a contested resource in the Hobbesian struggle of each against all; it is a structure of intersubjective relations that expresses a certain form of moral regard (or disregard) for those who can (or cannot) participate in it, and that is constitutively tied to individuals' potential for healthy and undistorted forms of personal integrity. Honneth's theory of recognition gives us powerful resources for making politically necessary distinctions between conflicts of interest and struggles for recognition, and between the three different forms of social recognition.[13]

3.2.4 The formal conception of ethical life

Honneth's account of the moral logic of recognition has a theoretical payoff as well: it allows him to put forward a "formal conception of ethical life" with a distinctive place in the landscape of contemporary practical philosophy. Recall that Honneth is primarily interested in articulating a social philosophy, as distinguished from the more common and narrower projects of moral philosophy or political philosophy. That is to say, the aim is to develop a theory that can address questions about the social conditions necessary for individual well-being, as opposed to addressing questions of individual obligation and right action as moral philosophy does, or questions of the state's legitimacy and function as political philosophy does. A necessary part of that social theory is a set of normative standards of undistorted or healthy social relations, to be used to gauge social progress and evaluate potential social pathologies. We need some picture or account of the social relations we ought to be striving for – at least a sketch of the contours of an anticipatory utopia – in order to render the social theory more than a mere description of reality, in order to be a normatively imbued social theory oriented toward human emancipation (Benhabib 1986).

Because Honneth takes the fundamental aim or purpose of social relations of recognition to be the facilitation of individual autonomy in a broad sense – the self-realization of individual personality – the normative standards for critical social theory must be formed around this central modern idea of human well-being. Thus Honneth's "formal conception of ethical life" consists of "the entirety of intersubjective conditions that can be shown to serve as necessary preconditions for individual self-realization" (SfR: 173). And, as we have seen in this chapter and the previous one, the various forms and media of intersubjective recognition are precisely those necessary intersubjective conditions of self-realization. Honneth's formal conception focuses on whether all individuals in society have equal opportunities to realize themselves in noncoercive and undistorted relations of reciprocal recognition.

To put this formal conception in a theoretical context, it may help to contrast it with rival contemporary theories. Like liberal and proceduralist theories inspired by Kant, such as those put forward by Habermas or Rawls, Honneth's theory prioritizes individual autonomy as the keystone value of modern life. As he puts it in his most recent book: "As if by magical attraction, all modern ethical ideals have been placed under the spell of freedom" (FR: 15). However, Honneth's formal conception is broader than Kant's moral deontology or contemporary political proceduralism since it goes beyond moral duties, owed categorically to all on a universal basis, or universally justified legal rights. It also encompasses particularistic obligations we have to concrete others in intimate relations of love and friendship and includes at least a structural account of the social relations required for self-realization in the light of substantive ethical values. As we'll see further in 6.2, Honneth also endorses a much richer conception of individual autonomy than that analyzed by Kant, one inspired instead by Hegel's account of the many dimensions of modern freedom. So Honneth's theory goes beyond a narrow form of practical philosophy that focuses only on what we morally or legally owe to others to encompass practical issues concerning what persons need (love and emotional support) and what persons find valuable (achievements measured against particular standards of esteemed social contributions).

This broader reach encompasses, then, matters of the good life. In this respect, Honneth's theory is more akin to teleological practical philosophy such as Aristotle's virtue ethics or contemporary communitarianism: the justification of normative claims about how society ought to be is ultimately grounded in the determinate goal of individual human flourishing. But it is a much thinner theory than virtue ethics or various forms of communitarianism since it does not recommend one hierarchy of virtues or one concrete form of life as supremely valuable. It is, instead, formal: it intends to specify the general social conditions necessary for a variety of potential avenues for individual self-development, not to recommend any particular form of self-realization. So Honneth's formal conception agrees with deontology and liberal proceduralism in aiming to respect the fact of modern value pluralism and the legitimate diversity of forms of life. However, it doesn't adopt the usual contemporary Kantian strategy for allowing for ethical diversity: it doesn't simply refuse to talk about needs and values. Rather, it takes a structural approach, abstracting from any particular substantive account of the good life, while indicating the social conditions necessary for undamaged self-realization within the different forms of life available in contemporary society. Thus it can productively address issues of the good life – especially in a negative form, in terms of social threats or obstacles to the opportunity for persons to achieve the good life – without being tied to any particular cultural form of life. As we will see especially in chapter 6, when philosophical issues involved in the justification of the normative standards for critical social theory come to the fore, Honneth's position is closest to Hegel's in attempting to combine the modern Kantian insistence on the centrality of equal autonomy of individuals with Aristotle's broader conception of the diversity of issues concerning practical philosophy. At this point, it is enough to see how his formal conception of ethical life intends to combine some of the respective advantages of Kantian and Aristotelian approaches while avoiding their respective problems.

3.3 Historical Progress

One of the central reasons for articulating a formal conception of ethical life is to get clear about the standards used in the theory of recognition's account of historical change. (Another main reason is to have standards to employ in diagnosing social pathologies; see chapter 4.3). In contrast to Honneth's model, the conflict-of-interest model will see history as, at most, a succession of battles between winners and losers in zero-sum struggles over limited resources. There may be some development in the direction of greater fairness in distribution of goods over time, or there may not be, largely due to historical contingencies and particular power dynamics. But when we consider the variety of different social recognition struggles, it becomes clear that we are not just here cataloging random and accidental episodes of social conflict. In and through these struggles, systematic changes occur over time: in the forms of recognition, in their institutional and culture realizations, and in who is accorded recognition. The question then becomes: is this history merely accidental with one recognition order being replaced with another randomly different order, or can we detect an underlying historical logic – a story of progress – in these transformations? Here Honneth makes the bold claim that we can indeed reconstruct the history of different recognition orders as a history of progress (even if not unbroken linear progress, but including periods of stasis, lag, and even backsliding). However, in order to tell this story of progressive modernization as the development of recognition orders, Honneth needs some normative standard of better and worse social situations: hence the formal conception of ethical life.

3.3.1 Inclusion and individualization

According to that conception, a society is to be gauged by the degree to which all individuals have equal opportunities for the undistorted self-realization of different aspects of their personalities afforded by the society's structures of reciprocal recognition. According to Honneth, there are two main dimensions along which we can gauge social progress using this standard: inclusion and individualization. Let me begin with a rough example to get a sense of these two dimensions. If we compare, say, thirteenth-century societies to early twenty-first-century ones using this ideal of equal opportunities for self-realization through reciprocal recognition, it quickly becomes obvious that the later societies fulfill this standard to a much higher degree than the earlier. For despite the institutional and cultural achievements of the high Middle Ages, it is clear that very few individuals had equal opportunities for receiving appropriate love, respect, and esteem, and what recognition was afforded to those few was not directly afforded on the basis of a broad diversity of each individual's traits and achievements. On the one hand, the great mass of the population – peasants, serfs, servants, merchants, artisans – had, for example, no legal protections that could be interpreted as expressing respect for their equal individual dignity or autonomy. By contrast, such legal rights are routinely afforded to almost all adult members of contemporary OECD societies. This difference is in the dimension of inclusion: later societies include more members in the scope of moral recognition. On the other hand, even those earlier few who were granted recognition, such as hereditary nobles, received honor because of their given position within a fixed and inherited status hierarchy. So the medieval duke receives high esteem on account of his higher social position, but this position is not his own achievement but an involuntary ascriptive status, one he gained by accident of birth. And if he was a member of the landed aristocracy, he might not have the legal right to sell his inherited real estate and so would not be able to see his autonomy vis-à-vis his property recognized by society. By contrast, the contemporary esteem order defined by the principle of meritocracy ideally restricts high regard to those who deserve it on the basis of their individual achievements. And contemporary legal subjects can see their individual autonomy confirmed not only in property rights, but also in their civil rights to due judicial process, political rights to democratic participation, social rights to the means necessary to realize their substantive freedom, and so on. Thus the moral logic of contemporary recognition is more inclusive and individualizing, even if it is repeatedly violated in practice. No one would defend the claims of Kennedys and Bushes to be US political leaders on the basis of their accidental status as dynastic scions, even if accidents of inherited social position explain much of the reality.

Thus the key measures for historical progress, applied across the three main forms of recognition, concern increases in inclusion – widening the scope of persons afforded the relevant type of recognition – and individualization – increasingly granting recognition based on an individual's own characteristics and on more numerous dimensions of an individual's identity. A morally superior recognition order, then, according to Honneth, displays increases in both of these criteria: "On the one hand, we see here a process of individualization, i.e., the increase of opportunities to legitimately articulate parts of one's personality; on the other hand, we see a process of social inclusion, i.e., the expanding inclusion of subjects into the circle of full members of society" (RoR: 184–5). Where such changes come about in a society in some particular set of recognition relations, and where those changes become stabilized over the long term, we are justified in talking of a social learning process, a directional moral development in social relations. Further, we are justified in using these criteria critically, pointing out those current social relations that do not measure up to the inherent developmental potential of reciprocal recognition.[14]

3.3.2   Progress in three domains of recognition

Just as with an individual learning different skills, different forms of social learning exhibit different developmental potentials. Learning how to tie one's shoelaces is not as complex as learning to construct geometric proofs, and each of these skills has still less developmental potential than learning to sustain and deepen friendships. Similarly,

Honneth claims that the three different forms of social recognition have different developmental potentials, and thereby also different degrees of historical specificity: whereas there is less learning to do across societies about the social recognition conditions necessary for the healthy development of self-confidence, the social recognition conditions for self-respect and self-esteem display a more robust historical profile of unfolding developmental progress. When new discoveries are made about the social conditions of personal integrity, and these discoveries are stably institutionalized in a society, we are warranted in saying that moral progress in the recognition order has occurred. In contrast, Honneth does not think that pure conflicts of interest have any developmental potential; they are merely episodic and contingent conflicts over the allocation of scarce resources.

We should note here an important change in Honneth's claims. Whereas in SfR he argued that there is historical learning evident in both respect and esteem recognition but none for love recognition, he has gradually weakened that distinction. By 2011, he explicitly historicizes in FR the development of recognition practices in the sphere of personal relationships. Thus in contrast to his earlier SfR thesis, he now agrees that, "the internal praxis of love can change and can even make progress" (Honneth and Marcelo 2013: 211). The intuition of his earlier position can be grasped when we consider that there is likely little variability across historical epochs in the destruction of basic self-confidence wrought by extreme violence. Torture and abuse destroyed personal integrity in the same way for ancient Mesopotamians as it does for us. In contrast, with regard to respect and esteem violations, there are certain harms that can only occur given specific social conditions in certain eras and societies. For example, the harm of being denied voting rights could only occur once some citizens have been actually accorded such rights in the first place. This seems to be the basic idea behind Honneth's older claim that there is no developmental potential with respect to recognition relations of love and friendship: "Whatever the construction of the system of legitimation that tries to justify it, the suffering of torture or rape is always accompanied by a dramatic breakdown in the reliability of the social world and hence by a collapse in one's own basic self-confidence" (SfR: 133).

However, as Honneth later acknowledges (RoR: 144 and 192–3), that thesis is somewhat overstated, for there does seem to be some real developmental potential in struggles for the social condition of self-confidence. This is clearest with respect to the criterion of inclusion: social progress is evident in the extent to which contemporary societies have extended the normative expectation of non-abusive treatment to more and more classes of persons over time. We no longer believe it is legitimate to physically abuse criminals in order to punish them, nor to employ indiscriminate corporal punishment on children, nor to enslave, rape, and pillage after battlefield victories. We are beginning to acknowledge that a marriage certificate is not a license for husbands to rape wives. All of these achievements, and more, were the results of social struggles for adequate recognitive bases of self-confidence, indicating clear moral progress according to the criterion of greater inclusion.

There is also progress here with respect to individualization. We have discovered (unfortunately through state experimentation) that psychological techniques of torture such as sleep deprivation or repetitive trauma simulation can be equally, if not more, destructive to basic self-confidence than traditional physical assaults on bodily tissues. Similar conclusions follow about new extensions of what we understand as severe emotional abuse within intimate relations between adults, extensions furthered significantly by feminist focus on the gendered power dynamics in personal relationships. These new social interpretations of abuse count under the criterion of individualization since they portend new forms of social relationships that allow individuals to experience more dimensions of their personalities. In summary, there is some real developmental potential with respect to the intersubjective conditions of self-confidence along both dimensions of inclusion and individualization.

At any rate, the most important developments for Honneth's theory of modernization are surely the changes from a feudal society of honor-based recognition, fusing together relations of respect and esteem, to a modern liberal society differentiating the principles and social spheres of respect and esteem and simultaneously individualizing both. We have already seen the basic idea above in the contrast between the honor due to the medieval duke and the law-based respect and achievement-based esteem due to modern bourgeois subjects. According to Honneth, the key development is the transformation in the notion of honor whereby that single form of recognition splits into two parts – a universalistic morality of respect and a meritocratic ethic of esteem – each following its own distinct moral logic. Whereas honor is afforded to persons on the basis of their group affiliation and a rigid status order, respect and esteem allow for the true individualizing of the two inherently different forms of intersubjective regard previously fused together. Respect as we now understand it is for the equal autonomy of each individual person, not respect for members of high-status groups determined largely along hereditary lines. Differential esteem as we understand it is afforded on the basis of a specific individual's valued social contributions, not for that person's mere membership in an ascriptive group. Thus, whereas honor is not distinctly individualized, modern respect and esteem both respond to different facets of individuals' own personalities. And, of course, whereas honor in chivalrous societies was limited to a select few, modern respect and esteem have both witnessed ever-increasing inclusion of more and more classes of subjects over time: all agents capable of rational autonomy deserve to be regarded with dignity and all members of society deserve an equal opportunity to achieve esteem for valued contributions. This crucial transformation of the concept of honor, then, represents the moral threshold between modern and pre-modern social relations, insofar as it allows for social relations of respect and esteem to realize the developmental potentials of their respective moral logics.

Of course, from the perspective of social history, it is not enough simply to witness a conceptual change in ideas alone; the change must be stabilized in social practices of intersubjective regard. As we saw above, for relations of respect-based recognition, the modern development of legal rights attaching to individuals is the crucial innovation. The legal practice of granting individual subjects rights is then itself a major step toward increasing individualization. And of course there is a long history of increasing inclusion where, through social struggles, some determinate right granted to a few – such as the right to buy and sell personal property – is granted to previously excluded persons – such as adult women. But there is a further complexity to the progressive history of rights. For as seen in T. H. Marshall's account of the three waves of rights development – civil rights, then political rights, then social rights – the expansion of the catalog of rights can be reconstructed as a series of discoveries of aspects of individual's personalities that deserve due regard in order to allow them to understand themselves as fully autonomous individuals. In the eighteenth century, it became clear that individuals could not regard themselves as freely acting subjects without legal protections against coercion by others, whether private subjects or the government itself. The democratic revolutions of the late eighteenth and nineteenth centuries demonstrated, however, that civil rights were not enough to secure full autonomy. For only when each member of society is recognized as having a legitimate claim to equal participation in legislating the community's norms can those members understand themselves as self-directing individuals. As Rousseau and Kant insist, only when individuals can understand themselves as co-authors of the laws they are at the same time subject to can they understand themselves both as free individuals and as obligated to obey laws. True individual autonomy under a system of coercive laws requires not just individual rights, but equal democratic rights as well. The progress of rights from civil rights to political rights can then be interpreted as an expansion of the dimension of individual's personalities that is formally recognized in legal structures: from individuals' capacity for self-directed freely willed action, to individuals' capacity to rationally reflect upon and legislate for themselves, together with others, the norms of their conduct.

A similar story can be told about the development of social rights in the twentieth century. While civil and political rights give formal legal recognition to each member's equal autonomy, economic mechanisms of boom–bust cycles and resulting cyclical massive social dislocations rendered the formal guarantee of equality merely aspirational for the dispossessed and the dislocated. As Anatole France sardonically puts the point, the poor are faced with "the majestic equality of the laws which forbid rich and poor alike to sleep under the bridges, to beg in the streets, and to steal their bread" (*The Red Lily*, 1925 [1894]: 91). So the move to the "materialization" of the law through social rights represents a learning process whereby the material conditions for the equal autonomy of each is given due recognition. In summary, progress in respect-based forms of social recognition can be reconstructed from the transformation of honor into (in part) a universalistic morality of respect, the individualizing anchoring of that respect in legal rights, the further individualizing of that respect through the concrete expansion of the catalog of legal rights due to persons, and the increasing inclusion of excluded categories of persons into the class of categorically rights-bearing subjects and citizens.

The historical development of esteem-based recognition practices and institutions is equally complex, although clear linear progress is perhaps not as discernible as it is with respect to rights. To be sure, history witnesses a similar individualization of esteem in that individuals' own traits and achievements are now at issue, rather than the traits of the social status groups they belong to. Furthermore, esteem also underwent a process of inclusion similar to rights: broader groups of people are afforded the equal opportunity to achieve esteem, rather than simply those select few who happen to have been born to the most exalted ranks of society.

However, there is another dimension of esteem individualization that is distinctive, making the history of social struggle even more complex than struggles over rights. Although Honneth does not explicitly name it as such, we can label this the "pluralization" of esteem. Simplifying a multifaceted history, one important aspect of modernization singled out by sociologists was the denaturalization and pluralization of evaluative standards. In the wake of the Reformation, the relatively rigid set of social values more or less imposed upon all through central church hierarchies in the Middle Ages lost the sense it reflected the unchanging order of the universe and thus had a claim to everyone's unanimous endorsement. Over the centuries, the conception that such a constellation of values was natural, unchanging, and univocal simply disappeared as the pluralization, diversification, and denaturalization of values led to our contemporary social situation. John Rawls memorably labels this as "the fact of reasonable pluralism": we have accepted that, as a result of the ordinary working of human reason, there is a diversity of legitimate, but incompatible, comprehensive conceptions of meaning, ultimate truth, and worthy ways of life. Recalling the moral logic of esteem claims – whereby differential regard is given to individuals based upon the degree to which their traits, abilities, and achievements are taken to make social contributions – the fact of reasonable pluralism entails that what counts as a social contribution and exactly how will inevitably be subject to controversy and disagreement. Contemporary societies are marked by persistent social conflicts over interpretations of individual achievement and social worth. For while at an abstract level we moderns might all be able to agree that the principle of individual merit is the key to all esteem assessments, the background horizon of evaluative standards that we use to assess merit in particular cases has been pluralized. This means that the diversity of forms of life and conceptions of the good available to modern subjects will enable greater individualization in the sense of generating esteem-supporting recognition in response to greater numbers of individual personality features.

Consider the ways in which various labor movements throughout the nineteenth and twentieth centuries sought to recharacterize manual and industrial labor from being the object of social disesteem to being seen as a potential avenue for dignified self-realization. This was a pluralization of esteem leading not only to greater inclusion but also to greater individualization. Or consider that, in a mere thirty years and thanks to the dogged social struggles of LGBT communities, western societies have witnessed a radical pluralization of the sexual identities and sexualities that may play a role in socially supported opportunities for self-esteem. With the transformation from universal derision of homosexuality to tolerant acceptance of the diversity of sexual identities, the scope of legitimate and viable esteem-generating communities of value has been pluralized and esteem structures have thereby been further individualized and made more inclusive. In summary, progress in esteem-based forms of social recognition can be reconstructed from the transformation of honor into (in part) a meritocratic ethic of individual esteem, the individualization of that esteem in three dimensions – individuals' own characteristics as the objects of esteem, equalized opportunities to experience esteem, and the pluralized horizon of values according to which social contributions are measured – and the increasing inclusion of subjects previously excluded from the moral circle of esteem-worthy individuals.

3.4 Critical Perspectives

We will return again to issues concerning social development in chapter 6, with a more detailed treatment of Honneth's deeply Hegelian accounts of freedom and justice. Section 6.4 will consider a number of objections one might have to this story of progressive modernization: e.g., the suspicion that this is an overly idealized "Whiggish" history or a general skepticism about the very notion of historical progress. Instead, in this final section, I would like to address a number of objections that might be made to Honneth's endorsement of the politics of recognition, that is, to the substantive policy aims and political techniques typically employed in struggles for recognition: that they are merely symbolic (3.4.1), that they undercut egalitarianism (3.4.2), that they endorse the claims of pernicious groups (3.4.3), and that they demand and enforce an unsavory form of group conformism (3.4.4).

3.4.1 "But that's just symbolism"

Consider the following political contretemps. Devout Sikhs demand and receive exemptions from laws mandating the wearing of motorcycle helmets so that they can maintain their religious practice of wearing the turban in the United Kingdom (Motor-Cycle Crash Helmets (Religious Exemption) Act 1976). The Canadian province of Quebec required outdoor commercial signs and billboards to be exclusively in French (Charter of the French Language 1974), until the Supreme Court of Canada ruled that Quebec could only enforce "marked predominance" of French language signage (*Ford v. Quebec (Attorney General) 1988*). The organizers of the annual St Patrick's Day parade in Boston, Massachusetts ban gay and lesbian groups from marching, a ban upheld by the Supreme Court of the United States (*Hurley v. Irish-American Gay, Lesbian and Bisexual Group of Boston 1995*), leading to the formation of an annual second peace parade following the first after a mile gap. An Italian law that requires the display of the Christian crucifix in state-run public school classrooms was upheld by the European Court of Human Rights (*Lautsi v. Italy 2011*).

These controversies all involve members of minority groups of one sort or another – religious, linguistic, sexual, nonreligious – protesting against policies that they claimed expressed forms of social disrespect toward them and demanding various forms of appropriate public acknowledgment or accommodation of their distinctive identities. Thus they are each clear examples of the politics of recognition, in particular one prominent contemporary form of such: the so-called "politics of identity." And importantly for the objection to be considered here, each of them revolves around the perception of harms to identity instigated by symbols, by markers of concrete identities: the turban, business signs, parade groupings, the Christian cross. One prominent objection to such political struggles is indeed that they are *merely* symbolic. This kind of suspicion of identity politics is rooted in two ideas. First, it is said that symbolic slights do not represent real harms to persons. Here the idea is basically akin to the old schoolyard adage: "Sticks and stones may break my bones, but words will never hurt me." Second, since symbolic slights are not real harms, even as contemporary society continues manifest forms of "real" harm to persons – physical degradation, loss of liberty, economic deprivation, starvation, and so on – mere cultural politics focuses on quite unimportant matters in comparison with more weighty political matters of individuals' objective material interests. Although not usually phrased in such unguarded and bald terms, such sentiments appear to me to undergird a number of intellectuals' and public figures' apparent unease with the increasing predominance of identity politics over the last forty years in western societies.

In response to such objections, Honneth's theory can begin with a straightforward denial of the notion that symbolic expressions of disregard and disrespect cannot constitute real harm to persons. If individuals' practical identities are of fundamental importance to them – as attested by the phenomenology of everyday experiences of moral outrage at assaults on the bases of one's self-regard – and if individuals' practical identities fundamentally rely on the character of the social environment of practices and institutions of recognition – as supported by the psychological, sociological, political, and historical evidence – then it is simply incorrect to believe that symbolic slights have no potential for individual harm. Sticks, stones, and words can all hurt me. Second, it should be clear that even such identity-based struggles are not "merely" symbolic. At stake in the four examples above are not just the cultural expressions of societal regard, but also legal freedoms, economic interests, social status hierarchies, and childhood education. And as we have seen in canvassing the variety of recognition struggles, they are by no means limited conflicts over intangible cultural markers but include any of the ostensibly "objective" material interests – money, power, jobs – an objector might point to as of fundamental importance for political struggle.[15]

3.4.2 "Shouldn't we all be treated the same?"

A more prevalent objection in political theory is that, because the politics of recognition asks society to affirmatively endorse the distinctive identity of various groups, it encourages various forms of sectarian, sectionalizing, and divisive politics in contrast to the proper focus of equal treatment for all persons. Prominent intellectuals have criticized various manifestations of the politics of recognition for acknowledgment and promotion of the differences between people, rather than highlighting and promoting all persons' fundamental equality (Gitlin 1995; Schlesinger Jr 1992). There has also been a spirited series of related disagreements in feminist theory pitting "difference" feminists against "equality" feminists.

One of the most sustained philosophical critiques of multiculturalism and, by extension, the politics of recognition has been put forward
by Brian Barry (Barry 2001). Although Barry does not specifically
address Honneth's theory (Charles Taylor and Iris Young are rather
prominent targets), because he presents one of the clearest attacks on
multicultural recognition politics from the perspective of egalitarian
liberalism, it is quite useful for understanding this widely shared objection to recognition theory. Barry in fact combines two different critiques
of multicultural identity: a worry about the displacement of the more
important politics of economic distribution, and a worry about the
balkanization of political communities through jingoistic group self-
assertion. The first worry is a more refined version of the concern
addressed briefly above: that recognition politics distracts from matters
of greater material import to persons' lives. As I said briefly there, it
should be clear that, at least on Honneth's account, recognition politics
fully includes conflicts over economic matters: class cleavages, massive
inequalities caused by capitalism, the division between paid and
unpaid labor, and so on. Because we will see this concern come up
again in chapter 5's discussion of the Fraser–Honneth debate, I will
defer further treatment of it.

The second concern is that demands by cultural and religious groups
for special legal treatment encourage social conflict, sectarianism, and
the potential split of nation-states into opposing cultural groups. Rather
than balkanizing multicultural policies, Barry favors (at least in the
abstract) strict liberal egalitarianism: universal and undifferentiated
legal and political rights, strict insistence on equal treatment for all
regardless of any difference (except economic difference), and economic redistribution through state welfare entitlements and social
insurance. Social conflicts between members of different cultural,
ethnic, and religious groups, according to Barry, would thereby be
ameliorated, leaving only the comforting old class conflicts as the main
source of social discord and political dispute. Without any legal and
policy accommodation in a strict regime of formal legal equality, the
politics of recognition would, apparently, simply recede as a bad
memory, the product of two or three decades of misplaced political
experimentation.

While this is not the place for a full-scale comparison of liberal egalitarianism and the political theory of recognition, a few points in
response to this critique are in order, especially given the frequent
voicing of such concerns. To begin with, note that recognition struggles
have been occurring for hundreds of years on Honneth's account. Thus
Barry's basic assumption that the politics of recognition is a new phenomenon – two or three decades old – is simply unconvincing. But
that also means that one of Barry's central causal predictions is also
unconvincing. For if, as seems evident, recognition struggles broke out

decades and centuries before legal and policy accommodations of cultural groups were made in the name of multiculturalism, it seems quite unlikely that we can confidently predict that further multiculturalist legal accommodation will lead to increased recognition-based social conflict whereas eschewing such accommodation will reunite society. In fact, these problems all point to a significant disagreement between Barry and Honneth over the definition of the politics of recognition. While, as we have seen, Honneth has a capacious understanding of recognition struggles spanning three different forms of recognition, diverse types of claims, and varied forms of envisioned sociopolitical changes, Barry effectively reduces all recognition struggles to the identity politics of groups defined by ethnicity, culture, language, and religion and then focuses only on identity-based claims for special treatment of groups according to their cultural difference from the mainstream of society. "My concern is with views that support the politicization of group identities, where the basis of the common identity is claimed to be cultural.... The views in question are known as the politics of difference, the politics of recognition or, most popularly, multiculturalism" (Barry 2001: 5). It seems to me that very many criticisms of the politics of recognition (including Fraser's as we'll see in chapter 5) also commit this same error of a radical narrowing of the notion to a specific form of group-based demand for special legal accommodation of minority cultures, effectively equating the wide diversity of recognition struggles with a much narrower identity politics of difference.[16] On the wider view, Barry's own preferred "egalitarian liberalism is in fact [one specific] form of the politics of recognition" (Thompson 2006: 13).

Furthermore, when we get to the consideration of specific cases, Barry's stark opposition between strictly universal rights and benefits, endorsed by liberal egalitarianism, and group-differentiated rights and benefits, endorsed by the politics of recognition, quickly breaks down. For example, Barry considers many different policies impacting Sikhs, and endorses a variety of approaches for them, ranging from exceptionless universalism to full-scale accommodation of difference. For Barry, there should be: no legal exceptions for turban wearers to mandatory motorcycle helmet laws, special time-limited exceptions for certain Sikh construction workers to mandatory hard-hat laws, general exceptions for Sikhs to laws forbidding public carrying of knives, and general exceptions from school dress-code policies for Sikh turbans (Barry 2001: 44–62, 152). Barry works through each case with special attention to the impact of the relevant policy for the equal treatment of citizens. But, note, this special attention to equality concerns is precisely what the theory of recognition endorses: attention to the equal autonomy of each and to the equal opportunity for esteem for each. The details of what particular policies and institutions will render each person the relevant form of equality are, as we well know, not predetermined by these abstract formulations.

That is precisely why we can and should expect ongoing social controversy and struggle about the appropriate standards of equal treatment and the policies that will sufficiently fulfill them. The theory of recognition does not take a one-size-fits-all approach to these controversies – always endorsing differentiated treatment – any more than liberal egalitarianism does – always endorsing non-differentiated treatment. The answer then to the critical question, "Shouldn't we all be treated the same?" is: "No, everyone should not always be treated the same; it depends." It depends on the relevant kind of equality at issue, the relevant standards of equality to be employed, the type of social institution or mechanism at issue, the impact of the various policy proposals on different persons, the particular social situation of the persons involved, the relevant histories of the society and groups involved, and so on. In summary, then, I believe Honneth's theory can confidently respond to the egalitarian objection to multiculturalism by pointing out that it does not refer to the full history and diverse panoply of recognition struggles, and it assumes a false dichotomy between a universal politics of equality and a recognition politics of difference, when in fact both liberal egalitarianism and the theory of recognition are centrally concerned with a context-sensitive and appropriate application of various norms of equality to particular cases and claims.

3.4.3   "Am I black enough for you?"

Another prominent concern about identity-based recognition politics, especially when it has sought to insulate or protect minority groups from assimilation or majority oppression, is that it may have the unfortunate effect of enforcing intra-group conformity amongst group members. For instance, in response to Taylor's promotion of policies protecting minority language communities in Canada, Anthony Appiah worries about whether one form of society-wide tyranny has been exchanged for another form of intra-group tyranny (Appiah 1994; Taylor 1994). Nancy Fraser's critique of Honneth's theory of recognition has repeatedly pressed a similar worry about the potential harms to individuals of the jargon of group authenticity. In seeking the social recognition of different groups, identity politics errs in several ways, she says: it reifies historically contingent, internally heterogeneous, and interacting collectivities into "natural," timeless, homogeneous, and hermetically sealed group identities; it fosters illiberal pressures toward conformity against supposedly "inauthentic" members; it perpetuates subordinating intra-group hierarchies whereby only some have the privilege of defining and speaking for the group's collective identity;

and, once again, it is liable to a kind of jingoistic group valorization that breeds increased inter-group conflict (Fraser 2000, 2001). Thus the politics of recognition leads, via its focus on group-based identities and the authenticity model of group identities, to new forms of injustice and discord.

Much of the response by Honneth to such concerns must begin where the response in 3.4.2 did: this critique reduces a broad and differentiated conception of manifold struggles for recognition to one narrow form of politics, an identity politics formed around ideals of separate, essentialistic, monolithic, and unchanging group identities which must force their own members to conform to authentic practices and expressions. In short, the politics of recognition as understood by Honneth is neither equivalent to nor exhausted by one potentially virulent form of the politics of identity.

The closest one could come to seeing this critique as justified – and it's not very close I would say – would be in certain passages where Honneth's formulations tended to portray an overly holistic and "siloed" conception of solidaristic groups. Thus, especially in his earlier works, one might say that there is an implicit assumption that each individual belongs only to one significant community of value and that those communities are relatively independent of one another. However, through the publication of his crucial essay on democratic social cooperation in 1998, it should have become clear that he in no way endorses a politics of authentic identity, even in the limited context of struggles for the bases of social esteem (Honneth 2007c). Instead, he explicitly adopts a more fluid and multidimensional account of group affiliations and identifications, for purposes of both social explanation and normative evaluation. Consider, for example, his strong endorsement of Dewey's ideals for a fully democratic form of social cooperation, which include, among others, multiple and diverse group memberships and identity for individuals, intra-group flexibility and democratic organization, and multiple sites of group interaction and cross pollination. According to Honneth, as the number and variety of one's social memberships increase – as they do in complex societies – the pressures for developing an integrated, post-conventional identity, which can coherently structure a number of potentially competing social roles, also increase. As Dewey often puts the point, a thief in a gang is less developed than an individual fully integrated into a complex, democratic form of social cooperation, since only the latter must develop a consistent identity and structure of roles and behaviors despite tensions across her memberships in diverse associations (Dewey 1984: 327–8). The authenticity model of identity politics is, then, not celebrated by Honneth but, rather, seen as more or less dynamically equivalent to Dewey's gang of thieves.

3.4.4 "*They* don't deserve recognition"

A final critique of the politics of recognition stems from what we might call the problem of "evil claimants." For, once we turn our attention to everyday social struggles, it seems there are any number of individuals and groups struggling for broader social recognition whose behavior, aims, and character lead us to think they deserve the exact opposite of positive recognition: namely, social scorn, shunning, and explicit disrespect. Whether reading the local newspaper's police blotter or the Southern Poverty Law Center's lists of hate groups, the variety of evil claimants to recognition seems limitless: persistent violent lawbreakers, neofascist and white supremacist groups, ideologically motivated terrorists, and so on. If the theory of recognition demands that we give them positive recognition, then the theory seems worse than worthless; it seems positively pernicious. But this appears to be at least one implication of the theory's insistence that positive recognition – in particular affirmative esteem-based recognition – is a vital need for individuals. Here is how Fraser once formulated the criticism of

> the view that everyone has an equal right to social esteem. That view is patently untenable, of course, because it renders meaningless the notion of esteem. Yet it seems to follow from at least one prominent rival account. In Axel Honneth's theory, social esteem is among the "intersubjective conditions for undistorted identity formation" which morality is supposed to protect. It follows that everyone is morally entitled to social esteem. (Fraser 2001: 28)

In other words, the theory of recognition is taken to have no normative standards for distinguishing between justified and unjustified claims to esteem-based recognition because it says that everyone deserves equal esteem simpliciter.[17]

Fraser is absolutely correct to point out that a truly critical theory of recognition requires robust normative standards for assessing concrete claims about how social relations ought to be structured and how they might be currently mis-structured. And she is correct to note that a normative standard insisting that everyone unreservedly deserves equal esteem is conceptually confused since esteem is precisely a standard sensitive to individual merit. Further, if that were indeed Honneth's claim, then it would seem that we owe just as much esteem to those who actively further white supremacy as those who actively further interracial justice.

Thankfully, there is no such implication in Honneth's account since – despite Fraser's uncited attribution – he never claims that all persons are categorically owed equal esteem. He does claim, as I explained above, that all persons deserve the social conditions necessary for an equal opportunity to realize self-esteem through reciprocal and symmetrical relations of intersubjective regard, depending on individuals' meritorious traits, abilities, and achievements as determined against standards of valued social contributions. Furthermore, that equal opportunity is violated when specific forms of life which are both viably and legitimately esteem-engendering are subject to generalized patterns of insult and denigration in the attitudes, cultural practices, and institutions of the wider society. In applying this complex set of standards to our examples of evil claimants, it should be clear that all of them violate one or more of the conditions built into the conception. Persistent violent lawbreakers (if they even constitute a requisite community of value) generate esteem through illegitimate means insofar as they violate the social conditions of self-confidence and self-respect that all are categorically entitled to. Various hate groups, male supremacist groups, and ideologically motivated terrorists can only become viable esteem-engendering communities to the extent to which they illegitimately deny others – through denigration and insult at the very least – an equal opportunity to achieve self-esteem in and through reciprocal and symmetrical relations of recognition. Furthermore, in the process they usually deny others their categorically owed social conditions of self-confidence and self-respect as well. In a nutshell, the complex understanding of normativity that Honneth articulates in terms of the formal conception of ethical life is precisely intended to provide his critical theory with the robust normative standards that the objection from evil claimants asserts is missing from that theory. The theory not only thereby has a clear response to the objection, but it has the resources for its broader purposes of insightfully differentiating between progressive and regressive social struggles and for articulating the degree of historical progress (and regress) that society has achieved through such struggles.

4

Diagnosing Social Pathologies

The previous two chapters have developed the substance of Honneth's moral anthropology – his account of the development of a practical identity through the four forms of intersubjective recognition – and his moral sociology – his account of the development of the normative infrastructure of modern social relations through progressive struggles for recognition. Along the way, we have also seen how his theory addresses many of the questions of traditional moral philosophy and political philosophy. Throughout there have also been hints of a more distinctive theoretical project as well: a social philosophy aiming at insights into the ways in which, even if sufficiently moral and just, contemporary social relations might nevertheless be troubled, unhealthy, deficient.

4.1 Social Philosophy as Social Diagnosis

It is perhaps best to start with some prominent examples of social philosophy to get a sense of its distinctive goals and methods. Honneth's key exemplars in his seminal 1994 article on social pathologies (Honneth 2007f) include: Rousseau's account of the origins of inequality in the beginning of human sociality; Hegel's account of the pathologies of modern merely subjective freedom generated by modern formal law and economic civil society; Marx's critique of the alienation of workers caused by the capitalist mode of production; Nietzsche's account of nihilism, the skepticism about all values, as arising from a degenerate culture; Lukács's critique of the reification of the everyday social world caused by the instrumental rationalizing tendencies of industrial capitalism; Plessner's account of the loss of potentials for free individual self-realization in the face of insistent pressures for communal authenticity; Horkheimer and Adorno's diagnosis of the domination of external and internal nature caused by the centrality of means–ends reasoning to the civilization process; and Arendt's diagnosis of the loss of individual freedom entailed by the destruction of a public sphere of joint communication and practice and caused by totalitarian social formations. Honneth also mentions other theorists who in some form developed a diagnostic social philosophy: Tocqueville, Mill, Freud, Simmel, Tönnies, Durkheim, Weber, Spengler, Dewey, Fromm, Marcuse, Bataille, Gehlen, Heller, Márcus, Habermas, Foucault, and Taylor.

What could hold together all of these disparate theorists, across two and a half centuries, with their widely disparate accounts of what ails society and what the causes of that are? For Honneth, all are engaged (at least in some part of their work) in the same basic task. "Social philosophy is primarily concerned with determining and discussing processes of social development that can be viewed as misdevelopments, disorders or 'social pathologies'.... Its primary task is the diagnosis of processes of social development that must be understood as preventing the members of society from living a 'good life'" (Honneth 2007f: 4). A number of elements in this understanding deserve amplification.

First, each theorist points to some malady or ailment that troubles their own society, and identifies some particular causes of that disorder which are specifically social. That is, the disorder is said to be rooted in the particular ordering or structuring or practices of the society. Further, the disorder identified is said to be a social problem or pathology because it impedes the ability of individuals to live fulfilling, or fully realized, or ethically praiseworthy, or happy lives. Thus the inability of individuals to live the "good life" according to the standards of the theory is said to be caused by particular features of the present social ordering.

Next, it's clear that, for all of the various theories, there is an important historical dimension. Even though each may not endorse a full-scale philosophy of history with some inborn aim or teleological structure, and some of the historical accounts are even self-consciously conjectural and nonempirical, each theory posits that the highlighted pathology arises at some determinate point in the society's history and then uses this historical inflection point to underwrite the causal story. And the fact that the pathology is historical shows that it is a contingent feature of social life, one that can be overcome through a different form of social ordering.

Another quite important point that Honneth stresses is that, even across the methodological diversity of social philosophies, all adopt a negative method of critique. That is, they do not first posit some imagined utopia and then measure up the deficiencies of contemporary society according to those ideal standards. Instead, they seek to identify particular social structures, practices, or understandings that are problematic in the actual society they find themselves in.

This then leads to the crucial question of how to justify the normative claims of social philosophy. For, at an abstract level, all must appeal to some either explicit or implicit ethical standards of the good life – or, at the very least, not deformed life – for humans. Just in using the medical metaphor of pathology, social philosophy must have some conception of social health and this will, according to Honneth, inevitably involve a conception of the social conditions necessary for individuals to live worthwhile or fully realized lives. For it is precisely when social conditions impede, block, or frustrate the achievement of the good life that we can speak intelligibly of a "social pathology." To be sure, there are enormous differences among the various theorists Honneth canvasses in the way each goes about justifying their normative perspectives. Some use a metaphysically loaded philosophy of history to justify their claims (e.g., Hegel, Marx, Lukács), some deny the possibility of any such justification even as they rely on determinate evaluative standards (e.g., Nietzsche and Foucault), and some rely on an implicit or explicit philosophical anthropology that can be at least subjected to empirical scrutiny (e.g., Rousseau, Plessner, Arendt). Honneth sides with the latter anthropological strategy, at least when its claims are not overly fulsome and contentious but refer only to a few very basic conditions of human life. We will return to this issue at the end of the chapter.

Furthermore, the disagreements between the social philosophies are not limited to such methodological concerns, for there are very significant differences in the substantive ideals or standards each employs. Some of this can be seen in the differing priority each gives to individualism (Rousseau, Nietzsche, and Plessner) or sociality (Hegel, Marx, Lukács, Arendt). Much of the substantive difference is in the underlying accounts of the good life and human self-realization: solitary self-contented freedom leavened with natural compassion for others for Rousseau, individual freedom through integration with a rational social totality for Hegel, self-realization through socially oriented labor for Marx, expressive life-affirming originality for Nietzsche, and so on.

Notwithstanding these deep methodological and substantive disagreements, it remains the case that all of these various theorists are engaged in a form of practical philosophy that is quite distinct both from mainstream forms of social theory and practical philosophy. Taking the contrast with other forms of social theory first, it is clear that the aim of social philosophy is not to simply describe accurately the social world as it is or has been. Sociology, social psychology, history, anthropology, economics, political science, and other social sciences all share empirical accuracy and categorial acumen – cutting social nature "at its joints" – as their central aims. While social philosophy surely has a descriptive element, that element must be combined with evaluative claims that the state of the social world is problematic, specifically, is pathological. Thus social philosophy is not limited to matters of fact about the social world, but is oriented by diagnostic and therapeutic goals, goals which essentially involve questions of value.

However, social philosophy is not simply pure normative analysis, the kind at the center of mainstream moral and political philosophy. Moral philosophy is organized around the articulation and defense of ideal principles of moral action and correct living that can be used to guide individuals in assessing their actions and forms of life. Ideal political philosophy intends to specify and defend principles of just or legitimate political arrangements that can be used in designing legal and political systems and guiding the development of legal and political policy. In a sense, then, moral and political philosophy deploys forms of positive utopia – the proper moral and political principles and ideals – that can be used to judge and correct that which is currently immoral, unethical, unjust, or illegitimate. But as we have seen, social philosophy starts not from a picture of ideal relationships that is then held up to a fallen world, but with society as it is and tries to identify deformations in extant social conditions which constrain the ability of persons to live fulfilling lives. So its method of pathology diagnosis is as distinct from moral and political philosophy as is its object: neither personal virtues and interpersonal obligations, nor legal systems and governmental policies, but rather the broader structures of social life to the extent that they form the conditions of possibility for the good life.

4.2   Social Pathologies as Second-Order Disorders

This section sketches five of the social pathologies that Honneth has recently diagnosed. It starts with the phenomenon of ideological recognition: that is, forms of positive social affirmation that serve to maintain existing systems of dominance or oppression. Before moving on to the other four pathologies, I will introduce my own terminology of "second-order disorders" to indicate a particular conceptual structure that underlies all of Honneth's pathology diagnoses. This conceptual structure, I believe, holds the key to seeing how Honneth's disparate pathology diagnoses are more than a collection of various observations on the contemporary state of society.[1] And it can also help to clarify the critical problems such a social philosophy faces, as discussed at the end of this chapter. Before that, the chapter discusses in turn four other social pathologies of invisibilization, instrumental rationalization, reification, and organized self-realization (4.2.3–4.2.6). Three of Honneth's most prominent pathology diagnoses are not discussed here. The pathologies of freedom that both Hegel and Honneth detect in social relations dominated by the anonymous formalism of either deontological morality or individualist legal rights will be discussed in 6.3. The pathologies of economic maldistribution are discussed in chapter 5, which takes up Honneth's debate with Nancy Fraser.

4.2.1   Ideological recognition

Theorists from many different perspectives have charged the theory of recognition with an unseemly and uncritical complicity with power (Allen 2010; Connolly 2010; Ferrarese 2009; McNay 2008; Petherbridge 2013; Rössler 2007; Young 2007). Reflect, for instance, on the many ways that recognition in an androcentric society can reinforce debilitating forms of gender identity that contribute to the ongoing oppression of women. The objection is that, in reconstructing the moral infrastructure of recognition relations from the inside out – from the structures of intersubjectivity to social structures – Honneth's theory renders an overly rosy but one-sided picture of subjectivity, a picture theoretically insensitive to the manifold ways in which the asymmetrical power of social structures is reproduced in and through individuals' actual subjectivities.

That charge is a version of the problem that motivates Honneth to reflect on the possibility of ideology recognition. How exactly is his theory to account for the disturbing possibility that an oppressive society grants positive respect and esteem to precisely those characteristics and achievements that serve to reinforce the very structures of individuals' oppression? Positive public recognition may always be beneficial to a person's practical relation-to-self, but it may be positively deleterious to that person's interest in the good life, if and when that positive recognition serves to reinforce social structures that oppress the person. Honneth's own examples make the problem quite clear:

> The pride that "Uncle Tom" feels as a reaction to the repeated praise of his submissive virtues makes him into a compliant servant in a slave-owning society. The emotional appeals the to the "good" mother and housewife made by churches, parliaments, or the mass media over the centuries caused women to remain trapped within a self-image that most effectively accommodated the gender-specific division of labor. The public esteem enjoyed by heroic soldiers continuously engendered a sufficiently large class of men who willingly went to war in pursuit of glory and adventure. As trivial as these examples may be, they do make strikingly clear that social recognition can always also operate as conformist ideology. (Honneth 2012j: 77)

In each of these cases, persons are induced to willingly accept and even welcome their subordinate position in a social hierarchy – and to take on the disproportionate burdens associated with that position – all through the use of noncoercive and relatively costless mechanisms: positive recognition of certain traits and behaviors. From our morally clarified vantage point of the present, we can easily see that the "Uncle Tom," the "good mother," and the "heroic soldier" suffer from forms of positive recognition which actually function to incorporate them into structures of oppression since we no longer endorse slavery, patriarchy, or the worship of war.

The problem of distinguishing between ideological and justified positive recognition, however, becomes much more difficult as we approach our own age. For we are witnesses to changing schema of evaluation, but we do not yet have the clear lens of history to be able to tell which new forms of recognition corresponding to them will ensue in moral progress and which, by contrast, simply reinforce existing patterns of oppression. It is important to note here that we are not considering openly or obviously negative forms of nonrecognition or misrecognition, such as are embodied in overt discrimination against certain groups. For however else such institutionalized patterns of disrespect might work, they will not induce their subjects to aspire to the demeaning values. Members of an openly despised group will not attempt to live up to the values embedded in discriminatory patterns of regard. Further, because the subjects of ideological recognition themselves must willingly accept the value standards that will make them unwitting participants in their own oppression, we cannot ask them to identify which patterns of recognition are progressive and which ideological. As new recognition patterns arise over time and as new subtle interpretations are given to older patterns, how then can we reliably tell which are ideological? After all, the subjects of the recognition do not themselves perceive it as problematic or oppressive: just the opposite, in fact.

Honneth's answer is basically that acts of recognition are ideological when there is a substantial gap between the evaluative acknowledgment or promise that the act centers upon, and the institutional and material conditions necessary for the fulfillment of that acknowledgment or promise. So for instance, the "Uncle Tom" is promised high evaluative esteem for adopting subservient and menial modes of behavior, but the institutional structure of slavery entails that such a promise of esteem can never be fulfilled insofar as no slave can have equal opportunities for achieving real esteem. Likewise, the "good housewife and mother" is promised esteem for activities that, according to the actual material division of labor in society, will never be accorded full reciprocal esteem. In a thoroughly sexist society with a strongly gender-coded division of labor, no man could ever expect to receive esteem for his impressive achievements in labor that is coded as feminine. Finally, in a militaristic society, the soldier is promised honor, even as the material conditions for realizing that honor entail his likely ignoble death. In short, ideological recognition can be distinguished from justified recognition by the irreconcilable gap between the evaluative promise of the recognition and the material conditions needed for realizing that promise.

Moving then to the present, Honneth investigates one new form of ideological recognition in the current economy. Coincident with major structural changes in the labor market over the past twenty years, he points to "current management literature [that] speaks no longer of 'wage-workers' or the 'labour force,' but instead of creative 'entrepreneurs' of their own labor, or 'entremployees'" (Honneth 2012j: 91). Here, workers are promised esteem to the extent to which they work ever harder, are flexible in job assignments, are not troubled by short-term jobs and the loss of career tracks within a single company, and, above all, are willing to see their own work life as a risky enterprise that they exercise all of their own unique skills and abilities in creatively realizing. All of this is not outlandish or unbelievable since it taps into strong currents in our culture that valorize ideals of self-realization through authentic originality and ideals of robust self-sufficiency through hard work, creativity, and risk taking. These resonances are what make the new understanding of being an entrepreneur of one's own labor something that workers could willingly accept without overt coercion or repression. But what then of the material conditions for the fulfillment of this promised esteem for treating one's own work life as an entrepreneurial venture? Here, Honneth's judgment is that the promise is simply not fulfilled by the institutions, indicating that we are dealing with ideological recognition. Rather than being esteemed for having made one's work into a flexible business plan, one is more easily discarded, downsized, outsourced, de-salaried, and generally subject to decreasing compensation and diminished job security. However much the recognition order evaluatively celebrates the worker as flexible entrepreneur of her own career, the structural and material conditions of the neoliberal labor market entails that such promised esteem can never be fulfilled.

4.2.2 Second-order disorders

I would now like to introduce the concept of "second-order disorder" as a way of unifying Honneth's various social pathology diagnoses and of getting increased critical insight into their promise and potential perils. A second-order disorder occurs where there is some social phenomenon that exhibits a constitutive disconnect between first-order contents and second-order reflexive comprehension of those contents, where those disconnects are pervasive and socially caused. The pathology of ideological recognition exhibits this disconnect. There is a first-order content of the evaluation promised by the form of recognition, but there is a significant, pervasive, and socially caused disconnect between this evaluative promise and, at a second-order of reflexivity, the material conditions needed to fulfill that promise. However, it is perhaps easier to see this structure in the classical theory of ideological beliefs and values.

Here I am not talking about ideology in the sense that it is commonly used in the media today: namely, to indicate a coherent set of political values held by individuals and political parties. Classically, "ideology" refers to a set of beliefs and values held by oppressed persons that serves to encourage them to willingly accept their oppression. The classical theory of ideology (whether Marxist or otherwise) investigates first-order beliefs, especially those about the basic structures, orders, and functionings of the social world, and argues that social actors suffer from a cognitive pathology to the extent that they are not cognizant of how those beliefs come about. In particular, the social pathology arises to the extent that persons are not aware, at a second-order level of reflexivity, that the current social consensus – one that exerts a tremendous orienting pressure on individuals' belief schemas – is to a significant degree sensitive to and shaped by predominant social powers and class-specific social interests. In the cases of both ordinary mistaken beliefs and ideological beliefs, there is an error at the first-order level: the person holds a false belief about something. However, only in the case of ideology is the mistaken belief systematically tied to social formations that affect belief formation and stabilization at the second-order level by hiding or repressing the needed reflexivity of social participants about the structures of belief formation and the connection of those cultural-cognitive structures to the material ordering of the social world. For instance, an ordinary mistaken belief that the morning star and the evening star are different celestial bodies is easily corrected when explicitly pointed out. By contrast, a belief that wealth in capitalist societies is dependent entirely on individuals' own initiative, rather than the amount of capital at one's disposal, is an ideological belief. It is rooted in a deformation of the second-order process of belief formation about the characteristics of the extant socioeconomic world; the first-order belief and the second-order deformation are both widely shared in society; those deformations systematically serve certain interests in society; and the mistaken belief is not easily corrected. And, of course, because the ideology naturalizes what is in fact a product of the way we have structured society, it functionally serves to reproduce inegalitarian social structures by hiding their essentially historical character and social causes. Ideology is a social pathology because it contributes to deleterious social outcomes through a kind of second-order disorder, a disorder socially patterned and thereby contributing to unwanted social outcomes.

Honneth's recent use of the concept of ideological recognition does not significantly differ from this theoretical pattern. As with the traditional concept of ideology, the social pathology crucially involves a second-order disorder. Only if persons subject to ideological forms of recognition are not able to understand – at a second-order level – that the required social conditions are lacking will they actually and voluntarily conform their beliefs and behaviors to a set of social patterns that nevertheless contribute to their oppression or domination. Ideological recognition is rooted in widely shared social deformations of second-order processes, that is, institutional processes of the formation and stabilization of interpersonal recognitional evaluation. These deformations systematically serve certain social interests by maintaining systems of oppression without overt coercion. Ideological recognition is not easily corrected but socially reinforced, even as its sources are hidden from view. The social theoretic critique of ideological recognition should then aim not only to expose the gaps in first-order positive recognition and the second-order material conditions necessary to fulfill them. More centrally, it should also expose the social mechanisms that promote and perpetuate the widely shared patterns of ideological recognition while simultaneously hiding the mechanisms of second-order recognitional disorders from society's members behind a functional veneer of naturalized patterns of class- and group-differentiated recognition.

4.2.3 Invisibilization

Another example of social pathologies as second-order disorders is Honneth's analysis, inspired by Ralph Ellison's novel *Invisible Man*, of the peculiar structure of social processes of humiliation that involve "looking through or past" another person (Honneth 2001a). Although Honneth's essay is largely devoted to working out the epistemological and moral structure of interpersonal acts of invisibilization, it also indicates one revealing form of social pathology evident in extremely stratified social contexts where there are clear social divisions between races, castes, classes, and so on, and where those social divisions are constantly reinforced through various practices devoted to publicly putting persons "in their place."

From a theoretical perspective, the interesting thing about social invisibility is that it involves an actual form of acknowledgment at a first-order level, but a non-acknowledgment of the person at the second-order level. Here, it is helpful to distinguish between cognizing the presence of a person and recognizing that person. With cognizance, one must perceive the physical presence of the other – for instance, because they are an object in one's visual field – and one must make some form of elementary individual identification of them as an individual – for instance, identifying them as a human adult engaged in a comprehensible activity. (In his essay on invisibility, Honneth uses the terminology of "cognizance" but in later work on reification he refines this analysis in terms of "antecedent recognition"; see 2.5 above). But antecedent recognition alone is not moral recognition, that is, the adoption of a positive stance toward the other person as a valuable being deserving of certain kinds of treatment. We can see this in looking through someone since the disdainful disregard of the activity – the nonrecognition of the other – can only be performed when they are, paradoxically, also given antecedent recognition as a human entity. Hence, the harmful, disdainful disregard of another is essentially *active* – purposefully ignoring or looking through another – and this presupposes that one has actually taken cognizance of the presence of another human in order to deny them the normal moral recognition that others are due as fellow persons.

Honneth gives a fair amount of attention to the expressive gestures, especially subtle facial gestures, employed in standard cases of greeting and interaction. These gestures publicly display the performer's readiness to engage with the other in a specific way. In general, they express a set of positive dispositions toward the other, thereby acknowledging the other's social validity. In particular, they express one's evaluative perception of the worth of the other, and thereby signal a disposition to limit one's own egotism and treat the other in a positive or benevolent manner. Following Kant's account of moral respect here, Honneth claims that such recognitional gestures indicate a future willingness to be obligated to treat the other as a being of moral worth. Of course, subtly different kinds of gestures may signal subtly different forms of readiness and different understandings of the worth of the other, ranging from broad smiles, indicating a disposition to care for a loved one's emotional needs, to a clipped nod, indicating the equal status of the other as an autonomous individual, to an agreeing nod of approval expressing solidaristic esteem of the contribution of an other. The act of looking through another involves actively withholding precisely such positive forms of recognition of one sort or another – thereby publicly signaling one's denial of the worth of the other – even while at the very same time antecedently recognizing the other as an identifiable individual. Invisibilization is then an active form of public humiliation, signaling a set of future dispositions toward mistreatment of various forms, a form of moral disrespect, and a deformation of the normal human capacity for the evaluative perception of others.

The activity of looking through another may of course happen in many contexts. Consider, for instance, vengeful invisibilization of

another after a breakdown in interpersonal relations. But, as the narrator of *Invisible Man* makes abundantly clear, the social invisibility he
suffers from is the result of a specific set of socially shared racialized
relations of subordination and oppression, rather than particular interpersonal relations he has with the perpetrators. Thus, to be a social
pathology, active disregard must be essentially connected to social patterns of group-specific denigration. And this social pathology clearly
exhibits the conceptual structure of a second-order disorder. There is a
constitutive disconnect between first-order contents – the cognizance
of persons as human individuals – and second-order grasp of those
contents – the moral recognition due to persons as human individuals.
Unlike the case of ideology, however, those who directly suffer from
the social effects of the social pathology are not the same as those
subject to the problematic form of reflexivity. Ellison's narrator is fully
aware of the disconnect between cognizance and recognition of others
– in fact, he tries to force others to match their cognizance with appropriate recognition – but he is the one who suffers from the pathological
gap between cognizance and recognition. Nevertheless, critical social
theory has a similar role in exposing and explaining the second-order
disorder as a social pathology.

4.2.4   Instrumental rationalization

The connection between social diagnosis and second-order disorders
holds for the social philosophy of the Frankfurt School critical theorists
as well, as Honneth has shown (Honneth 2009d). A crucial claim of his
intellectual history is that, in their different ways, all of these theorists
consider present social pathologies to be fundamentally connected to
distortions in reason or rationality. As he puts the point in the preface
to *Pathologies of Reason*, a collection of articles on the legacy of the
Frankfurt School:

> Through all their disparateness of method and object, the various authors
> of the Frankfurt School are united in the idea that the living conditions
> of modern capitalist societies produce social practices, attitudes, or per-
> sonality structures that result in a pathological deformation of our capac-
> ities for reason. It is this theme that establishes the unity of Critical
> Theory in the plurality of its voices. (PR: vii)

In particular, each gives a type of social diagnosis that highlights the
disconnect between the latent potential of reason, as disclosed at a
particular level of historical development, and actually existing social
structures, practices and modes of thought. Furthermore, this disconnect between existing reason and its developmental potential is caused
by particular social features of modern capitalism and/or technology.

For instance, Horkheimer and Adorno identify the dominance of means–ends rationality over all other forms of reason to be the characteristic root of contemporary social deformations, a dominance that in turn leads to the subjugation of nature and other humans. Although as they concede, instrumental rationality is evident in societies as least as far back as the ancient Greeks – witness their account of the single-minded cunning of Odysseus – it is only in contemporary societies that instrumental reason crowds out all other forms of reason. And the root cause of this is to be located in the supremacy of the economic institutions of capitalism and the rational organization of bureaucracies over all other social forms in contemporary societies. Even though the process of the Enlightenment should have made possible emancipatory forms of reason, the depressing dialectic of enlightenment for Horkheimer and Adorno is that, due to social causes, the potential of reason is deformed by the dominance of instrumental rationality.

In a quite different vein and with a quite distinct underlying social theory, Habermas also points to a socially caused pathology of reason. On the one hand, through the various processes of the rationalization of the lifeworld, the different underlying types of validity claims raised in communicative action are separated out from one another – meaningfulness, truth, rightness, and sincerity – and give rise to specialized forms of discourse with their own internal logics. On one side of the ledger, modernization processes can be seen to have disclosed new potentialities of reason that could enable more emancipated forms of social life. On the other hand, however, technical and economic progress in meeting the material needs of persons has entailed the separation out of anonymous, functionally integrated systems of social action – capitalist economies and state bureaucracies – that operate through anonymous mechanisms coordinating the purely strategic actions of individuals calculating their own best interests against the strict imperatives of increased profit and power. On the other side of the ledger, functional social systems, despite their undoubted efficiencies, have a tendency to take over functions of communicative socialization. When they do so, there result distinct social pathologies arising from the "colonization of the lifeworld by functionalist systems imperatives."

Whether considering Horkheimer and Adorno's dialectic of enlightenment or Habermas's colonization thesis – or the various other diagnoses of the present put forward by critical theorists – it is clear that each reflects a similar intuition. A one-sided development of human powers of reason leads to pathologies inhibiting the pursuit of the good life for humans, and that distorted development of reason can be traced to particular features of contemporary social life. Although Honneth frames his treatment of these themes in terms of a history of ideas, I think it quite clear from both the tone of the various articles and the frequency with which he has returned to the themes that Honneth himself regards the diagnosis of pathologies of instrumental rationalization to be a compelling and more or less accurate portrayal of a central deformation of contemporary social life. In other words, I think it warranted to ascribe this particular pathology diagnosis not only to earlier Frankfurt School theorists, but to Honneth as well.

If we now take a step back and look at these diagnoses from the vantage point of second-order disorders, we can notice another important set of similarities. The disconnects between the first and second levels are twofold. The first disconnect is that the first-order level of the extant social institutions – Horkheimer and Adorno's totally administered society or Habermas's colonized lifeworld – does not reflect the potential of the second-order level of historically available rationality – Horkheimer and Adorno's mimetic reason or Habermas's communicative reason. The second disconnect is that, even though there is an available potential of reason in contemporary society, it is not widely shared and accepted by society members, at a second-order level of reflexivity, as socially relevant precisely because of the structure of society. As Honneth puts it, we are dealing with "a system of convictions and practices that has the paradoxical quality of distracting one's attention from the very social conditions that structurally produce that system" (Honneth 2009d: 30). There are thus two forms of pathologies: the disconnect between extant social institutions and the available level of reason, and the disconnect between the broadly accepted sense of what rationality consists in and the latent potential of reason, which is not yet understood by society's members as available and potentially emancipatory. A critical social theory is oriented toward opening the eyes of society's members to the particular character of the second-order disorders and enabling them to see how the broader emancipatory potentials of reason have been obscured by current social conditions. This, in the end, is the crucial connection between theory and practice. Even though, for the Frankfurt School theorists, reason is one-sided and distorted, it is also the vehicle through which subjects may see the social world more clearly and take up their latent interest in emancipation, seeking to overcome the sources of social pathology and the suffering it causes.

4.2.5   Reification

One of Honneth's most substantive and intriguing analyses of a social pathology arises in his multifaceted endeavor to rehabilitate and reformulate Georg Lukács's concept of "reification." Very briefly put, Lukács contended that modern commercial society tends to treat everything as discrete, commensurable, interchangeable, priced objects – including not only raw resources and manufactured products, but also labor power, persons, artistic creations, ideas and ideals, social relations, politics, and so on. Because a capitalist economic system forces everything it comes into contact with into the commercialized model of a priced commodity, it tends to dehumanize, to reify, the social lifeworld and all within it. Honneth's goal is to see how the concept of reification might be productively reformulated in the present intellectual context, in particular when detached from Lukács's unconvincing overly totalizing critique of capitalist reification.

Whatever the deficiencies in Lukács's social theory, Honneth is convinced that an analysis of reification – of the complete and thorough dehumanization of others involved in treating them as things, as objects in the natural world to be manipulated or destroyed as one's own prudential calculations determine – is still practically relevant. It is important to note at the outset that Honneth's account of reification significantly narrows its scope and so makes it a much rarer phenomenon than Lukács believed. In fact, rather than Lukács's claim that reification is involved in any form of instrumental or calculative approach to social phenomena, Honneth claims that reification refers only to those rare situations where humans adopt an objectifying stance toward others while simultaneously forgetting their antecedent recognition of the others as human persons.

In order to unpack Honneth's analysis of reification, we'll need to recall the notion of antecedent recognition, contrast it with cognitive objectification, show the differences between objectification, instrumentalization, and reification proper, explore different causes of reification, see how both oneself and one's objective world can be reified, and explain the second-order disorder structure of reification.

Recall from 2.5 that Honneth first identifies antecedent recognition as a fourth form of recognition in his Tanner Lectures on reification. The fundamental idea is that, before any normatively substantive form of interaction with others can occur, interaction partners must become aware that they are dealing with persons – and not, say, insects or things or machines. Honneth conceives of such antecedent recognition as the "spontaneous, nonrational recognition of others as fellow human beings" (R: 152). Antecedent recognition concerns a kind of sympathetic engagement with the interaction partner, where the other is encountered as an emotional and intentional creature with his or her own desires, goals and projects. This differs fundamentally from interacting with the world of things which cannot have their own desires and goals, their own emotional responsiveness, and their own perspectives which can be taken up by others. In short, this form of primordial sympathetic engagement with an interacting *alter* involves the recognition of the other's existence as a human being.

Honneth highlights two different stances that individuals might adopt toward others, the world, and themselves: a stance of practical,

interested involvement and a stance of detached, cognitive objectification. One central ambitious thesis put forward in *Reification* is that the
stance of practical, interested involvement – antecedent recognition – is
both ontogenetically *and* conceptually prior to the objectifying, cognitive stance. For instance, the mode of formal, objectifying and calculative cognition of the facts of the social world and of social actors within
it that is often required in the economic sphere *presupposes* a prior act
of what might be called fully humanized recognition of the other, a
moment of interested involvement with the other as an other. The
thesis is supported by a set of fecund readings of diverse theoretical
and empirical sources – from Lukács to Dewey, Heidegger, Adorno,
Cavell, and developmental psychology – all pointing at similar phenomena, and all tending to support the claim that qualitative relations
to others have priority over objectified relations to others and, in
fact, that the former are a condition of possibility for the latter. Once
we understand the stance of interested involvement with another
as a stance of recognition, it is then a short but momentous step to
seeing the diverse theories as all supporting the bold claim that intersubjective recognition is a condition of possibility of even monological
cognition.

Despite the interest of these epistemological claims, we should turn
to their use in diagnosing reification pathologies. Honneth argues that
the concept of reification can be productively reanimated today under
changed theoretical and historical conditions by understanding acts of
reification as actions in which an objectifying stance – to the others, to
the world, or to the self – is adopted, while simultaneously *forgetting*
the constitutive connections that such an objectifying stance has to our
practical, interested, and normatively laden interactions with others.
For Honneth, in distinction from Lukács, an objectifying stance can be
benign when it serves to promote cognitive values in a normatively
permissible manner – say a naturalizing stance that promotes rational
problem-solving within a morally delimited sphere of permissible
objectification of others. A cost–benefit analysis of different governmental health policies, for instance, does involve the objectification of
various human "costs" such as human suffering and "profits" such as
human health, so that comparative monetary figures could be calcu-
lated for policy analysis. But this need not be a reifying form of objectification, at least if the constitutive connection of the calculations to
the antecedent recognition of society's members as humans is not systematically forgotten. In fact, even a non-benign stance of objectification of others need not be reification for Honneth. Consider, for example,
what is involved with the instrumentalization of another person for
one's own ends. In such a case, we make use of the other's human
characteristics in order to get what we want without their consent: for

instance, where we deceptively play on another's emotions in order to get them to carry out some social task we ourselves do not want to do. Thus, even with the objectification involved in non-benign instrumentalization, we must give antecedent recognition to the other in order to treat them as a mere means to our own ends. With reification, by contrast, we simply treat the other as a thing without any human characteristics whatsoever, forgetting entirely that sympathetic engagement with them as humans is a condition of possibility of treating them as mere things. Under extreme conditions where social practices have become thoroughly twisted, we might simply calculate how much soap could be produced from fat rendered from humans we were weighing in a prison camp, treating them simply as natural resources for our own ends. What is distinctive of reifying objectification, then, is that it involves an active forgetting of the priority of intersubjective recognition to cognition, where that forgetting is socially pervasive and systematically or institutionally reproduced, and where it serves to deform the networks of intersubjective recognition that are essential conditions for maintaining any ethical form of social life. Thus the reification of others involves a disregard of the structures of normatively imbued and meaningful recognition of others, where that disregard is located in distorted forms of sociality that serve to dehumanize participants and thereby perpetuate pathological social structures.

More extreme examples of reification – ones I believe that furnish a sort of paradigm for Honneth – are witnessed in the Holocaust and other genocides and mass slaughters of the twentieth century. In order to comprehend the possibility of such terrifying action, we would need to understand the complete and thorough dehumanization of others involved in treating them as things, as objects in the natural world to be manipulated or destroyed as one's own prudential calculations determine. While it is true that such atrocities are gravely immoral, mere appeal to routine human immorality cannot be the story, for industrialized or mass slaughter cannot be achieved without the desensitization of the perpetrators to the very existential character of the victims as persons with human characteristics. This involves a kind of conceptual or category error that can only be achieved, according to Honneth, through extensive social practices that de-habituate persons from the existential acknowledgment of others they ordinarily and automatically afford to all persons. While it is not Honneth's intention to provide a full social psychology explaining the pathologies of genocide, he does want to point out that it must involve a form of forgetting of the antecedent recognition of the very personhood of the victims, forgetting an elementary form of non-moral recognition that is itself a precondition of the other three main forms of morally substantive recognition.

Nor is it his intention to proffer a full sociological account of the causes of reification. In fact, he acknowledges just how tough a nut he must crack sociologically: if both the ontogenetic and conceptual arguments for the priority of recognition over cognition are correct, it would seem quite difficult for this fundamental human relationship to be forgotten. Honneth is careful to note that different kinds of reification will likely have different causes and that it is most likely that single-cause accounts of reification will be inadequate. The general suggestion throughout *Reification* is that some specific combinations of widely shared social practices, institutional incentives, and skewed cognitive schemata and evaluative patterns can often overcome the anthropological fundamentals of recognition and ensue in reifying second-order disorders. In sum, social reification involves a widely shared disregard of the primordial recognitional structure of intersubjective interactions in favor of objectification, where that forgetting is socially caused in some particular way and leads to social pathologies: specifically, pathologies that distort fully humanized interactions, thereby impeding the necessary social conditions for an ethical form of the good life.

Social interactions are the centerpiece of this analysis, yet it is not restricted to intersubjective phenomena, for Honneth also develops a categorial framework for understanding what it would mean to have reifying relationships both to the objective, nonsocial world, and to the inner world of subjective self-relations. The surprising concept of reification of the physical world, for Honneth, means systematic forgetting of the significance that objects and relations in the physical world might have for humans. The idea here follows Adorno's claim that, when we fully recognize another, we must have some grasp of the other's meaningful, emotionally imbued relationships with both persons and objects in the physical world. If that is so, then the notion of a "'reification' of nature... would consist in our failing to be attentive in the course of our cognition of objects to all the additional aspects of meaning accorded to them by other persons" (R: 63). Reification of nature and our physical environment would then be, according to Honneth's analysis, a sort of derivative phenomenon of the reification of others.

Reification of one's self involves a distorted relation to one's inner states, where one forgets that one's relation-to-self is chiefly a practical relation, a kind of qualitative recognition of one's self first made possible through the variety of intersubjective relations of recognition one experiences. The analysis identifies two varieties of such self-reification pathologies evident in contemporary culture. On the one hand, there is a form of self-objectification that Honneth labels "detectivism," where individuals take their inner states as brute empirical givens, not subject to transformation through acts of self-reflection, but rather only given states of affairs to be accurately detected and cataloged. Exemplary here is the kind of reification that occurs when individuals are required to take a disinterested stance toward their "personality type" and adjust their detached observations of their inner states to standardized grids for self-profiling. Think for instance of the reification potentially involved in articulating one's identity profile in online dating forums, particularly where one distances oneself from one's own characteristics and reports on one's character traits as though they were unchangeable facts of life unaffected by one's own choices or life experiences, in the same way as birthmarks or natural hair color.

At the opposite extreme, there is a kind of reification of self that Honneth identifies as "constructivism," where individuals take up an instrumentalizing stance to their inner states, believing in essence that those inner states are fully under the control of acts of will, and thereby represent wholly plastic material to be remolded in the light of socially defined norms and goals. Think, for instance, of the need to repeatedly transform one's personality to meet various job-specific character traits in contemporary "flexible" economies, devoid of lifelong careers. The reification involved in such treatment of one's own self as a willfully manufactured persona might in fact be reinforced through insistent practices of ideological recognition: one is esteemed as an "entrepreneur" of one's own life. In this case, the reification reinforced by the ideological recognition can be traced back to new imperatives of the current neoliberal labor market. In all these cases of self-reification, we forget this essential recognitional relationship to ourselves. We end up reifying our inner states, either believing that we can instrumentally remake ourselves in the interest of selling ourselves to others, or that our inner states can be calculatingly reduced to standardized schemas of categories, thereby locating ourselves in an abstract grid of personality types.

In the terms I have developed here, it should be clear that the social pathologies of reification represent second-order disorders: first-order objectifying cognitions and interactions (whether of and with other persons, one's own practical identity, or the objective world) are disconnected from a second-order grasp of them as temporally and conceptually dependent on a prior act of recognition, yielding reifying cognitions and interactions properly speaking. The metaphor of forgetting here essentially refers to a second-order disorder. Yet reification is a *social* pathology, not a mere self-misunderstanding, psychological peculiarity, or individual psychopathology. The analysis aims therefore at diagnosing socially widespread features and practices in our collective life, caused by specific mechanisms located in the extant forms and institutions of social life that thereby deform the prospects for a good life.

4.2.6 Organized self-realization

The last social pathology diagnosis to look at here is what Honneth calls "organized self-realization." In the inaugural volume of a new series intended to reinvigorate the distinctive Frankfurt School tradition of closely linking sociological and critical-philosophical research (Honneth 2002b), Honneth argues that a new, paradoxical form of individualism has developed since the 1960s (Honneth 2012h). According to the diagnosis, starting some forty years ago, claims to self-realization vastly multiplied in developed western nations. Consider, for instance, the explosion of various lifestyles and subcultures set off by the cultural revolutions of the 1960s. A decisive change in broader culture occurred when the hippie slogan of "let your freak flag fly" was domesticated into the idea that each and every person ought to consciously pursue his or her own individuality and authentically realize her or his own unique nature.

Although from an objective standpoint such an increase in conscious individualism would appear to be an increase in the qualitative possibilities for individual freedom, paradoxically, from a subjective standpoint, the expectations for self-realization increasingly strike individuals as insistent, inescapable demands. This form of institutionalized individualism in turn has led to pathological symptoms: psychological feelings of individual emptiness, meaningless, and purposelessness on the one hand, and sociological symptoms of a pervasive ideology of personal responsibility that lead to neoliberal deinstitutionalization on the other. The pathologies of socially required and organized self-realization clearly count as second-order disorders. Conceptually, a claim to authentic self-realization requires that one's own mode of self-realization – the first-order contents – be grasped, at a second-order level of reflexivity, as arising autochthonously out of one's own specific appropriation of one's life history and character. Yet the very claim to authenticity is itself rendered invalid – inauthentic, as it were – either when the first-order contents are not really one's own, in some significant sense, or when the second-order grasp of those contents is demanded from the outside as a condition of normalcy in contemporary capitalist culture or even as a job requirement in a neoliberal economy encouraging employees to become independent creative entrepreneurs. Thus, in the contemporary paradoxical form of institutionalized individualism, there exists a series of disconnects between the first-order contents – often enough, vacuous forms of consumer self-identification and "fulfillment" that are supplied as pre-given templates for individuality – and the second-order reflexivity required of adequate claims to authenticity – often vitiated by the fact that the demand for individualized self-realization is itself a productive force, playing an important functional role in neoliberal economic transformations.

What is particularly striking in Honneth's development of these theses is that, more so than in other works focusing on his own diagnoses of contemporary social pathologies, they are supported by substantive and explanatory socio-theoretic claims. Methodologically, the point is made that the symptoms of emptiness and purposelessness arising from institutionalized demands for authentic self-realization are *not* to be explained in a monocausal fashion, much less as ensuing from deliberate manipulations by economic powers of contemporary forms of social life. Honneth goes beyond these negative caveats to argue that social theory can identify elective affinities between distinct developmental processes, each with their own logic and dynamics, which nevertheless coalesce in a certain social formation. Thus, without falling prey to the errors of explanatory monism that plague not just Marxist economism but also Hegelian idealism, social theory is used to identify in piecemeal fashion the similar directional tendencies of distinct and often unrelated societal transformations.

This methodological idea is operationalized in a social theory that identifies six different developmental processes, giving rise to paradoxical institutionalized individualism, a social theory providing explanatory support to the social pathology diagnosis. First, of course, are the general structural transformations identified as definitive of modernization over the last several centuries by the founding sociologists (Durkheim, Simmel, and Weber, and carried forward in Parsons). In modern societies, individuals are increasingly released from the set bonds and life patterns of traditional societies, and experience tremendous increases in freedom to determine their own lives and thereby pursue self-realization. Second, and more recently, the move from a Fordist form of industrial economic organization to a post-Fordist form of capitalism after World War II, where employees are increasingly required to become self-responsible, creative inventors, and promoters of their own careers, has made self-realization into a productive force in economic development itself. Honneth adds two cultural transformations to these socio-structural and economic changes. On the one hand, the upheavals and social movements of the 1960s and 1970s brought to preeminence Romanticism's ideal of individual authenticity as a central orienting value. On the other hand, transformations in electronic communications media increasingly diffuse celebrity-centered models of authenticity that delimit available lifestyles and blur the lines between fiction and reality. Finally, two other changes also play explanatory roles. As a response to the way consumption-focused capitalism requires an ever-increasing turnover of new consumer goods, the advertising industry has instrumentalized the ideals of authenticity by packaging consumer items as aesthetic resources for each person's development of their "own" lifestyles. Finally, there is a dialectical interplay between the neoliberal political program of dismantling the welfare state and the increasing prominence of ideals of self-responsible, atomistic individualism, ideals that get channeled into and realized through pre-organized forms of "authentic" self-realization. In all then, a series of distinct social changes with elective affinities have led to increasing pressures for authentic self-realization even as they have simultaneously undermined the possibility of truly authentic and truly self-directed realization, thereby impeding or distorting the potentials for the good life for society's members.

4.3 Critical Perspectives

We've now seen what Honneth intends in promoting social philosophy as a distinctive and important endeavor within practical philosophy: it entails the attempt to diagnose pathologies in our current social relations and institutions that negatively impinge on individuals' opportunities to live fulfilling lives. We have also encountered here five of Honneth's substantive diagnoses (chapters 5 and 6 add three others), and we have seen how they all display the structure of second-order disorders. However, there are two large methodological issues which deserve further consideration. First, if we are to work with Honneth's definition of social philosophy, we ought to have a clearer idea of the various tasks involved in a diagnosis of social pathologies and the diverse sociological, historical, psychological, and philosophical work that would be needed to fulfill those tasks. This will enable me to present a general assessment of the degree to which Honneth has made good on the various tasks required for social philosophy. Second, we must deal again with a question that has repeatedly come up in this book: the status of the normative standards employed here. Other concerns – for instance about the persuasiveness of one or another of the specific diagnoses – will have to await another day. Nevertheless, consideration of these two general issues should put us in a better position to make an overall assessment of the fecundity of Honneth's social philosophy since the prospects for all the diagnoses stand or fall together on these basic methodological issues.

4.3.1 Tasks and tools of social diagnosis

Throughout 4.2, I have argued that the different social pathologies that Honneth has analyzed can be productively understood as exhibiting the conceptual structure of second-order disorders. In each case, there is a pervasive disconnect between first-order contents and second-order reflexive modes of grasping those contents, and that disconnect is claimed to be widely shared in contemporary society, caused by determinate social practices, institutions, and cultural patterns, and leading to deleterious consequences for society's members by blocking opportunities for the realization of an ethically intact form of collective life. Surely this is not the only way Honneth's social diagnoses can be reconstructed, but I do believe that it is particularly helpful in illuminating the various tasks a critical social theory must fulfill if it is to vindicate and put to use its proposed social diagnoses. I now turn to articulating four such tasks, and indicate the kinds of theoretical tools that would be needed to accomplish them.

The first task – what we might call symptomatology – is to identify and explain the symptomatic phenomena of the social pathology in a revealing way. An important achievement of social philosophy is in fact clearly naming and illuminating some problems or symptoms that we might not otherwise have noticed, or perhaps only had inchoate hints of. Honneth's own diagnoses employ tools of careful phenomenological description, sociological accounts of modernization and rationalization, as well as appeals to findings from action theory and psychology, though other tools might also work well. Literary evocations, illuminating metaphors, or perhaps even strategic exaggerations and distortions of social reality could also have a role here.[2] The key is that a symptomatology must be able to revealingly articulate the feelings of suffering, disorientation, or meaninglessness that the analyses take as their primary data. It should be noted that this task is not merely descriptive, however, for describing symptoms relies on substantive background assumptions concerning health and normalcy. In the case of social philosophy, in fact, the assumptions concern tricky judgments about the health or normalcy of a social form of life, in the light of which the identified phenomena can be said to be pathological.[3]

Analyses of social pathologies need to take on a second task: establishing that the described phenomena are pervasively experienced throughout contemporary society. Here, the theory must vindicate the claims that the symptoms really exist in a population, and in more than an accidental, episodic, or individualistic manner. For instance, if organized self-realization is really a *social* pathology, it is not enough to point out that a few persons in a given society suffer from the sense that they are forced, rather than free, to realize their unique individuality. This second task, supporting the claim that we are dealing with socially pervasive pathologies, is then a kind of epidemiology. Here, I would think that the standard tools of the social sciences would be directly relevant, particularly if we include more sophisticated tools than simple statistical analyses of polling data or other self-reports. For an epidemiology of social pathologies will need to document the pervasiveness of maladies that are not often acknowledged as such by those who suffer from or are subject to them.[4]

The third task is etiological: a diagnosis of social pathologies must supply convincing explanations of their social causes. As I have argued here, this will involve giving explanations for the second-order disorders in a way that shows them to be not only socially experienced, but also causally rooted in social structures, institutions, normative patterns, cultural schemas, and so on. Etiology is a crucial task for the viability both of social philosophy in its broad sense, and of critical social theory as a particular form of social philosophy. First, unless a social philosophy can establish that it is dealing with a pathology that has determinate causes in the structures of a specific society, whatever pathological symptoms it ostensibly identifies in its symptomatology and etiology may very well not be caused by social forces. Perhaps the suffering is a universal fact of human life, or perhaps it occurs in a specific society only because of environmental or geographical contingencies. Neither human susceptibility to death nor the Philippines' susceptibility to natural disasters is a social pathology – even though social conditions will influence the impact of both mortality and natural disasters. Only a convincing causal account of a putative social pathology can reliably indicate that it is in fact one. Second, since critical social theory intends to further emancipation, it must be prepared to explain the root causes of the social pathologies it diagnoses. That is because progressive social change requires that the real causes of maladies are addressed, rather than adopting ill-directed reform strategies. To be sure, causal accounts in the various social sciences are enormously contested at both substantive and theoretical levels. Any particular causal story told about some social phenomenon almost inevitably faces substantive objections, counter-stories and counterevidence, given the complexity of the phenomena studied. And methodological disputes are endemic in the social sciences: about the cogency of various explanatory strategies, about the propriety of modeling tools, and even about the very possibility of isolating relevant causal variables and factors. Such substantive and methodological disputes, rife in each of the social sciences – economics, psychology, sociology, political science, history – are magnified when a pathology explanation combines several disciplines. Nevertheless, despite its daunting nature, it seems to me that both social philosophy in general and critical social theory in particular cannot avoid wading into these choppy waters in order to attempt to justify the causal claims they need to make in order to support their diagnoses.

A social theory with only descriptive and explanatory ambitions might rest content with fulfilling these three tasks of symptomatology, epidemiology, and etiology, but a critical social theory – an interdisciplinary social theory fundamentally oriented by an emancipatory intent – will need to go further and begin to fulfill, fourth, the tasks of therapy: prognosis and treatment recommendations. Prognosis involves a reasoned assessment of the likely potential courses of the pathology with, and without, intervention or social change. Giving a recommendation or social prescription involves a reasoned assessment of different strategies for addressing, ameliorating, or eliminating the social pathology, while reducing unintended consequences of the treatment. Critical theory will need to provide theoretical resources for transformative social change, which may (non-exhaustively) include: resources for evaluating the likelihood and feasibility of social change; resources for consciousness-raising about the relevant second-order disorders; resources for strategizing, centrally including convincing accounts of the correct targets for social struggle; and normative resources for collective evaluations of current conditions, goals, and strategies. Given the variety of issues here, it seems to me that critical social theory will need to call on all of its tools: not only descriptive tools, but also epidemiological and etiological tools, as well as its normative and philosophical tools for classification, analysis, and evaluation. It will need, as well, to be able to communicate its results to relevant social actors in a clear and convincing way.

With this fourth set of clinical tasks, we touch on a distinctive issue in the history of the Frankfurt School: the fraught relationship between theory and practice. However critical social theory carries out its description and explanation of social pathologies, if it intends to make good on its inherent therapeutic tasks, it cannot help addressing a series of pointed questions that were part and parcel of that history. What is the best way to translate theory into everyday terms useful for social actors and social movements? Is theory sufficiently rooted in the ideals and problems of the actual social lifeworld, or is it an esoteric form of philosophical reflection? What of the potential elitism and anti-democratic character of theorists preaching what to do to subjects who might be modeled in the theory as too benighted to understand their own problems? Is the acceptance and employment of a social diagnosis by ordinary actors a condition of the truth of the diagnosis? Even more stringently, is progressive social change itself a criterion of the truth of the theory? These and allied meta-theoretical questions cannot be avoided, but I would say that they should also not overwhelm attention to the substantive center of the therapeutic endeavor: prognosis and recommendation.

Surely it is ambitious to envision a social philosophy carrying out all four of these theoretical tasks, but it seems to me that they follow organically, as it were, from the attempt to actualize critical social theory in the form of diagnoses of contemporary social pathologies.

I have argued elsewhere that Honneth has fulfilled these tasks with varying degrees of success (Zurn 2011); here I simply summarize my assessment.

The symptomatologies are phenomenologically well developed and often convincing in articulating subjectively felt experiences of second-order disorders, and the existence of those feelings are good prima facie evidence for the existence of underlying social pathologies.

The epidemiological claims – the claims that the feelings are suffi-ciently similar and prevalent throughout a given social population – are not directly vindicated by Honneth himself, but this is not a serious problem for the theory. Such vindication is a matter of empirical social research, and in many places evidence from various areas of the human sciences is provided. Even where evidence is not explicitly cited or indicated, it seems reasonable to understand the diagnoses as promis-ing hypotheses to be tested through well-designed sociological and social-psychological studies. In summary, then, there seems little concern with respect to the epidemiological tasks.

However, when we turn to the etiological task – the task of explain-ing the social causes of pathologies – the results are more variable across Honneth's different diagnoses. Let me indicate where I think things stand with the particular diagnoses before turning to a consid-eration of some more general methodological concerns. With respect to the pathologies of modern reasons, there are too many causal stories to choose from, as it were. It is unclear which of the several different and incompatible versions of the thesis Honneth intends to endorse: Habermas's earlier technocracy thesis, his later colonization thesis, Horkheimer and Adorno's thesis of a 3,000-year dialectic of Enlighten-ment, or Lukács's commodification thesis.

In comparison, the analyses of ideological recognition, invisibiliza-tion, and reification appear to suffer from a lack of substantive socio-logical details concerning institutional, structural, normative, cultural and/or functional explanations for the social causes of the pathologies. The two brief essays on invisibilization and ideological recognition are largely concerned with issues of how to conceive the relevant patholo-gies in relation to recognition rather than how to explain them. In the Tanner Lectures, Honneth offers an admittedly "general, rather vague hypothesis about the social etiology of reification" in "a highly one-sided form of praxis that necessitates abstraction from the 'qualitative' characteristics of human beings" (R: 155). But this beginning of an explanation sketch leaves open myriad substantive and methodologi-cal issues.

When we turn to organized self-realization, by contrast, there is a causal story that is clearly articulated, suitably complex, and pro-mising for further research. The six factors it isolates seem to account for the phenomena and could be further investigated for empirical correctness. Also, importantly, with this diagnosis there is an explicit statement of etiological methodology, namely, the invocation of Weber's elective affinities between multiple causal factors of several different kinds. Each of the causal factors has followed its own distinct historical pathway, but together they have coalesced into the specific pathological formation of contemporary institutionalized individualism. The causal picture here is that each of the six factors is jointly contributive to the phenomena, even though it may be difficult or impossible to isolate any one of them as absolutely necessary or to identify some set of them as jointly sufficient.[5] In summary, there is much room for further work on the etiological tasks associated with the diagnosis of social pathologies. The most promising route seems to be, then, to follow up the other diagnoses with causal accounts as clear and rich as that given for organized self-realization. A good example here is Honneth's multicausal account of the pathology of legal freedom: the rigid juridification of all personal relationships (FR: 86–94).[6] For only when we have traced the social symptoms to social causes do we know that we have a true social pathology.

Finally, I would suggest that without a well-developed causal account of a social pathology, the therapeutic task of prognosis and recommendation cannot even begin to get off the ground. Unsurprisingly, this fourth set of clinical tasks has not yet been acknowledged as such by Honneth, let alone brought to fruition. As I mentioned before, doing so will involve not only the substantive issues of how to change society in order to ameliorate social pathologies, but also the tricky methodological issues involved in thinking through the relationship between theory and practice. To be sure, there may be compelling moral concerns about intellectuals dictating reforms to members of society, as well as about transforming the theoretical search for truth into practical advocacy, but I would suggest that additional research must attend to and negotiate such issues explicitly.

In summary, then, I would suggest that Honneth's social diagnoses have generally carried out the task of symptomatology impressively, and have indicated clear paths for further empirical vindication of the epidemiological claims. However, in my opinion more attention should be paid to etiological, prognostic, and therapeutic concerns. A sufficient diagnosis of social pathologies must do more than simply take note of a complex of related social symptoms. It must also develop a convincing explanation of the social pathologies precisely so that social members can productively engage in the manifold social struggles necessary to overcome their causes. Said simply, a critical social theory of social pathologies needs not only an accurate explanation of pathological disorders at the level of personal experiences, but also insightful sociological explanations of the causes of those pathological distortions in order to really further emancipatory interests. My sense is that the current theory of recognition has managed the former tasks of description better than the latter tasks of social explanation and recommendation.

4.3.2   "Pathological according to what?"

Consider a claim that an aggressive form of cancer, say pancreatic cancer, is pathological for humans. This is uncontroversial since we have robust standards of measurement for healthy biological functioning. At the least, anything that results in long-term severe pain, organ failure, and premature death can be clearly labeled as dysfunctional, as a disorder of the human biological system. In contrast, defining the boundaries of pathological and non-pathological for issues of individual mental health and adequate mental functioning may be more difficult. For instance, is an individual's distrust toward others a healthy form of skepticism or unhealthy paranoia? Is another person's temporary euphoria a destructive mania or productive enthusiasm? Nevertheless, at least in cases of severe mental disorders – e.g., untreated schizophrenia – it is clear that the conditions so significantly impede individuals' ordinary functioning that we can uncontroversially label them as pathological. In the cases of individual somatic and mental health, then, the problems seem to be largely twofold: defining the human functionings that are relevant to individual health, and making useful distinctions on a continuum between pathological and non-pathological based on those functionings.

Things become more difficult still when we turn to the notion that a society, its practices, concepts, and institutions, might be "pathological." How exactly can Honneth explain and justify social philosophy's standards for distinguishing pathological from non-pathological features of a society? Here, analogous questions about defining the relevant functionings of any society and about making useful distinctions on a continuum will arise. But these questions become much harder to track in concrete terms, and much more subject to controversial assumptions and claims, particularly since defining the proper functionings of a society is a fraught normative endeavor. In order to get some traction on the problems, I will treat two different groups of challenges to the normative component of the project of social philosophy as Honneth understands it. First, there is a set of challenges that claims about social pathologies cannot be normative or evaluative in any of the standard ways we understand normativity in practical philosophy. Second, there are various skeptical challenges that the universal ethical standards Honneth invokes cannot be justified. At both levels, then, we are faced once again with the problem of grounding the critical standards of social critique.

In his response to Honneth's *Reification*, Raymond Geuss agrees that there is a distinctive tradition of social philosophical critique that Honneth's diagnosis of reification continues. But Geuss, himself no fan of standard forms of moral philosophy, points out that this alternative tradition of social criticism cannot and does not adopt the usual apparatus of moral philosophy. Such diagnoses of social disorders "do not intend to be moralizing – that is they do not discuss the defects in society relative to subjective failings of individual agents or relative to notions of responsibility, guilt, regret, or any of the rest of the Christian and post-Christian apparatus. If the criticism is *not*, however, moralizing, then to what can it appeal?" (Geuss 2008: 123).[7] Geuss's challenge could be extended to standard forms of political philosophy as well. After all, the social pathologies involved are not directly injustices against subjects committed by states, or illegitimate procedures employed for political decisions, or usurpations of political authority, or any of the other standard deformations of state action attributable to particular political regimes or political systems. Thus, even though well developed and clearly understood, the usual apparatus of standard political philosophy will also be unavailing here. We can get a sense of the difficulties by contrasting everyday responses to moral or political wrongs on the one hand and to social pathologies on the other. Standard violations of norms clearly evince responses in terms of normatively informed outrage on the parts of both those affected and sensitive observers. But in the case of some social pathologies, while individuals may feel inchoate discomfort or unease, it is not usually the case that there is a sense that either specific persons or specific institutions have violated legitimate expectations. They may even accept the discomforting feelings as ineliminable facts of life.

Honneth's response to this first challenge agrees with Geuss that standard modes of normative criticism – employing ideal norms of either morality or justice – are simply misplaced where we are concerned with assessing the degree to which social relations might be "pathological." But he also rejects the contention that social diagnosis might be able to do without normative standards altogether. The very concepts of pathological and non-pathological ineliminably refer to standards of health, normalcy, or proper functioning. In the case of social philosophy, the standard has to be that of a healthy society, or at least a society that is not seriously deformed. Although one might try to use strictly sociological, nonevaluative definitions of social normalcy, Honneth argues that such attempts inevitably end up surreptitiously invoking evaluative standards arising out of the sociologist's own culture. Thus, he insists, social philosophy must appeal to transcultural standards against which it can justify its distinctions between pathological and non-pathological. And for Honneth, the basic normative standard of any healthy society is set by his formal conception of ethical life: "A paradigm of social normality must, therefore, consist in culturally independent conditions that allow a society's members to experience undistorted self-realization" (Honneth 2007f: 35). Social pathology then involves socially prevalent and socially caused conditions that impede the full development of individuals' personalities in all their dimensions.

The general standard supplied by the formal conception of ethical life also resolves another related problem that arises in light of the diversity of pathologies analyzed: each diagnosis seems to appeal to different standards of social normality. Some are more or less directly normative in their critiques of contemporary social relations: invisibilization is pathological because it is a social relation that arbitrarily selects those who are to receive the moral disrespect of being treated as invisible; and institutionalized individualism violates the normative ideal that authentic forms of self-realization ought to be self-instigated and self-directed. Yet other diagnoses criticize practices for failing to live up to their implicit conceptual structure: ideological recognition supports institutions of regard that fail to live up to the recognition they themselves promise, instrumental rationalization leads to a one-sided advance of means–ends rationality despite reason's fuller developmental potential, and reified practices render individuals forgetful of the antecedent recognition of others as humans that is a precondition of recognition and cognition. Finally, some of the diagnoses also employ indirect normative critiques: instrumental rationalization also leads individuals to treat others as mere means to their own ends, organized self-realization has an ideological role in supporting neoliberal labor markets and vacuous consumer culture, and, reification deforms networks of intersubjectivity that are necessary conditions for ethical life. At first glance, then, the various diagnoses appeal to a number of distinct types of standards. However, a moment's more reflection will show that, in fact, all of the diagnoses refer, in a negative way, to Honneth's formal conception of ethical life. For each of the pathology diagnoses demonstrates a different way in which social conditions can impede the pursuit of human flourishing, where flourishing means the full development of the different aspects of persons' personalities and practical identities in and through social relations of recognition.

As soon as this move to a putatively universal and culturally invariant ethical standard is made, however, a second barrage of skeptical challenges arises. These challenges can be organized into two families: those based on neo-Kantian suspicions of universalist claims concerning the good, and neo-Nietzschean suspicions of any transcultural universals whatsoever. To understand the Kant-inspired challenge first, we need to understand the distinction between "the right" and "the good." In its briefest and simplest form, this is a distinction between two kinds of evaluative standards, two kinds of ways that actions can be valued. While the right concerns what duties individuals or institutions owe to other persons, the good concerns what is worthwhile for individuals or collectives to pursue as goals. According to the standard liberal interpretation, issues of the right may be settled from an impartial perspective, considering any and all persons simply as free and equal rational agents. Issues of the good can only be settled from the perspective of ethical agents sharing a thick ethical tradition, capable of realizing themselves in the light of the substantive values they esteem as most worthy. The traces of this basic distinction are detectable in Honneth's own account of the difference between respect and esteem recognition, and in his continuation of Hegel's critique of pure morality for ignoring the substantive background of ethical life. For instance, in FR, Honneth argues that Hegel was correct: the right and the just cannot be understood without seeing how freedom is valuable, how freedom is the predominant good for modern individuals (see chapter 6).

Although there is a voluminous philosophical literature on this distinction, for our purposes the key issue is that those in the liberal tradition insist, in one way or another, on two things: questions of the right can be given culture- and time-transcending answers universally valid for all persons; and answers to questions of the good are ineliminably restricted to distinct and culturally specific conceptions of human flourishing. When practical philosophy seeks to employ universal normative standards, according to this Kant-inspired line of thinking, it must then restrict itself only to issues of the right. Whether it be Rawls's argument that the "burdens of judgment" in practical reasoning entail that there will always be a diversity of incompatible and rival "comprehensive doctrines" of the good life (Rawls 1996: 47–71), or Habermas's argument that issues of the good are always embedded in distinct historical traditions yielding a plurality of incompatible ethical identities and self-understandings (Habermas 1993), Kantians agree that the ancient project of a universally valid ethics is no longer compatible with a modern pluralistic world. Perhaps surprisingly, many contemporary defenders of the so-called Hegelian response to these ideas – e.g., communitarians – have agreed with the liberals that issues of the good cannot be universally justified but are indeed context-bound. They simply argue against the liberals' account of the right, claiming it too is culture-bound, particularistic, and non-universalizable (MacIntyre 1989; Sandel 1982; Taylor 1989).

Thus from both prevalent sides of the debate between the right and the good, Honneth's attempt to provide a universalistic ethics appears doomed to fail. It seems frankly unbelievable that a practical philosophy today, in any form, could articulate one convincing and correct picture of the good life for individuals, or presuppose that there is one universally valid form of flourishing for persons. There is a buzzing, blooming diversity of substantive conceptions of ethical life in modern, complex, and pluralistic societies. Not only is this ethical plurality apparently ineliminable – there is no hope of going back to putatively homogeneous societies with one hegemonic comprehensive doctrine – but this ethical plurality is positively attractive to us – we wouldn't want to go back if we could. How then can Honneth employ a universalistic ethics as the underlying standard for his pathology diagnoses, not to mention for his theories of recognition and freedom?

The key move is to focus on a *formal* conception of ethical life. Rather than articulate specific determinate substantive values or ways of living as universal, Honneth claims universality only for the *general social conditions* required for the realization of any number of different substantive ways of life. Thus at a stroke the theory is able to accommodate much of the diversity of contemporary ethical pluralism since it does not aim to choose or champion any particular form of self-realization. It is oriented more to the social structures and relations that enable – or disable – any and all persons' opportunities to realize themselves. "Thus what constitutes the standard according to which social pathologies are evaluated is an ethical conception of normality tailored to conditions that enable self-realization. This ethical background condition is formal in the sense that it only normatively emphasizes the social preconditions of human self-realization, and not the goals served by these conditions" (Honneth 2007f: 36). Thus, for instance in the theory of recognition, different forms of intersubjective recognition are shown to correspond to different forms of practical relation-to-self, such that Honneth can assert that specific forms of social regard are the formal social conditions for the development of practical identity of corresponding kinds. Although this provides a teleological account of human morality – as oriented toward the promotion of individual human development – it need not posit any particular positive ideal of human development or flourishing.[8] Furthermore, the diagnosis of social pathologies need rely even less on any positive vision of the good since its method is essentially negative: it articulates current, concrete social conditions that impede individual's self-realization. It is true then that social philosophy refers to normative standards of social normality, but the focus is on negative social conditions impeding individuals' pursuit of the good life, however they might understand or pursue the good life.

The ultimate justification for the formal conception of ethical life that serves as the normative backbone to Honneth's social philosophy is, finally, what Honneth calls a "weak formal philosophical anthropology." This enterprise is intended to reconstruct universal features of human life – say, social recognition structures, the contours of individual identity development, the spheres of human freedom, and so on. But it is not intended as a full catalog of all universal features of human life. It focuses only on those that impinge on the opportunity of each person to develop his or her personal identity in its various dimensions. Thus, for instance, because intact social structures of inter-subjective love, respect, and esteem can be empirically shown to be necessary conditions for free individual self-realization, these recognition structures must be included among the general conditions a formal anthropology articulates. In these various ways – invoking a formal rather than substantive conception of ethical life, restricting itself to negative impingements on self-realization, and referring to an empirically supported but thin philosophical anthropology – social philosophy, according to Honneth, is able to make universal claims about ethical life, thereby answering to the Kant-inspired concerns about ethical pluralism.

Skeptics of any universal claims whatsoever about humanity will, of course, be unconvinced by these moves. Whether it is Nietzsche's insistence on the perspectival character of any evaluative claims, or Richard Rorty's admonitions that talk of universal features of human nature is little more than a way of expressing our own contingent and particular sentimental attachments to those features identified, or Michel Foucault's and Judith Butler's relentless suspicions that purportedly human universals turn out to be veiled vehicles for normalizing, subordinating, and/or excluding some persons taken not to possess the requisite human nature – all agree that sensitive historical genealogies show the futility, and potential perniciousness, of universalistic normative projects. Honneth himself recognizes the worry posed by a simple inductive inference: since each past attempt by social philosophers to identify human universals has turned out, in hindsight, to be little more than "an arbitrary expression of a culturally contingent point of view" (Honneth 2007f: 38), why shouldn't we expect the very same to be true of the formal conception of ethical life and the thin philosophical anthropology supporting it?

In responding to the neo-Nietzschean suspicions, the greatest burden of argument will be shouldered by the strength, coherence, and diversity of evidence justifying Honneth's general theory of recognition and therefore its philosophical anthropology. Much of this is culled from diverse domains of social science: developmental psychology, moral psychology, social psychology, sociology, political economy, social history, political science, and so on. Thus the response to abstract skepticism will largely be made in terms of the cross-cultural and trans-temporal validity of the particular social scientific research employed in supporting the philosophical anthropology. Support for the empirical cogency of Honneth's anthropological claims comes not only, however, from the cogency of isolated research studies. It also arises from the overall coherence of the different studies with one another.

When, for instance, the findings of psychoanalytic object relations theory cohere in an illuminating way with the findings of social conflict histories, the overall ideal of a formal conception of ethical life based around struggles for recognition gains significant support. And all of this straightforwardly empirical support is further validated to the extent it coheres with diverse research trajectories in philosophy and social theory broadly construed. Said in the briefest way, the justification for the truth of recognition theory is that it can coherently systematize a great deal of diverse findings from a great deal of diverse fields of thought, and all in a manner that productively illuminates "the struggles and wishes of the age."

One might worry in the abstract about hanging one's theory on empirical evidence,[9] but it seems to me that this is in fact a real strength of the account. Rather than the standard philosophical move of jumping to a very abstract level in order to vindicate the universality of claims – for instance, that humans are "rational animals" – Honneth's theory descends to the details and attends to psychological and social reality as revealed in our best investigations. Applied to the particular question at issue here, this means that Honneth's response to the genealogists' suspicions is that the standard for gauging social pathologies – social relations that negatively impact individuals' abilities to fully realize their practical personalities – is not itself restricted to one contemporary form of society, as shown by the diverse, justified research results it is reliant upon.

With that weak formal anthropology delineated and the support for it clearly indicated, the burden of argument, it seems to me, shifts from Honneth's theory and toward the genealogical skeptic: she must explain exactly where and how some putative universal is not in fact universal. Is love not a vital human need, and is it not required for the development of basic self-confidence? Does the development of self-confidence not depend in fact upon a specific form of unconditional love and support that negotiates the boundaries between intersubjective dependence and independence? Is it false that the historical differentiation of social relations of honor into two distinct forms of regard – respect for autonomy and esteem for traits and achievements – represents the realization of an implicit and important conceptual division in the very idea and practice of honor? And is it false to say that this differentiation represents an improvement in the overall social conditions necessary for individuals' realization of distinct dimensions of their practical identities? The proof for such questions, I would say, is in the pudding: Honneth has presented his, and the skeptic's critique needs to specifically address that pudding. After all, it is not as if recognition theory is hiding its ethical values.

As for the genealogical suspicions that universal normative standards are particularly suspect for complicity with unsavory forms of power, perhaps these worries can never be dispelled fully. Consider, for instance, Lois McNay's argument that "at a conceptual level, the idea of recognition is constraining for an analysis of gender because it remains committed to a face-to-face model of power that obscures the systemic ways in which sexual and other inequalities are produced" (McNay 2008: 196). Her idea is that Honneth's empirical account of subject formation – upon which his normative account of recognition is based – whitewashes those power asymmetries of gender that are always already at play in subject formation in the first place, thereby yielding a normative account (unintentionally) complicit in gender oppression. My suspicion here is that such a critique is both on and off target. It is correct to highlight the lack of a sufficiently developed account of the interrelationships between the structures of recognition, gender assumptions, subject formation, and asymmetrical structural power in Honneth's work (Allen 2010). As we will see in 6.4, the absence of a fully developed theory of power in Honneth's recent theory of social freedom raises allied concerns. But it is wide of the mark in suggesting that such an account is necessarily or conceptually unavailable to the theory of recognition, particularly in arguing that this is due to recognition theory's exclusive reliance on an analysis of face-to-face interactions. As I've emphasized, the normative standards employed in Honneth's pathology diagnoses are justified in a broad-based account of the coherence of a number of distinct lines of empirical and theoretical argument.

4.4 Recapitulation

With the specific interpretation of social philosophy as the diagnosis of social pathologies, Honneth has made a number of significant contributions. First, this interpretation makes a major contribution to the history of thought. On the one hand, it shows how a number of quite disparate forms of practical reflection on contemporary society over the last two hundred and fifty years can be seen as engaged in one overall project: social philosophy. Whether it be Rousseau, Marx, Weber, or various other critical theorists, each pursues a form of social analysis quite distinct from either descriptive social theory or ideal moral and political philosophy: namely, the detection and critique of pathologies that undermine the social conditions necessary for human flourishing. Second, Honneth has shown how Frankfurt School critical theory differs from other forms of critical social theory, such as feminism, critical race theory, or postcolonial theory. While all the broader critical theories are oriented toward emancipation, the Frankfurt School in particular has highlighted the diagnosis of social pathologies rooted in the specific form of rationality characteristic of modern capitalist societies. Third, Honneth has given us a number of enlightening substantive diagnoses. And, fourth, he has articulated the underlying conceptual issues and methods involved in productively carrying forward social philosophy. Although I have argued that more work needs to be done in many of the specific diagnoses, particularly in supplying causal accounts sufficient to explain the second-order disorders and in exploring prognostic and therapeutic possibilities, I have also argued that, despite challenges, the endeavor is not conceptually flawed from the get-go. I would maintain that the idea of social philosophy as pathology diagnosis is a particularly distinctive and promising area of research.

5

Recognition and Markets

What can the political theory of recognition say about the distribution of material resources such as income, wealth, power, or health care? Doesn't it counsel moving away from the social theory of conflicts of interests toward struggles over recognition? And doesn't this mean that recognition theory overlooks unjustifiable inequalities of material resources, as well as the political economic structures that cause those inequalities? In focusing on the injuries of disrespect to identity, what about the injuries of deprivation and dispossession? This chapter considers these and allied questions by way of an account of an extraordinary exchange between Honneth and Nancy Fraser in their co-authored 2003 book *Redistribution or Recognition?* While both of these contemporary critical theorists agree that political theory must address distributive injustices, they fundamentally disagree about the adequacy of the recognition paradigm for conceptualizing economic relations, contemporary capitalism, and diverse struggles for social justice. But this is not just a debate between Honneth and Fraser, for it reveals a number of crucial fault lines in recent political philosophy more broadly: between liberal egalitarianism and multiculturalism, between a politics of individual rights and entitlements and a politics of group identity and accommodation, between equality and difference, between Kantian proceduralism and Hegelian substantialism. In working through the issues raised in RoR, then, it is important to keep these broader intellectual contexts in mind.

To set the stage, the chapter will first develop a crucial point: as analyzed by Honneth, struggles for recognition have never been restricted only to what is called "identity politics" (5.1.1). In fact, Honneth's substantive concerns have always been wider than identity politics, and he has consistently tied his recognition theory to issues of political economy: the division of labor, wealth inequality, neoliberal privatization, and so on. Thus the chapter will provide an overview of Honneth's account of the constitutive connection between economic injustices and a society's underlying recognition order (5.1.2). We can then turn to Fraser's specific critiques of Honneth (5.2) and a critical assessment of this unfinished debate (5.3).

5.1   Work and Recognition

5.1.1   Beyond identity politics

Recognition theory, as it has developed in the last thirty years, has been most closely associated with social movements focused on identity-based forms of injustice, that is, injustice affecting persons on account of "who they are": female, nonwhite, immigrant, homosexual, and so on. This is a natural – if misleading – association given, to begin, the tight connections between recognition theory's account of the inherently social formation of individual selves and its account of injustice in terms of social forms of disrespect and denigration. Further, the appearance of recognition theory in the late 1980s and 1990s fit an understandable temporal pattern for practice and theory: "the owl of Minerva begins its flight only with the onset of dusk" (Hegel 1991: 23). Here Minerva's owl – political theory – seemed to fly some twenty to thirty years after the flowering of the so-called "new social movements" in the 1960s and 1970s, movements seeking to move traditional oppositional politics away from class conflicts and toward issues such as discrimination against racial and ethnic minorities, anti-patriarchalism and the women's movement, pacifism, ecological stewardship, gay and lesbian rights, and self-determination of indigenous peoples. Recognition theory provides a particularly apt language for articulating the aspirations and distinctive moral concerns of many of these new social movements.

Finally, of course, the normative concept of recognition is not solely the province of Honneth's particular theory but was powerfully articulated by many other theorists, who tended to tightly associate recognition with identity politics, and only multicultural state policies at that.[1] Charles Taylor in his famous 1992 essay (Taylor 1994) used his version of recognition theory to argue for the need to give special political and societal regard to the identity-based claims for a cohesive linguistic community, claims put forward by francophone Quebecois Canadians. Following Taylor's lead, "recognition" became a central keyword – usually denoting only multicultural policies of state accommodation of indigenous, ethnic, religious, and cultural minorities – in 1990s' debates in political philosophy (Barry 2001; Benhabib 2002; Habermas 1994; Kymlicka 1995; Okin and respondents 1999). The focal concerns in these debates were whether the liberal framework of equal individual rights could accommodate group-differentiated rights and whether such "recognition" of groups might perversely facilitate the internal oppression of group members. Fraser herself often conceptualizes recognition struggles in terms of identity-based claims for the acknowledgment of group difference, thereby virtually reducing the theory of recognition to the practice of multiculturalist identity politics.[2]

When we look only to identity politics as the paradigm of recognition politics, however, we are doing a serious disservice to Honneth's theory. In fact, one might say that such narrowing is a problem in political philosophy more generally, foreclosing a proper appreciation of the diversity and scope of recognition relationships. To begin, as we have seen in chapter 3, this is a much too narrow construal of the variety of actual social struggles for recognition: they can focus on inclusion under universal norms as well as pluralization through differentiated norms; they can be waged on behalf of individuals or of groups; they can aim at overcoming or affirming identity-based differences; they can aim to change familial, legal, and political institutions as well as cultural patterns of evaluation; and so on. More importantly for this chapter, the identity politics construal of recognition is too narrow for Honneth because he has consistently, throughout his thirty-year academic career, been concerned to theorize economic, class, and distributive struggles in terms of his developing recognition theory. A brief look at the history of Honneth's writings makes his long interest in economic struggles clear, especially those focused around work and the conditions of labor in contemporary capitalist societies (Smith 2009). His third article, published in 1980, was a critique of Habermas's way of conceptualizing the relationship between work and instrumental action (Honneth 1995j). Because Habermas identified labor with merely technical questions about instrumental rationality, according to Honneth his theory missed the protest potential embedded within experiences of alienated labor. In other words, for Honneth of 1980 – and, it should be said, also for Honneth of 2011, as we will see in the next chapter – treating labor as a mere technical activity entails missing the potential for moral protest against the status quo that is embedded in contemporary capitalist conditions of work. Similar concerns are raised in a 1981 article (Honneth 1995g) and 1985's CoP. To be sure, this early work is not yet formulated in terms of recognition theory, but they clearly show Honneth's interests in treating labor and work experiences as a crucial starting point for engaged social theory.

Furthermore, that normative consideration of economic issues – the division of labor, class conflicts, protest against economic degradation, social welfare rights, just wages, and just distributions – are all represented in *The Struggle for Recognition* as well. For instance, Honneth argues that Hegel and Mead showed, in broad strokes, that an acceptable modern form of ethical life must be based around a thoroughly democratic division of labor. Marx's early work on the alienating character of work under capitalism is also taken to have "succeeded...in showing labour to be a central medium of mutual recognition" (SfR: 158). The work of English historians E. P. Thompson and Barrington Moore is used to show how class conflicts are not merely struggles over material resources, but are also recognition struggles, deeply motivated by the actors' morally encoded sense of disrespect (SfR: 165–8). Furthermore, Honneth argues that the expansion of social welfare rights in the twentieth century – in particular, rights to a degree of economic security and a basic standard of living – should be understood as resulting from moral arguments founded on respect-based recognition since each person deserves the social bases of full membership in the political community. And struggles over esteem recognition are explicitly tied to struggles over economic arrangements: "since...relations of social esteem are...indirectly coupled with patterns of economic distribution, economic confrontations are also constitutive for this form of struggle for recognition" (SfR: 127).[3] Finally it should be noted that Honneth published an important essay on Dewey's theory of social democracy in 1998 which centrally revolves around the internal relationships Dewey theorized – and Honneth largely endorsed – between distributive justice, the division of labor, and social relations of esteem recognition (Honneth 2007c).[4] In short, recognition theory as developed by Honneth was never restricted only to identity politics; along with a broad focus also on the conditions of socialization, individual legal rights, and the structures of esteem, it always kept a keen eye on the justice of economic relations.

5.1.2   Recognition and political economy

Starting in 1995, the American political theorist Nancy Fraser – a pioneer in feminist critical social theory – began to develop a critique based upon the idea that economic injustice had received too little attention in recent radical political practice and theory.[5] In contemporary radical politics, according to Fraser, focus had shifted too exclusively toward issues of identity politics (chiefly gender, sexuality, and ethnicity) and environmentalism. Political movements seemed indifferent to the ravages of distributive injustices, even though the rise of neoliberal capitalism and the consequent diminishment of the welfare state in the 1980s and 1990s should have alerted movements to such economic concerns. She detects a similar insensitivity to issues of distributive justice in the newly prominent political theories of recognition. While she is broadly sympathetic to the kinds of harm and injustice articulated in recognition theory – and so is not wedded to the notion that *only* economic injustices matter – she argues that the extant paradigms of recognition theory had not and could not develop an adequate critique of political economy that would comprehend economic injustices alongside recognitional ones. Even as the details of Fraser's arguments have changed and developed, her central claims are powerfully summarized – and directed specifically at Honneth's theory – in her contributions to *Redistribution or Recognition?*[6]

Honneth's RoR chapters are thus structured in response both to Fraser's various critiques of recognition theory and to her own preferred version of critical social theory. This chapter addresses only Fraser's most potent critiques of Honneth's recognition-based approach to political economy, leaving aside his critiques of her preferred theory. This will help to show the kind of work that Honneth leaves unfinished in RoR but attempts to rectify in his latest magnum opus, *Freedom's Right*, treated in chapter 6.

The central ambition of Honneth's RoR account of the capitalist economy is to show the plausibility of a theory that is thoroughly grounded in recognition, rather than in other nonrecognitional normative principles or in functionalist accounts of the economy. Thus the account aims to show how issues central to distribution-focused theories of justice – e.g., systematic impoverishment, increasing material inequality, structural unemployment, the concentration of oligarchic power, global economic inequality – can be comprehended and normatively evaluated with the same recognitional concepts applied to other forms of injustice, misrecognition, and social pathology. Honneth sees no need to develop a different set of theoretical tools for the economic domain of society. Accordingly, he must develop a social theory of modern capitalist economies that rejects the methods of functionalism and systems theory, where economies are theorized as amoral, norm-free domains of interaction with more or less automatic processes happening behind the backs of participants, largely out of their control and understanding. On Honneth's account, economic phenomena are seen as thoroughly shot through with normative content, subject to human control and guided by moral concerns, in particular, moral concerns that can be traced back to the structures of intersubjective recognition. In short, the ambition is to show the capacious reach of a single normative and social theory built around demands for recognition. This ambition is realized through two main arguments: one about the normative determinants of economic outcomes, and another about the normative preconditions of functioning markets.

The starting points of the first argument, as in Honneth's general theory of recognition, are everyday experiences of misrecognition, in particular those felt by those subject to economic dislocations. When individuals fail to achieve fair pay for their labor, or lose their job to "downsizing" by their employer, or cannot find any work in a stagnant job market, or have inadequate resources for education and retraining needed to keep up in a changing labor market, they experience these dislocations as affronts to their sense-of-self, affronts generated by distorted or inadequate appreciation of their own worth and contributions. Economic harms are thus experienced morally, as forms of disrespect or of denigration of one's achievements. Building on a moral phenomenology of such maldistributive harms, Honneth then endeavors to show that such harms are best conceived in terms of a normative analysis of violated expectations of legitimate intersubjective recognition. Of the three main forms of mutual recognition, Honneth focuses on two as crucial to evaluations of economic injustices: self-respect and self-esteem. In particular, he argues that in capitalist societies the demand for recognition supporting self-respect is specifically interpreted in terms of a principle of equal opportunity: because each person can legitimately demand to be treated as equally autonomous, in practice each person deserves fair equality of opportunity to achieve their own goals and life projects. Capitalist societies also interpret the demand for recognition supporting self-esteem in terms of a specific principle of achievement: in specifically capitalist societies, where each person is esteemed in part for his or her individual work contributions and accomplishments, each deserves to be fairly compensated in line with those contributions and accomplishments. Economic dislocations in our society are, on this account, experienced in terms of violations of the principles either of equal opportunity or achievement.

Of course, there have always been very significant disagreements about what the principles of equal opportunity and achievement actually mean in practice and what they specifically require from society. On Honneth's interpretation of struggles over economic issues like wages, distributive equality, and the division of labor, these disagreements are precisely the substantive content of these struggles. So, for instance, following T. H. Marshall's periodization of the expansion of citizenship, Honneth argues that historical struggles for the expansion of the content of rights should be understood in part as struggles over the practical requirements for fully realizing the principle of fair equality of opportunity. From the eighteenth-century focus on negative rights such as private property to the nineteenth-century focus on positive rights such as political participation in decisions about economic relations, and on to the twentieth-century focus on social welfare rights such as social insurance against the calamities of cyclical economic crises, such struggles over economic issues are best understood as struggles over the meaning and social entailments of the principle of fair equality of opportunity. For an example relevant to the achievement principle, consider feminist struggles over the last fifty years over androcentric denigration of unpaid reproductive labor such as child rearing and housework. Criticizing Marx for focusing only on paid labor, Honneth argues that feminist scholarship in favor of the social provision of adequate day care or for the remuneration of housework shows that these are not merely struggles over pay and monetary equality, but are in fact moral struggles over the degree to which such activities and their necessary qualifications are to be socially esteemed in the first place. They are struggles over the proper scope and application of the recognitional principle of achievement and its practical realization in our society.

Honneth then generalizes these kinds of examples to claim that, for any specific society, there is a specific respect and esteem "dispositive" or "recognition order." This recognition order is a reigning set of interpretations of the specific principles that society uses to accord respect and esteem – fair equality of opportunity and merited achievement for capitalist societies – and institutional structures that more or less imperfectly realize those interpretations of the moral principles – e.g., social welfare rights and merit-based remuneration. In this way, we can interpret contemporary economic relations as the specific outcome of a society's struggles over the meaning and institutional embodiments of its respect and esteem order. So, for instance when we look at claims about the unequal distribution of work or about inadequate wages for some jobs, we are considering claims about misrecognition, claims that may underlie socially organized struggles for a more just system of work and remuneration. The current economic situation can then be interpreted as a specific economically relevant order of respect and esteem, one that has resulted from past struggles for recognition waged in the economic sphere. The crucial idea is to think of the extant distribution of remuneration and the division of labor in any society as an expression of current patterns of social esteem concerning individual task types, the abilities required to perform them, and their overall social contribution. Thus struggles over a fairer distribution of goods and resources should be thought of as recognition struggles. As Honneth put the argument in an earlier article:

> Conflicts over distribution, as long as they are not merely concerned with just the application of institutionalized rules, are always symbolic struggles over the legitimacy of the sociocultural dispositive that determines the value of activities, attributes and contributions. In this way, struggles over distribution, contrary to Nancy Fraser's assumption, are themselves locked into a struggle for recognition. The latter represents a conflict over the institutionalized hierarchy of values that govern which social groups, on the basis of their status and their esteem, have legitimate claim to a particular amount of material goods. In short, it is a struggle over the cultural definition of what it is that renders an activity socially necessary and valuable. (Honneth 2001b: 54)

The same point goes for other economic patterns and outcomes beyond the distribution of goods: the specific division of labor, the remuneration schedule for different jobs, the redistributive effects of social welfare rights, the progressivity of tax schedules, and so on. All these are not merely economic phenomena determined by the anonymous, economic laws of supply and demand and the like. They also reflect the outcomes of morally imbued conflicts of interpretation over appropriate modes of intersubjective treatment of persons. According to Honneth, then, struggles over the principles of equal opportunity and achievement – the very motors of major economic transformations in capitalist societies – can best be reconstructed in terms of the underlying moral logic of mutual recognition. This first argument claims, in sum, that, because a given society's particular economic outcomes are conditioned by contests over normative meanings, issues of economic justice must be understood in recognitional terms.

Honneth's second main argument claims that markets – the central organizing feature of capitalist economies – are not themselves autonomous, but have instead a thick set of irreplaceable normative preconditions, preconditions that can be reconstructed in recognitional terms (RoR: 135–50 and 250–6). Some examples of various preconditions of markets will help to make the point here. To begin with law, no capitalist economy is possible apart from those legal arrangements that: establish and secure private property; create and regulate corporations; enforce the actionability of contracts; establish the legality of commodity markets for some entities but not others; establish the parameters of employability; protect against fraud and deceit; regulate labor contracts; establish fair procedures for bargaining between firms and employees; set the limits of monopoly power; correct for negative externalities that firms would otherwise costlessly impose on others; and provide for public goods. Notably, all of these legal arrangements are thoroughly imbued with moral content: conceptions of rights, fairness, justice, merit, and so on all play a role in convincing individuals of the acceptability of these arrangements. Said another way, if individuals were to lose their belief in the legitimacy of these legal arrangements and so withdraw their support for them – say, because they believed that they embodied seriously egregious forms of misrecognition – then markets would simply not be able to function. This is what it means for these legal arrangements to be irreplaceable *preconditions* of markets.

Like points can be made about other normative preconditions. Markets presuppose well-socialized individuals with certain specific capacities for appropriate interpersonal behavior and comportment: specific habits of interaction are required to establish and maintain social networks, intersubjective trust, and stable relations of authority. Furthermore, markets cannot work efficiently without substantial numbers of participants who have internalized behavioral controls that prevent them from engaging in covert but egregious relations of coercion and fraud, even when it may be strategically beneficial to do so. Without such dispositions, markets may barely function, but their enforcement costs will become unsustainable. At the same time, individuals must have internalized dispositions to strongly prefer material self-interest over all other goals and values they might have, at least when interacting in specifically market-mediated spheres. Without *homo economicus*, markets may function, but they will not efficiently connect available products to individual preferences. These specific patterns of interpersonal norms and psychological dispositions are, furthermore, systematically tied to moral conceptions and so connected to society's general acceptance of the worth of those norms and dispositions. In sum, because capitalist markets depend on the acceptance, by society's members, of the moral legitimacy of some irreplaceable legal, interpersonal, and psychological preconditions, and those preconditions are anchored in recognitional judgments, capitalist economies are in fact embedded in normatively structured social orders. Further, because these preconditions obtain only to the extent that social actors continue to accept their legitimacy, and because this acceptance depends on normative attractiveness, markets would collapse as soon as social actors ceased to believe in their legitimacy and thereby withdrew their support from them. Capitalist markets cannot then be analyzed as purely functionalized or norm-free domains of society. There is no integration of social action by means of markets without there already existing a moral consensus on market preconditions: social integration through recognitional norms has primacy over other forms of social action coordination.

With these two main arguments – the first concerning the normative determinants of economic outcomes, the second concerning the normative preconditions of functioning markets – Honneth intends to forge tight moral and socio-theoretic connections between recognition and political economy. However, this is not a mere exercise in descriptive theory sensitive to the social world's normative infrastructure, but is ultimately aimed at clarifying and articulating justified calls for greater economic justice. On this view, justice in the political economy is a demand arising from individuals' legitimate recognition expectations to the appropriate social bases of self-respect and self-esteem. Here, for Honneth, it is crucial that critical social theory not lose sight of work as a central site for self-realization through intersubjective recognition, and as a central site for developing a progressive theory of a just division of labor. As he puts it ruefully in a later article, "Never in the past two hundred years have there been so few efforts to defend an emancipatory and humane notion of work as there are today ... the hardships of all those who not only fear losing their jobs, but also the quality of their jobs, no longer resonate in the vocabulary of a critical theory of society" (Honneth 2012g: 56, 58). And it should be emphasized that Honneth's methodological arguments against functionalist or systems theory perspectives on political economy – arguments directed at not only Fraser but also Habermas[7] – are motivated as much by substantive moral concerns as purely theoretical ones. "We can only grasp the fact that people suffer under the currently existing circumstances [of work], and are not merely indifferent to them, if the market continues to be analyzed as a part of the social lifeworld," and not as an autonomous, norm-free subsystem (Honneth 2012g: 72).

Honneth further speculates that the best way to approach justice in the political economy, particularly given the interpretive difficulties of the achievement principle, might be to look at the flip side of justice: economic injustice. Injustice in general consists in institutionalized recognition interpretations and relations that block the progressive development of increasingly individualized and inclusive relations of mutuality, relations within which social members can have increasing opportunities to develop their individuality and realize themselves.[8] Take for instance Honneth's repeated invocation of the way in which one-sided, masculinist interpretations of the achievement principle lead to unjust material deprivation of women in comparison with men. The problem here is not some particular operation of anonymous economic processes or laws of the invisible hand of the marketplace. Rather, a clear material injustice follows from a specific form of misrecognition – the denigration of women and "women's work." This is why he says, for instance, that social justice "in the recognition sphere of social esteem...might mean radically scrutinizing the cultural constructions that, in the industrial-capitalist past, saw to it that only a small circle of activities were distinguished as 'gainful employment'" (RoR: 188).

In sum, Honneth aims to ground a thoroughgoing critique of current economic conditions in capitalist societies from the point of view of a moral and socio-theoretic monism. Recognition theory, he claims, can articulate the moral feelings of disrespect and denigration suffered by those harmed by the current political economy; it can reconstruct the normative infrastructure of the recognition order that provides the reference point for claims of injustice; it can show how that recognition order both furnishes the preconditions for market mechanisms and plays a significant, determinative role in the distributive outcomes of economic processes; it can reconstruct the historical transformations that led to our current political economy in terms of struggles for expanded conditions of recognition; and it can ground claims for a more just political economy and division of labor in terms of the recognitional relations needed for full self-realization.

5.2   Fraser's Challenges, Honneth's Responses

Fraser has been advancing arguments against monistic recognition theory since 1995, claiming it is inadequate for developing a critical social theory appropriate to the manifold forms and causes of contemporary injustice. Her basic conviction is that we need a social theory that is at least bivalent, that is, a theory where the causes and remedies for cultural and economic injustices are distinguished from one another and analyzed using different tools. For Fraser, as for Honneth, recognition struggles and distribution struggles are both important arenas for progressive political action. An adequate critical theory must attend to both. But on Fraser's account, because the social causes of recognitional and distributive injustices are different, neither can be reduced to the other. Each must be kept distinct in order to theorize correctly both the causes of and potential remedies for injustice. By contrast, if Honneth is right that market dynamics can be conceived of as the results of institutionalized recognition relations, then Fraser is wrong to claim that distribution and recognition are irreducibly different. Although Fraser has employed many arguments to support her multivalent social theory, I focus here on five argument types she has advanced specifically against recognition theory, attempting to indicate how cogent they are as critiques of Honneth's theory.

5.2.1   Displacement

Fraser's first charge is that the cultural focus of recognition theory simply distracts attention away from the depth and prevalence of economic injustice in contemporary capitalist societies. The idea is that, by focusing so relentlessly on injustices that are rooted in cultural patterns of evaluation which treat some persons as unworthy of respect and esteem – for example, invective and vilification directed at discrete minority groups – recognition theory has simply displaced legitimate concerns about distributive injustice. I think this argument has merit when applied to some recognition theorists. Consider, for instance, that Taylor's formulation of recognition theory simply does not touch upon issues of political economy and distributive justice.[9]

When we ask whether this argument has merit against Honneth's theory, it should be clear by now that it does not. As I adumbrated earlier in this chapter, many issues concerning political economy and the legitimacy of contemporary capitalist societies have been part and parcel of Honneth's theorizing throughout his career, and, he clearly continues to foreground such issues in his most recent work.[10] When recognition theory is construed as a narrow theory of identity politics

– worse as a theory only of multiculturalism – there may be legitimate complaints of inattentiveness to material injustices, not to mention all kinds of other injustices. But if Honneth's theory displaces questions about the justice of the political economy, it cannot be because of a simple lack of attention; it would have to be because of specific methodological and substantive theses in Honneth's social theory.[11] And this is precisely what Fraser argues in her second line of critique.

5.2.2 Inaccurate social theory

Fraser argues that accurate social theory needs to acknowledge at least two different kinds of causes of injustice in contemporary society. On the one hand, there are injustices causally rooted in the evaluative patterns that shape the status order institutionalized in a society. So, for instance, systematic denigration of gays and lesbians or vilification of foreign-born citizens is caused by cultural patterns of evaluation that grade some persons or groups as lower status than others. These evaluations are then reflected in the institutionalized status order whereby some are systematically treated worse than others across a manifold of social institutions. According to Fraser, such recognitional injustices are rooted in culture: for instance, in the evaluative patterns of homophobia or xenophobia. On the other hand, there are injustices causally rooted in the anonymous workings of economic processes and institutionalized in society's class structure. So, for instance, rapidly increasing unemployment or rapidly decreasing wage labor rates are caused by the autonomous workings of capitalist market dynamics. According to Fraser, such distributive injustices are rooted in economics: for instance, in the response of labor markets to boom–bust investment cycles or financial globalization. Thus, on Fraser's account, misrecognition and maldistribution are different in terms of their causes and resulting social dynamics. She then criticizes recognition theory for a deficient causal account of capitalist economies, in that it is not able to analyze adequately maldistributive injustice.

To support these claims, Fraser argues first that individuals may suffer from two distinct causes of injustice – cultural patterns institutionalized in the status hierarchy and economic mechanisms institutionalized in the class structure – where neither form of injustice can be reduced to, nor is a result of, the other form. Consider the scenario of an "African-American Wall Street banker who cannot get a taxi to pick him up" (RoR: 34). This is a situation where the injustice results from patterns of cultural value prevalent in American society that systematically code blacks as dangerous and untrustworthy. Yet, since he is a banker, he cannot have suffered the harm because of any characteristics tied to his class position or economic standing. Hence, it seems we have a misrecognition injustice that is independent of, and irreducible to, the distributive arrangements of society. In another case, consider the harm suffered by a "skilled white male industrial worker who becomes unemployed due to a factory closing resulting from a speculative corporate merger" (RoR: 35). Here, the injustice results purely from economic imperatives, as the status position of a skilled, white male worker is not symbolically or culturally devalued. Therefore, the maldistribution is independent of, and irreducible to, misrecognition. From these two examples, Fraser claims that recognitive and distributive harms are independent of one another precisely because their causal origins are different and so should not be reduced to one another. This is directly contrary to Honneth's claim that economic injustice should be interpreted within the comprehensive and monistic framework of recognition theory.

Fraser's second kind of argument rests on empirical phenomena that cannot be explained only in terms of underlying evaluative patterns. So, in contrast to the claim that wage labor rates and other schedules of compensation are fully determined by a society's esteem order, Fraser points out that, in addition to cultural factors, remuneration rates are also dependent on evaluatively independent

> political-economic factors such as the supply of and demand for different types of labor; the balance of power between labor and capital; the stringency of social regulations, including the minimum wage; the availability and cost of productivity enhancing technologies; the ease with which firms can shift their operations to locations where wage rates are lower; the cost of credit; the terms of trade; and international currency exchange rates. (RoR: 215)

Because these kinds of purely economic factors have a major role in determining actual economic outcomes, and because those outcomes occur independently of any changes in society's morally imbued patterns of intersubjective evaluation, Fraser argues that maldistribution is a distinct form of injustice that cannot be reduced to misrecognition. It is important to note here that Fraser's distinction between cultural and economic orderings of society is supposed to be merely an "analytic" distinction. That is, it should not be taken to imply that cultural and economic injustices are entirely separate in the actual social world. In fact, Fraser argues, most forms of social subordination will involve different proportions of both misrecognition and maldistribution. Thus women suffer from both an unjust androcentric status hierarchy and unjust exploitation of unpaid reproductive labor; African Americans suffer from both an unjust racist status hierarchy and an unjust class structure of urbanized poverty. Nevertheless, Fraser insists that it is important to keep the causes of injustice distinct if we are to analyze accurately our society's actual social problems. So although Fraser agrees that recognition can *influence* some economic outcomes, recognitional factors alone do not fully – or even mostly – *determine* those outcomes.

Are these arguments compelling against Honneth's theory? Honneth certainly rejects them as based upon fundamental misunderstandings. Against Fraser's attributions, he claims that he is not giving a full explanation of economic developments, nor dismissing the role of economic imperatives such as profit and utility in accounting for economic outcomes. Much here depends on how one interprets Honneth's original claims, which are not entirely clear and univocal. To begin with, there is a conspicuous ambiguity centering on words such as "determines" and "determinants": do they mean "dictates" – as the sole or overwhelmingly significant causal factor – or do they mean "influences" – as one among several significant factors? On the one hand, Honneth appears to be making the strong claim that a society's specific interpretations of the equality and accomplishment principles of recognition dictate ("determine") the division of labor and its attendant pay schedules. On the other hand, he repeatedly retreats from such a strong claim, moving to the weaker and more abstract claim that recognition structures are but one variable among others in influencing or constraining economic processes and outcomes. Consider two remarkably opposed passages. "Definitional patterns and evaluative schemas, deeply rooted in the culture of bourgeois-capitalist society, determine not only which of the various spheres of activity and action performances in general are to count as 'work' and so are open to being an occupation, but also the current degree of social return for each occupational sphere of activity" (RoR: 153–4). Yet, in his rejoinder to Fraser, Honneth denies that his theory of recognition operates as an explanatory account of the underlying causes of market dynamics. "I do not wish to be understood as a representative of the cultural turn in the social sciences, nor do I want to make any claims about the determinants of market occurrences themselves, nor do I think an analysis of globalizing capitalism could be adequate if it ignored considerations of corporate profitability and utilization" (RoR: 248).[12] Thus we have stronger and weaker forms of Honneth's claims, sometimes considering recognition as fully determining economic outcomes and sometimes as only operating as an outer constraint on broad structures of the political economy (Thompson 2005, 2006: 113).

I have argued elsewhere, and still maintain, that this ambiguity is not merely accidental nor the result of sloppy formulations, but arises from warring desires on Honneth's part: to develop a capacious, integrated theory of society with only the categorial resources of recognition theory; and to develop an accurate and insightful social theory (Zurn 2005). Without pursuing that further, it is worth noting here that the weaker and stronger versions of the thesis roughly correspond to the two broad argument strategies we saw above in 5.1.2. The stronger version claims basically that the reigning recognition order of a society is responsible for that society's economic distributions. Correlations, for instance, between the division of labor and the sex–gender system, between the relative status of various occupations and pay rates, and between the specific conception of equal opportunity and levels of social welfare rights benefits are all results of the economic institutionalization of a given recognition order. In contrast, the weaker version claims merely that the recognition order is one among several causal determinants of capitalist markets in general since there are recognitional preconditions for the very functioning of markets – laws, social norms, psychological dispositions – preconditions that could be withdrawn should social actors no longer be convinced of their legitimacy.[13] Here there are no specific claims about recognition directly *determining* economic outcomes, but rather that, at an abstract level, recognition must be counted as one of several different ineliminable variables relevant to explaining market dynamics.

Consider again the industrial worker who loses his job due to a speculative merger. It surely seems false to follow Honneth's stronger claims and insist that his unemployment is directly traceable to some specific evaluative pattern that has changed in the reigning recognition order – say that industrial jobs used to be seen as esteem-worthy achievements but are no longer. It is more accurate to say that his unemployment is directly traceable to market factors – say concerning the prospects of short-term profitability for the stockholders of the merged company. Beyond this thought experiment, it is also quite worth recalling the variety of factors that Fraser cites as actually at play in determining employment, labor rates, distributions, and so on, and considering that they are not, as an empirical matter, directly tied to recognitional norms: for instance, supply and demand for labor, costs of labor-saving technology, costs of relocating businesses, interest rates, international currency rates, and so on. Even if recognitional norms are one causal factor in determining employment, labor rates, and distributions, it seems a stretch to say that those norms are the only – or even the overwhelmingly determinative – causal factors.

Honneth's weaker thesis, however, may well be sustainable. Perhaps in the industrial worker's case, we could point to changes in union and corporate law – changes rooted in society's new normative consensus about what is worthy of recognition – that have made industrial jobs increasingly precarious, strengthened the power of finance capital, and weakened workers' collective bargaining rights. For at a sufficiently abstract and general level, Honneth is correct: patterns of economic distribution are partly the result of "institutionalized patterns of cultural value." To begin with, there are legal and political institutions that guarantee private property, establish corporations, set tax policies, carry out redistributive policies, create administrative regulations, and so on. There are also requisite interpersonal patterns of trust, norms of interaction, and *homo economicus* psychologies. Insofar as the ostensibly autonomous logic of market relations is only made possible by being anchored in such preconditions – a stable, rule-based structure of positive law, predictable interpersonal norms, and broadly established personal dispositions – patterns and outcomes of a specific political economy are, at some remove, partly the causal results of normative preconditions that can be clearly understood in recognitional terms. In this weaker sense, then, it is not at all implausible to give a recognitional account of (some) important aspects of capitalist economies. At this point, in order to fully adjudicate the cogency of the weaker thesis – the thesis that recognition structures are ineliminable variables in economic explanations – we would need to look at a much fuller, more detailed, and multivariable account of the determinants of political economy than Honneth has produced, or is willing to produce.[14] What we can say is that, faced with the apparent falsity of the stronger claim that the specifics of a recognition order fully determine all maldistributive injustices, Honneth rightly retreats to the more defensible claim that markets are ineliminably embedded within normative structures and that those structures have an important, but not dispositive, causal role in economic injustice.

Fraser advances a third form of argument against Honneth's social theory of capitalism, one I will only flag here. She claims that recognition theory yields an inaccurate historical picture of modernization processes. On her account, capitalist modernization was achieved precisely through processes that increasingly disconnected economic relations, which are structured by anonymous impersonal markets, from social relations, which are structured by moral norms. Said another way, the key structural transformation that marks the move to capitalism is the social differentiation between marketized arenas of social life, where instrumental and strategic interaction predominates, and non-marketized arenas of social life, where value-regulated interaction predominates.[15] On Honneth's account of modernization, by contrast, the key developments are the differentiation of three spheres of recognition, each responding to distinct normative principles, and their internal normative development, as we've seen in 3.3. Contrary to Fraser's claims, according to Honneth, the way in which markets are embedded in and constrained by recognition structures shows that capitalism has not developed as a norm-free, automatic process beyond the reach of intentional, evaluative action. Rather, struggles for recognition have decisively shaped the contemporary form of capitalism and recognition-based values form the normative preconditions for its continued existence.

The evaluation of these grand and ambitious claims about modernization will have to await another day. It should be noted, however, that neither Fraser nor Honneth provide the extensive backing that would be needed to fully support their contrasting accounts. Yet the stakes are clear: the Fraser–Honneth debate is not just about how to understand the relation between misrecognition and maldistribution but also about fundamental questions of history and social theory.

5.2.3   Impractical critical theory

Fraser's third main charge follows directly on her critique of Honneth's social theory. If recognition theory does not put forward an accurate causal account of the drivers of economic outcomes, then, according to Fraser, it will also be deficient when it comes to the guidance it can provide in orienting political practice aimed at overcoming maldistribution. According to Fraser, to the extent that recognition theory promotes cultural and evaluative changes in response to market-based ills, it will, at best, promote ineffective remedies. More worrisome yet for Fraser, recognition theory provides an inappropriate account of how to mediate the tensions between misrecognition and maldistribution and thereby may well recommend political responses that actually foster either further cultural backlash or economic marginalization. When rendered practical, recognition theory may, in her phrase, "add insult to injury." In short, Fraser's charge is that a faulty diagnosis of distributive injustice will lead to faulty therapeutic insights.

This charge is perhaps best evaluated by looking at examples. In his defense, Honneth cites as a paradigm feminist struggles to expand the definition of socially useful labor beyond work for pay. Here a recognition-based analysis of one of the main causes of women's comparative impoverishment indeed seems apropos since a main reason that reproductive "women's work" is unpaid, even though socially essential, appears to be a deeply entrenched esteem order encoding androcentric values and interpretations. In addition, Honneth's theory is clearly able to justify claims for changing this order – and so changing its resultant distributive patterns – in terms of the social requirements for egalitarian individual self-realization. Finally, the theory is also well suited to showing why at least some potential remedies are not recommended. Thus programs for an immediate legal mandate requiring remuneration for all reproductive labor, without a substantial cultural change, would likely be not merely ineffective but positively regressive by means of strong backlashes. Also, remedies oriented at restructuring the wage labor market would miss the real causal target: the extant institutionalized hierarchies of value concerning socially useful work.

Recognition theory also seems appropriate to evaluating legal remedies, for example those aimed at overcoming discrimination against the physically and mentally disabled in the labor market, such as that effected in the United States by the landmark 1990 Americans with Disabilities Act. Here, such a theory could: show that the causal roots of maldistribution are in the misrecognition of traits and abilities; show the efficacy of formal legal remedies given the experience of previously successful anti-discrimination legislation; and justify such remedies in terms of the social conditions all persons need to ensure an equal opportunity for full self-realization. In short, in these two cases, recognition theory seems to provide an accurate causal account of distributive injustice, combined with convincing normative and practical guidance concerning potential political responses.

Such an analysis seems causally misguided, however, when considering Fraser's example of the white male industrial worker who was laid off because of a speculative corporate merger. Since he is not a victim of any form of identity-based disrespect or status subordination by hypothesis, the injustice is better attributed to the structure of unconstrained market mechanisms. Furthermore, the theory's strategic guidance, oriented in general toward changing patterns of value and interpretation, would operate at such a high level of abstraction that it could not usefully differentiate between proposed legal, political, economic, or sociocultural remedies. Finally, given that the worker has not suffered a recognition injustice, it would be strange to justify calls for change in terms of his and all persons' needs for a social environment conducive to personal integrity.

Consider further the phenomenon of widespread and multipronged protests against capitalist globalization. As Honneth claims, it is quite likely that the multiple and often conflicting underlying motivations for antiglobalization protests – jingoistic unease with the loss of nation-state sovereignty, protest against the inegalitarian consequences of capital mobility both within and across nation-state boundaries, outrage at environmental degradation, unhappiness with ineffective state financial regulation, even self-interested dismay at direct personal harms – could be systematically reconstructed in terms of the recognition framework. It may well be, furthermore, that a sufficiently differentiated account of legitimate intersubjective norms of recognition may be able to sort justified from unjustified claims amidst the welter of motivations for these protests. However, it is unlikely that insufficient realizations of recognition principles are actually the single – or even a directly relevant – cause of the economic dislocations whose effects are protested against. The causes of the dislocations are to be found in variables specific to the global political economy: currency rates; disproportionate supply and demand; asymmetrical regulatory environments; capital flows; stratified availability of technologies; differential natural resources; diverse interest rates; differential regimes of private property; and so on. This means that recognition-based remedies will likely be simply ineffective against the root problems.

Consider, alternatively, another phenomenon arising from the fact that national borders don't really matter to multinational corporations: skilled white-collar jobs requiring a great degree of specialized professional training are being increasingly outsourced from the United States, Canada, and Europe to Southeast Asia and India. Here we seem to have a pretty clear example of careers enjoying high esteem – not just customer service, but personnel relations, payroll, computer programming, business-to-business sales, and product development – where, nevertheless, many workers face downward spiraling wage pressures, if not outright unemployment. Harmed workers may feel that they are being disrespected and their achievements denigrated, and we may be able to evaluate whether in fact these feelings point to instances of injustice in terms of a robust normative analysis of legitimate recognition expectations. However, again, the evident explanation for the cause of these changes in the global division of labor and the remuneration schedules has little to do with changing recognition relations. It is that when choosing between paying a programmer US$120,000 and US$20,000 per year, market imperatives simply dictate the "choice." In such a case, it is implausible to claim that society's recognition order directly determines either the division of labor or the comparative wage rate of different occupations. Moreover, specifically counseling recognition remedies may compound the harms: any increases in one locality's social-rights schedule or labor-market regulation may cause employers to shop elsewhere even more readily. In a similar fashion, attempts to reinterpret androcentric value patterns that contribute to the sex-gap in earnings may induce employers to seek more patriarchal and traditional societies where the impoverishment of women can be exploited.

Of course, the critical force in these last three examples (concerning industrial laborers, antiglobalization, and outsourcing) comes from employing the strong version of Honneth's political economic thesis: namely, that the reigning esteem order has a direct causal impact on maldistributive injustices. So one may be tempted to defend Honneth by retreating to the weaker thesis: that is, that there are legal, interpersonal, and psychological preconditions of market systems, preconditions based in recognition structures which can be withdrawn when they lose their normative legitimacy. The basic problem with this move is that, even though it may be able to save the truth of the theory's empirical economic explanations, it is so abstract as to be of little practical use in evaluating potential remedies and orienting political action. Should antiglobalization activists, for instance, seek to overturn international private law, change interpersonal norms concerning authority and trust relations between economic elites, or inculcate more altruistic dispositions amongst corporate decision makers through publicity and education? Perhaps all of these and more, or perhaps none. However, recognition theory in its weaker form will not be able to shed much productive light on such questions since the recognitional elements of the political economy it points to are but some of the many indirect causal variables operating to structure the broad framework of market economies. Avoiding a direct causal account of market dynamics or processes, but only highlighting their multivariate character, the weaker version cannot point out which of the possible "determinants" is most important in any particular example or distributive outcome.

Thus I would argue that Honneth's rejoinders to Fraser's critique are caught in a dilemma. His theory either must retreat to a high level of abstraction in order to save the empirical phenomena under the recognition analysis, or it must descend to a sufficiently substantive level of social analysis in order to provide strategic guidance. However, in the former case, the theory loses requisite practical guidance, while in the latter case it cedes empirical accuracy. Another way to put this dilemma is that it is one between empirically accurate but strategically impotent theory, and strategically promising but empirically inaccurate theory. I conclude that Honneth may be right that most distributive harms are experienced by individuals in recognitional terms, and that his theory's concept of society-specific interpretations of respect and esteem recognition may be productively used to evaluate competing claims about distributive injustice. However, Fraser is correct that, as presented in RoR, Honneth's theory of political economy has difficulties linking theory back to progressive social and political practice since it yields either causally misleading recommendations or unhelpfully abstract indeterminacies.[16]

5.2.4 Sectarian teleological standards

Another issue prominent throughout the Fraser–Honneth exchange concerns the proper kinds of evaluative standards to use in moral and political philosophy. In particular, Fraser argues that deontological normative theories are better suited to the very broad range of ethical pluralism witnessed in contemporary societies than are teleological and perfectionist theories like Honneth's. There are a number of tricky issues here, once again, about recognition theory's understanding, justification, and use of normative standards. I briefly describe Fraser's most serious critiques of Honneth's theory and indicate how he responds; similar issues arise in the context of Honneth's latest work on Hegel (see 6.4.2).[17]

Simplifying away from Fraser's support of her own preferred form of normative theory – a "thick deontological liberalism" that conceives of justice in terms of "participatory parity" – we can see that she has three main critiques of political theories like Honneth's that are based around the values of self-realization. In particular according to Fraser,

Honneth's teleological theory: (1) cannot make universally justifiable claims; (2) is unacceptably sectarian concerning the wide diversity of conceptions of the good acceptable in modern societies; and (3) is insufficiently determinative when assessing actual social and political controversies.

Fraser's first charge is rooted in a standard Kantian contrast developed in Habermas's moral theory: that between questions of *ethics* on one side and questions of *morality* or justice on the other. When we are thinking ethically, we ask questions like "What is good for me, given my identity and value commitments?" and "What are our conceptions of the good life and how do we best realize our shared values?" When we are thinking morally, by contrast, we ask questions like "What is the right thing to do for anyone in this context?" and "What kinds of policies are in the equal interest of all people affected by them?" In short, ethical questions are about the good – teleology seeks to answer those – while moral questions are about the right – deontology seeks to answer those. Fraser then points out that Honneth's theory of recognition, since it is founded around the notion of self-realization, is a teleological theory. Finally, Fraser simply insists on Habermas's (controversial) contentions that, while no ethical claims can be justified as universally applicable across different cultures, deontological claims concerning morality and justice are universally justifiable across diverse horizons of value. When it comes to ethical life, we simply run out of argumentative resources to convince others who do not already accept our own conception of the good life that our view is correct and theirs is mistaken. For Fraser, the claims of recognition theory, because they are ethical, cannot be universally justified across different cultures and horizons of value.

We have already seen that Honneth is sensitive to the problems of making context-transcending claims concerning ethical life in 3.2.4 and 4.3.2. In fact, the central thrust of his attempt to articulate a "formal conception of ethical life" is precisely to make universalist claims about the social conditions of the good life. By abstracting from specific conceptions of the good, and attending to the kinds of social and political relations needed for anyone to realize themselves, whatever their preferred conception of the good, Honneth is attempting to make a universalist teleology possible. These claims about the social conditions of the good life are, in turn, supported by the philosophical anthropology of recognition theory itself. Finally, it should be remembered that Honneth – like Fraser – is here only concerned with universal justifiability within the context of modern, complex societies. In other words, neither is making the claim to temporal transcendence – their respective claims are formulated for and in the light of social conditions in modern liberal societies. One may or may not agree that this approach is convincing – I have argued that in the end it is not (Zurn 2000). But

its cogency cannot be determined by simply stipulating that any teleological theory is – just for being a teleological theory – irredeemably
contextually bound. Furthermore, one cannot simply ignore Honneth's
contrary claims to have put forward a teleological theory with universalist capacities and his specific arguments backing that theory.[18] In
other words, Fraser's charge here is not much more than an unsup-
ported form of guilt by association. We will return to the question of
context transcendence of Honneth's theory in the next chapter.

Fraser develops her second charge at greater length: because it is
concerned with self-realization, recognition theory is inappropriately
sectarian and, hence, insufficiently liberal. The idea here is that a theory
which prioritizes one form of the good life – self-realization through
social relations of reciprocal recognition – also, by implication, denigrates other acceptable forms of the good life. But modern complex
societies evince tremendous value pluralism – there are many distinct
and incompatible conceptions of what is worthwhile in life, what the
true virtues are, and what the most important goals in life are. As long
as adherents of these different forms of life agree to abide by some
basic interpersonal duties for the just treatment of others, social and
political theory should allow for as much "reasonable pluralism"
(Rawls's phrase) as possible. Individual liberty requires that the state,
for instance, cannot tell people what the best form of life is but only
require that people do not violate one another's rights. But, according
to Fraser, Honneth's theory takes sides amongst the different and contending reasonable forms of life, and so is inappropriately sectarian.
Because recognition theory relies on thick accounts of individual
autonomy and self-realization, it valorizes one specific form of life
while impinging on the right of members of a liberal society to endorse
for themselves whatever conception of the good life they identify with,
as long as that conception stays within the constraints of just treatment
of others.

In response to this second charge of sectarianism, Honneth's central
response is to argue that supposedly pure deontological theories of
justice – like the one that Fraser proposes or those of Rawls and Habermas – cannot help but surreptitiously smuggle in the very same teleological content that recognition theory explicitly endorses. The central
principles of such theories of justice revolve around rights, political
procedures, and social arrangements that anybody can claim as due to
them in virtue of their individual autonomy. But when asked why
individual autonomy is so important, such supposedly non-sectarian
deontological theories must inevitably smuggle in a fair amount of
substantive teleological content about the preeminent values of individual autonomy and self-realization. The question to ask procedural
theories is, for Honneth: why are individual liberty and justice

important? At this point, however, such theories become either silent or obfuscatory. For, if they explicitly spell out the basic values that justice is intended to serve, they will be hoisted by their own petard, being overly partial to a particular modern conception of the good life formed around the values of self-realization. But if they do not spell out these values, then it is simply unclear what the point of justice-ensuring rights, procedures, and institutions are in the first place.

For Honneth, in contrast, recognition theory has the forthrightness to specify its animating values, even as it attempts to carefully spell those out in an abstract enough manner that many different (modern, liberal) conceptions of the good life will be compatible with them. "I take it that the reason we should be interested in establishing a just social order is that it is only under these conditions that subjects can attain the most undamaged possible self-relation, and thus individual autonomy.... Here we have a weak idea of the good, without which a conception of justice would have no aim" (RoR: 258–9). In short, then, the theory of recognition is indeed sectarian in its partiality to autonomy – just as, Honneth claims, are rival deontological conceptions of justice like Fraser's, Habermas's, and Rawls's – and it is this partiality that forthrightly explains the point of justice in the first place. We will see in chapter 6 that this response is at the core of Honneth's impetus for revivifying Hegelian political philosophy in the current theoretical context. I think it at the very least a quite plausible response to the charge of sectarianism.

Fraser's third main critique is that Honneth's teleological theory is insufficiently determinative in contrast with deontology. She claims, for instance, that theories focusing on claims of equal justice can simply note that, since denying same-sex partners the right to marry effects a status subordination of them, same-sex partners are unjustly denied parity of participation by being excluded from marriage. There is no need to evaluate the worth or value of homosexuals or homosexuality. In contrast, a theory focused around facilitating autonomous self-realization, according to Fraser, cannot avoid first making a controversial value judgment that homosexual relationships are valuable. But such value claims for Fraser are not ultimately justifiable since they are tied to one particular conception of the good life, one that might not be shared by all members in large pluralistic societies. So, on this charge, teleological theories cannot justify claims for expanded recognition of same-sex marriage without controversial premises, whereas deontological theories can justify such claims while relying only on the shared principles of rights and justice.

I have real doubts about whether deontology can actually prescind from controversial value judgments in such cases and about the how determinative Fraser's own theory is (Zurn 2003a, 2012). But more importantly, same-sex marriage clearly falls within the ambit of Honneth's conception of respect-based recognition, and in particular should be clearly covered by principles of legal equality. Thus he does not need an elaborate justification of the wrongness of heterosexual-only marriage beyond the simple appeal to the principles of nondiscrimination, equal protection, and equal freedom at the heart of modern legal systems. It is true that such principles of legal equality need to be justified, but as we have seen, this is accomplished by showing how such legal principles represent moral progress in the historical development of modern societies, moral progress measured as the advancing discovery of the exacting social conditions needed to secure to each person, qua autonomous person, the social conditions needed for undistorted realization of self-respect.

In summary, we can say that the issues about the universalizability of recognition theory's normative claims and about whether its teleological basis is sufficiently compatible with value pluralism are live issues. As major issues concerning the basic orientation of moral and political theory, they cannot be easily assessed in a few pages, and they continue to be focal concerns driving Honneth's theory toward its Hegelian roots and away from his earlier gestures toward Kantianism. On the third issue of determinativeness, the devil is in the details: whether or not a theory needs to invoke controversial premises to make substantive claims about social and political controversies can only be decided case by case. As Fraser is not convincing with respect to same-sex marriage – in part because her own theory cannot prescind from value judgments and in part because she overlooks substantial resources in Honneth's theory of modern law – we should be suspicious of her general claim that teleological theories are less determinative than deontological ones.

5.2.5   Insufficient left-Hegelianism

Finally, let me flag an intramural methodological critique that Fraser levels against Honneth: namely, that there are problems developing a left-Hegelian theory based in psychological experiences of violated recognition expectations. To understand this, we should note that both Fraser and Honneth share a commitment to carrying out a particular kind of critical social theory, one inherited from Hegel and Marx, worked up further by the theorists of the Frankfurt School and continued by various theorists since. In particular, both agree that critical social theory must be able to identify some morally laden content immanent in the actual social word, which also points toward a transcendence of current, pathological forms of social order. The critical social theorist thus needs a point of reference that is simultaneously extant in social reality, morally structured, concerned with the social character of life, and capable of indicating a better form of life than the present social formation. As Honneth puts it, both agree on "the idea that a critical analysis of society needs to be tied to an innerworldy instance of transcendence" (RoR: 238).

The dispute between them is then where to find this point of immanent transcendence. Fraser claims that it is better to find it in language – specifically in "folk paradigms of social justice" (RoR: 207) employed in contemporary social movements – than to find it, as Honneth does, in psychology – specifically in the morally laden feelings and recognition expectations of social actors. Although she deploys a number of arguments against Honneth, I only note one here. Because recognition theory starts from subjective feelings of violated expectations and works up from there, she claims that it does not sufficiently scrutinize those feelings to see whether they are in fact justified. In other words, it risks having no transcendent potential, no ability to take up a critical stance toward contemporary reality, since the theory understands wrongness simply as what is in fact experienced by subjects as wrong.[19]

Contrary to Fraser, Honneth argues that his theory does have the requisite critical potential for social transcendence. Although the theory starts from the recognition principles embedded in current society, it is able to critically evaluate that society in the light of the criteria of historical progress, in particular, progress toward recognition structures that facilitate greater individualization and broader inclusion (see 3.3). This occurs by overcoming limited interpretations of extant recognition principles and tapping the "surplus validity" of those principles that has not yet been realized in social reality. Experiences of violated recognition are then the detectors of surplus validity. When such experiences coalesce into social movements, the possibility exists for struggles for expanded social relations that transcend society's current limited forms. Here Honneth argues that psychological experiences have an advantage over explicit discourses of justice extant in a society. For, while linguistic discourses of justice can be distorted by ideology, inchoate psychological experiences of moral discomfort can detect social problems where they have not yet coalesced into explicit understandings, especially where that coalescing is blocked by prevailing ideological interpretations of a society's recognition principles. However, experiences of moral suffering *themselves* do not warrant justified claims to expanded recognition (see the discussions in 3.2.3 and 3.4.4). Such justification only comes through showing to a broader society that current social practices, interpretive schemes, and social institutions are not making good on their promises of facilitating intact intersubjective relations that can provide the social conditions necessary for healthy self-realization. In other words, it is the social structure of interaction – not subjective experience – which bears the normative weight, and current forms of social interaction can be gauged against normative criteria that point toward the transcendence of the status quo. We will see in the next chapter that questions of exactly how to structure his theory in order to fulfill the dual left-Hegelian criterion of transcendence and immanence occupy a central place in Honneth's latest work.

5.3   Assessing an Unfinished Debate

At this point, it is worth taking stock of the state of this remarkable, but unfinished debate between two major critical theorists who share so much in terms of broad political sympathies and theoretical ambitions. To begin, it is quite striking that, even though Fraser and Honneth both consider themselves to come out of the same traditions of critical social theory and both are fundamentally concerned with contemporary issues of social justice across a broad range of issues in contemporary capitalist societies, their RoR exchange so often seems to evince a kind of talking past one another. My guess is that this is a result of the fact that both are centrally concerned to put forward their own "grand theories" of contemporary society, such that the task of clearly articulating their own views overshadows due attention to finer points of interpretation of the other's work. Viewed now in the light of what Honneth has published in the last decade, and whatever its flaws in details of dialectical interchange, it is clear that the debate had a decisive effect in clarifying for him the kinds of issues recognition theory still needed to address. In fact, some of the most contentious and unresolved points reviewed above become central foci for Honneth's reanimation of Hegel's sociopolitical theory in FR.

Starting from Fraser's first charge that a critical theory built around recognition eclipses or displaces important social justice issues concerned with material equality and economic justice, we can confidently say that Honneth's theory is innocent. Redistributive justice is, and has been, a central concern of his theory. When we turn to the second question of whether recognition theory has an adequate social theory, one that can sufficiently comprehend the structures and dynamics of capitalist political economies, the results are more mixed. I argued that Fraser is right in her critiques of the stronger version of Honneth's political economy: contrary to his occasional claims, recognitional factors do not solely determine the substance of economic processes and outcomes such as labor rates or material distributions. But Honneth does have a more plausible claim that there are ineliminable normative preconditions of capitalism – law, norms, and dispositions – such that those preconditions should be counted as causal factors – some among many causal factors – in the explanation of market processes at a general level. Furthermore, it is quite plausible to spell out those pre-conditions in terms of recognitional structures, even if it is not the only way to do so. In the end, however, neither theorist has produced the kind of well-developed, in-depth, and empirically testable explanatory account of capitalist political economies that would be able to settle some of their larger disputes: that is, the degree to which – and exactly how – cultural and evaluative content interacts causally with more anonymous market forces; and, the best account of modernization processes. This is, then, a significant area for further theoretical development.

I also argued, concerning Fraser's third major charge, that recognition theory has real challenges stemming from its underdeveloped causal social theory when it comes time to make interventions into practical policy debates and assessments of different policy proposals. In particular, I would contend that his theory faces a kind of dilemma between overly abstract but accurate claims and sufficiently concrete but inaccurate claims. It may be that, in the end, Honneth believes that such interventions are not the job of theory but, if that is his conviction, then he will need to abandon or reconceptualize the traditional critical theoretic link between theory and practice. At any rate, this is another area calling for further development.

On the questions concerning normative standards and strategies, I would say the debate between Fraser and Honneth is unsettled. Fraser raises serious issues for teleological theories, in particular with respect to universalizability and to the degree to which such theories illiberally prefer certain conceptions of the good over other incompatible but reasonable conceptions of the good. Her claims about the indeterminacy of recognition theory are, however, less persuasive. Assessing the seriousness of the issues for teleological theories is, nevertheless, impossible to do by just looking at potential problems. One must also consider the strengths of teleology, particularly in comparison with the weaknesses and strengths of rival forms of theory. It should come as no surprise that the opening section of *Freedom's Right* is a methodological brief on behalf of the Hegelian mode of doing social and political philosophy, a brief advanced by contrasting that mode with the deficiencies of rival forms of ideal theory: proceduralism and deontology.

Finally, I would say that Fraser's reading of Honneth's project in 2003 raises real problems concerning how to square the left-Hegelian circle of immanent transcendence, a desideratum of adequate theory construction shared by Fraser herself. Much of the methodological work and substantive sociohistorical analysis in FR is dedicated to working out in greater detail and with more care his fundamental intuition that individuals' moral experiences of intersubjective recognition provide the most promising starting point for critical social theory. Thus a final assessment of Fraser's critiques and Honneth's responses can only be made in the light of his ongoing theoretical development. It is surely the case that the debate with her sharpened the issues and highlighted the challenges that recognition theory must meet to remain a compelling project.

6

Social Freedom and Recognition

6.1 Introduction

This chapter presents an overview of some of the substance and methods of Honneth's most recent major work, *Freedom's Right* (FR). In this extensive monograph, Honneth outlines a theory of social freedom indebted to Hegel but updated for the early twenty-first century. Even as this book builds upon the irreplaceable foundations of *Struggle for Recognition*, I think it should be seen as Honneth's new magnum opus. Not only does it have the ambition to rewrite one of the classics of social and political philosophy – Hegel's *Philosophy of Right* – but it also reorients Honneth's theory around the theme of freedom rather than recognition.[1]

This chapter summarizes three new or newly deepened central ideas Honneth introduces in FR. First, it sketches the leading idea of a *social* conception of freedom, one Honneth develops in contrast to competing negative and reflexive conceptions of freedom (6.2). Second, it gives an overview of the rich new theory of society that Honneth develops in terms of distinct institutionalized spheres of social freedom (6.3). Third, it sketches some of the theoretical innovations Honneth makes here and raises critical questions about these new directions (6.4).

6.2 Social Freedom

6.2.1 Focusing on freedom

Perhaps the first and most obvious new element in Honneth's latest book is simply the overwhelming prevalence of the concept of *freedom* and, correlatively, the apparently diminishing focus on the concept of recognition. The main reason for this arises from the basic aim of the book: to update the project of Hegel's *Philosophy of Right*, understood as grounding a theory of justice in and through an analysis of the social institutions as they have actually developed in contemporary society. With Hegel, Honneth shares the ambition to show how moral-practical reason is historically embodied in social reality. As soon as this theoretical ambition is entertained, the question arises of which moral values are central to contemporary social life (whether of the early nineteenth or early twenty-first centuries). Honneth is convinced, as is Hegel, that the keystone moral ideal of modernity, the central value around which all other values are arranged, is simply: freedom. Honneth puts this quite dramatically near the book's beginning:

> Of all the ethical values prevailing and competing for dominance in modern society, only one has been capable of leaving a truly lasting impression on our institutional order: freedom, i.e. the autonomy of the individual....As if by magical attraction, all modern ethical ideals have been placed under the spell of freedom; sometimes they infuse this idea with greater depth or add new accents, but they never manage to posit an independent, stand-alone alternative. (FR: 15)

Even the ideal of equality according to Honneth – the singular central and sovereign virtue according to some (Dworkin 2000) – "can only be understood as an elucidation of the value of individual freedom, as the notion that all members of modern societies are equally entitled to freedom" (FR: 337, n. 1). Furthermore, he claims that all modern conceptions of justice – whether embodied in political philosophy or proclaimed at the forefront of social movements – revolve around the ideal of freedom.

While he gives little in the way of quick and decisive abstract philosophical arguments in support of these extremely strong claims for the preeminence of freedom, I think one should understand the bulk of FR – Honneth's extended, 300-year history of the central social institutions of modern western societies, including law, morality, the family, the market, democracy, and the state – as vindicating these claims through extended, concrete, historical-sociological analysis. The claims, then, are not the abstract ones that freedom is ideally the most important value of all values, or that all other values ought to be conceptually subsumed under freedom. More exactly, the claim is that our actual social institutions, as really practiced in contemporary societies, are in fact all deeply structured to develop, facilitate, and realize individual freedom above all. Furthermore, to the extent that they realize other modern values such as equality, romantic expression, or the sacredness of nature, our social institutions do so only by submitting these other values to the sway of individual freedom. In addition, only those conceptions of justice which centrally incorporate some conception of individual freedom have remained legitimate and viable, whether we are speaking of the history of modern political thought or the history of modern social movements for emancipation and justice.

Of course, what exactly is meant by individual freedom is a deeply contested issue. For his purposes, Honneth distinguishes three main models of freedom evident in modern thought and society: negative freedom, reflexive freedom, and social freedom. He discusses the meaning of each model, as well as the specific model of justice each leads to. A further dialectical discussion of the insights and limitations of negative and reflexive models leads to an endorsement of social freedom as the proper and preeminent – even if often obscured – modern model of freedom. Thus another central new element in this book is the elucidation and defense of the *social model* of freedom as the real meaning of freedom structuring modern social institutions – the central normative ideal that these institutions aim to realize – and so the core value of a normative theory of justice.

6.2.2 Negative freedom

The negative model of freedom is familiar across a range of modern theories of justice, from the seventeenth-century authoritarianism of Thomas Hobbes to the contemporary libertarianism of Robert Nozick. Freedom on this model indicates that an individual faces no external impediments to action but is free to satisfy any and all idiosyncratic desires. An individual is not free when she is externally prevented from satisfying her contingent desires. There is in this model little consideration of mutual bonds of affection or obligation to others; individuals are seen instead as isolated monistic actors seeking egoistically to satisfy their own whims. There can be, of course, a conception of moral obligations to others corresponding to negative freedom: simply, individuals ought to interfere as little as possible with the negative freedom of others.

The model of justice usually paired with the negative model is an instrumentalist version of the social contract. As disconnected, egoistic monads, individuals calculate that it is in their own interest to have as little interference as possible from others. The best way to secure this non-interference is to engage in a one-shot prudential contract with others to establish equal individual rights for each to the maximum amount of non-interference possible, rights that are then to be enforced by a state given a monopoly on coercive power in order to make it unprofitable for individuals to violate those rights. Justice, in other words, is merely the enforcement of subjective rights to non-interference and is justified as being in the egoistic interest of each actor. There is no sense that justice is connected to social cooperation, for actors are assumed to be interested only in their own goals. And there is no need for political engagement or democratic citizenship since justice is secured simply by the enforcement of individual subjective rights, an enforcement achievable by any government securing the basic rule of law, whether authoritarian, oligarchic, or democratic.

The limitation of this model of freedom can be clearly shown when we consider various exemplary cases: the addict, the manipulated person, the coerced person, and the wanton.[2] In each case, we can clearly see that their actions may be free in the negative sense, but they are unfree in a very important sense at the same time. Thus the alcoholic may face no external impediments to another drink, but his inner compulsion to drink more is itself a source of unfreedom. A person manipulated or brainwashed in such a way that her desires are implanted by others may act without interference, but we wouldn't want to call her actions free – likewise for someone coerced into performing some action. Finally, a wanton may well be able to satisfy all of the contingent, natural desires he may find himself to have, but we should be wary of calling him free since on due reflection he does not fully approve of those desires as products of his own sincere endorsement. The wanton is simply "free" to be jerked around by whatever desires nature or socialization happens to implant in him. In all these cases, the problem with the negative model of freedom, according to Honneth, is that the individuals do not autonomously determine their own desires. Instead, their actual aims are simply left up to the capricious play of natural causes or social forces – causes and forces outside of the control of the individual. While the action may be free of external constraints, the contents of the action – the actor's desires or aims – are not themselves the product of the actor's own free, conscious willing.

6.2.3 Reflexive freedom

This basic limitation of the negative model has been a frequent theme since at least the mid-eighteenth century, when thinkers like Rousseau and Kant began to stress the importance of notions of authenticity and autonomy as central to any individual freedom worth having or aspiring to. Accordingly a new model of freedom – or, rather, a number of new models of freedom – arose which Honneth describes under the term "reflexive freedom." Across all the differences of specific conceptions, the central idea of reflexive freedom is that an individual's actions are free when they are guided by that individual's own intentions. Freedom requires a free will: a free person must live her life according to her own reflectively endorsed motives and reasons. Hence, freedom requires not only that actions not be interfered with; it also requires one to reflect upon and autonomously or authentically decide upon the contents of one's own aims. Real freedom demands that one's actions

arise from a will suitably refined and purified, rather than from accidental desires one happens to have at any moment.

In reconstructing the various reflexive models of freedom, Honneth
traces out two main lines of thought. The first is a moral autonomy
version of reflexive freedom. As articulated by Kant, a person is free
when he gives himself a rule of action that can survive rational scrutiny
and follows that rule as the real motive for the action. While Kant
famously explains rational scrutiny in terms of moral universalizability
– modeled in the various formulations of the categorical imperative –
other thinkers in this tradition have proposed other formulations of the
requirements of rational scrutiny. Of special import to Honneth is the
thoroughly intersubjectivist notion introduced by Karl-Otto Apel and
Jürgen Habermas of an unlimited communication community, whereby
rational scrutiny cannot be carried out by the individual actor in isolation. Instead, rationally justified rules must, ideally, meet with the
reasonable assent of all affected persons in an open and unlimited
discursive process of coming to a mutual understanding. When a
person acts on a discursively justified rule, according to this version of
reflexive freedom, she is morally autonomous.

A second main model of reflexive freedom runs through the notions
of authenticity, personal integrity, and individual self-realization made
prominent in the writings of early nineteenth-century Romantics.
According to this general model, a person is free when she acts only
on those desires and aims that are truly reflective of her deep, authentic
self. This model of freedom was first articulated clearly in various writings by Rousseau – his *Confessions* and several of his novels – where
an individual only truly becomes who she is through a long period of
reflection on her own experiences and feelings in order to articulate the
deep, authentic core of her personal identity. Only when that authentic
core is the true source of her actions can she be regarded as freely
willing her actions. Like the autonomy-based strand of reflexive
freedom, the authenticity strand has a long history, stretching from
theorists such as Herder and Nietzsche to Harry Frankfurt. In each
case, the idea is that the contents of one's will must be suitably purified
in order for one's actions to be considered authentically one's own
actions and so free actions.

Honneth explains three main types of theories of justice centered on
reflexive freedom. On the one hand, corresponding to the autonomy
strand, there is a range of proceduralist theories of justice. Most prominently represented by theorists like Rawls and Habermas, proceduralism posits that the legitimacy of collective political decisions is
ultimately a function of whether those decisions have been made under
ideal procedures for structuring collective cooperation, procedures that
ensure that each individual is treated as a free and equal citizen. Justice
is then a feature of political arrangements that can ensure the equal

freedom of each in a reflexive process of collective willing. On the other hand, corresponding to the authenticity strand, Honneth analyzes two main families of theories. First are theories like John Stuart Mill's that insist that justice names those social and political arrangements enabling the greatest number of persons maximal freedom for authentic self-development over the course of a life. A second family of authenticity-influenced theories is represented by various forms of republicanism, for instance Hannah Arendt's theory in which it is claimed that justice requires individuals to realize themselves in and through collective forms of self-realization. Despite this diversity across liberal proceduralism, liberal perfectionism, and republicanism, all of these theories of justice share the central feature that they take the realization of individuals' reflexive freedom to be the point of – the basic purpose for – just social arrangements.

Despite his evident belief in the superiority of the reflexive model of freedom over the negative model, Honneth argues that even the reflexive model has essential limitations. Expounding and updating Hegel's arguments to the same effect, he argues that the model fails to recognize that individual freedom cannot be achieved unless there is already a surrounding context of social institutions and meanings which provide individuals with potential content for their moral and ethical aims. While reflexive freedom requires individuals to reflectively purify their wills in order to arrive at morally self-determined or authentically self-realizing aims for their actions, these aims are themselves only candidates for such freedom if they are already instantiated in an accommodating social context. While reflexive freedom improves on the negative model by focusing on the content – the aims or goals – of an individual's actions, it fails to see how those potential contents must first be available socially before an individual can endorse them. And, further, an individual's action can only succeed to the extent to which an at least partially accommodating social, cultural, and political context exists that acknowledges the action as free. Hence, social institutions and practices are not external to an individual's freedom: they are constitutive elements of freedom itself.[3]

To clarify with an example, consider the way in which the idea of a professionally rewarding career was not even a live possibility for a woman in an eighteenth-century western nation – "professional woman" was not an intelligible role in that society's social practices – nor would a woman have been able to freely realize a professionally rewarding career there, no matter how reflectively she had determined herself to do so in accordance with her autonomy or authenticity. In short, negative freedom's non-interference and reflexive freedom's self-endorsement of ends are necessary conditions of freedom, but are insufficient without the compliant social context of social freedom.

6.2.4 Social freedom

In response to the limitations of the negative and reflexive models, Honneth proposes the model of social freedom as embodying the widest and most important sense of modern individual freedom. According to this model, free actions require an accommodating social environment from which those actions derive their sense and purpose, and within which those actions fit into a cooperative scheme of social activity. As Honneth puts the basic intuition:

> For modern subjects, it is obvious that our individual freedom depends upon the responsiveness of the spheres of action in which we are involved to our own aims and intentions. The more that we feel that our purposes are supported and even upheld by these spheres, the more we will be able to perceive our surroundings as a space for the development of our own personality. As beings who are dependent on interacting with our own kind, the experience of such a free interplay with our intersubjective environment represents the pattern of all individual freedom. (FR: 60)

Persons may be free from external interference and may in fact act on an autonomously or authentically purified will, but if their actions are seriously incompatible with the social world in which they find themselves, then they cannot experience themselves as free. Real freedom, according to Honneth, requires not only certain subjective conditions within an individual's control but also certain objective social conditions not directly within an individual's control.

It is important to realize here that Honneth is denying neither the reality nor the normative importance of the freedom conditions picked out by the negative and reflexive models. Modern individuals rightly value the capacity to be able to pull back from, to withdraw from, the intersubjective obligations and social roles they find themselves enmeshed with. Sometimes, we value that simple, unhindered space to realize our contingent desires that negative freedom enables. At other times, reflexive freedom is crucial so that an individual can take a step back from her given social expectations, and evaluate the validity and worth of those expectations in the light of her own sense of morality and personal integrity. Such experiences of detaching from the sometimes overweening power of social roles are of course central to the worth of modern freedom. Nevertheless, Honneth argues, the movement of detachment necessarily comes only after our immersion in social life. The detachment at the heart of negative and reflexive freedom is therefore secondary to our social entanglements which we already find ourselves in the midst of. To define and understand freedom aright, therefore, we cannot refer only to the withdrawal from social roles and obligations; we must understand the value of that withdrawal within a broader notion of freedom that comprehends our social interactions as well. In sum, for Honneth, negative and reflexive freedom are essential elements of modern freedom, elements within a broader conception defined by a more capacious conception of social freedom.

Following Hegel's more exacting specification, Honneth claims that social freedom involves at least three conditions. The most important condition is the first: a person must be realizing his own individual purposes in and through social institutions whereby others are reciprocally enabling or promoting his purposes. Honneth puts this point in a number of ways. In an institution facilitating social freedom – what Honneth calls a "relational institution" – individuals' various role obligations must "interweave with each other in a way that would enable subjects to view each other's freedom as the condition of their own freedom" (FR: 176). "Free activity...consists in the fact that others do not oppose our own intentions, but enable or promote them" (FR: 60). The social model involves "normative practices in which subjects seek to realize their individual freedom in the experience of commonality... the reciprocal satisfaction of individual aims" (FR: 62). A relational institution makes social freedom possible by structuring its roles reciprocally: individuals can act freely within the institution and get the uptake from others required only to the extent that other individuals also fulfill their respective role obligations. In this sense, individuals acting within relational institutions complete and fulfill the freedom of others in an irreplaceable and constitutive way. Returning to my stylized example, an eighteenth-century woman's autonomous and authentic choice to seek personal fulfillment through a professional career simply cannot be realized without accommodating relational institutions – e.g., institutions of gender roles, educational opportunities, career structures, labor markets – in which the actions of others enable or promote her preferred form of self-realization. Her negative and reflexive freedom is not enough to secure her full freedom. Her freedom also requires that her ambitions receive social uptake in accommodating intersubjective institutions.

The next two conditions for social freedom follow organically from this first condition. Secondly, the roles and expectations of relational institutions gain their persuasive power and their validity from the relations of mutual recognition that they enable. Since social freedom involves the reciprocal satisfaction of individual aims, the relationships between the actors will involve some forms of intersubjective recognition. It is not enough, according to Honneth, for a social institution to simply structure interweaving paths of individual action. Participants must be able to be aware that they are involved in enabling and promoting the actions of other participants. It is precisely this way in which individuals can self-consciously realize their socially free actions "in the experience of commonality." Relational institutions are not then mere agglomerations of anonymously integrated individual actions. They are systems of action integrated through participants' awareness that they are players in social contexts enabling the freedom of others. Thus, in a truly relational institution, individuals are persuaded that their obligations and roles are valid and appropriate because individuals gain recognition in and through those roles and expectations. Perhaps the clearest example of this is Hegel's model of friendship: a relational institution in which I realize my own freedom only insofar as I can freely be with myself in and through another, in and through my friend. The expectations of friendship receive their power, their attractive character, and so their validity for me because friendship structures a particularly powerful form of mutual recognition.

It is also worth noting that this deep, inseparable connection between social freedom and recognition helps to link Honneth's latest book to his foundational work on struggles for recognition. Thus what seemed an initially surprising change in Honneth's keywords – from "recognition" to "freedom" – turns out to be more a matter of conceptual extension rather than deep substantive change. As Honneth puts it simply in a recent interview, "as Fichte and Hegel demonstrated, all forms of individual freedom depend in an elementary way on practices of mutual recognition" (Honneth and Willig 2012: 148).

The third condition of social freedom is that the role obligations and expectations of relational institutions must be ones that all participants can agree to from a reflective point of view. Social freedom thus incorporates the central insight of reflexive freedom: freedom requires not only space for individual spontaneity (as negative freedom insists), and not only that individual actions compatibly intermesh with the objective social world (as social freedom insists), but also that those institutions of the objective social world can withstand rational critique. Institutions of freedom must be compatible with the demands of morality as determined in intersubjective, discursive, and critical processes of justification. (Here Honneth follows the Habermasian model of reflexive freedom as the most defensible version.) It is not enough that an extant social institution structures reciprocal roles and expectations; those expectations must be able to survive the critical scrutiny of reflexive detachment and evaluation central to moral discourse.

It is precisely here that the actual eighteenth-century system of careers fell flat. It may have structured a set of reciprocal role expectations and relations of mutual recognition but, in the end, it could not convincingly give any justification for why esteemed roles and their corresponding recognition relations were restricted to males alone. Of course, according to Honneth (following Hegel), individuals can only take up such a critical distance on extant practices and institutions because of the already extant modern form of social freedom they find themselves within. "These institutions of recognition within which subjects can achieve social freedom must be designed before the subjects, in a further step, come to a considered position on that order. In short, recognition within institutions must precede the freedom of atomistic individuals and discursive subjects" (FR: 59). Finally, it is important to note that this third condition of rational acceptability allows Honneth to describe moral progress in a straightforward way. By incorporating the distantiating moves of negative and reflexive freedom, the modern form of social freedom insures that the freedom provided is not just a semblance of freedom, a dressed-up form of institutionalized oppression or social control. Modern freedom allows for agents to exploit the inherent but untapped normative potential of an institution in order to change that institution.[4]

We come finally to the relationship between social freedom and justice. Honneth defines justice in a straightforward way: "justice must entail granting all members of society the opportunity to participate in institutions of recognition" (FR: 61). More specifically, justice requires an actual social order in which all of the institutions necessary for individuals' intersubjective freedom are present and working well. As Honneth puts it in a recent interview, "our societies can therefore be judged as 'just' to the extent that the corresponding spheres are organized in a way that allows each person actually to exercise the freedom promised by that respective sphere" (Honneth and Willig 2012: 147). Those institutional spheres must then embody practices of reciprocity and institutions of mutual recognition. And they must provide the social context necessary for individuals to realize the diversity of their individual ends "in the experience of commonality."

In terms of its abstract content, this conception of justice is not that different from those associated with reflexive and negative freedom, where a just institutional order is simply one that allows for and promotes individual freedom. Abstractly, then, Honneth defines justice in terms of maximal promotion of social freedom. But in terms of the method of a theory of justice, social freedom demands a quite different kind of approach. Unlike liberal proceduralism, liberal perfectionism, and liberal republicanism, the meaning of justice cannot be an ideal, philosophical procedure or standard of justice that is justified abstractly and then applied to social reality to see whether it measures up. For, according to Hegel and Honneth, there must first be an actual, more or less just social order enabling freedom before subjects can participate in any distancing legitimation procedure such as the ideal social contract, the abstract notion of personal perfection, or democratic proceduralism. The meaning of justice is then to be derived from investigating actual social relations. In particular, it is those real relational institutions securing social freedom themselves which make room for individuals to take up the detachment of negative and reflexive freedom and question the worth of those institutions in the first place.

It turns out then that a theory of social freedom and justice must employ history and sociology to uncover the actually existing "normative practices in which subjects currently satisfy their purposes so as to realize their individual freedom in the experience of commonality" (FR: 62) I will return to Honneth's method of "normative reconstruction" in 6.4. For now, it is enough to emphasize that such a method must proceed from sociological and historical analyses of the actual institutions securing the possibility of social freedom in modern western societies. The content and meaning of justice cannot be generated through conceptual analysis, ideal theory, transcendental reflection, pure ratiocination – it can't be dictated or determined by philosophy alone – and then applied to our fallen social reality. Taking their cue from Kant's methods, most contemporary theories of justice first seek an abstract, trans-contextual justification of pure principles and then attempt to apply them, in a second step, to "non-ideal" conditions to detect where injustices might be. In contrast, inspired by Hegel, Honneth is convinced that a theory of justice, as a theory of social freedom, must arise from and be realized through an analysis of actual social institutions. "A theory of justice must be based on social analysis" (FR: 1).

6.3   Social Spheres

The bulk of *Freedom's Right* is concerned with such a social analysis of the history and current state of those central relational institutions in modern societies that enable and promote individuals' social freedom. Like Hegel's *Philosophy of Right*, Honneth's new book intends to articulate each of the crucial social spheres of individual freedom in modern societies: to explicate each sphere's central purpose, the specific aspect of freedom it enables, and its basic principles of legitimacy. Such an articulation is in part sociological – it aims at a perspicuous description of the structure and content of the various spheres of freedom – and in part historical – it aims to describe the emergence, change, and development of such spheres. But the project is not simply empirical, for Honneth (following Hegel) intends the reconstruction of the spheres to be at the same time justificatory: the reconstruction of a sphere of freedom also demonstrates its value for individuals and so contributes to justifying it for participants as a necessary condition of their social freedom.

Finally, it should be noted that Honneth intends it to be normative in a different way as well: the reconstruction of the contemporary state of the social spheres of freedom is also critical. Here, departing from at least the standard "right-wing" interpretation of Hegel, Honneth insists that his account is not a smug or satisfied legitimation of the present as the more or less perfected apex of human history. Instead, for each sphere, Honneth attends in detail not only to its underlying principles of normative legitimacy but also to the ways in which each has exhibited certain limitations, misdevelopments, injustices, or even pathologies. In other words, the reconstruction of the social spheres is intended as a contribution to a critical theory of the present: an inter-disciplinary theory of society with emancipatory intent. In thus real-izing a theory of justice through a social analysis, Honneth intends to simultaneously display the reality of just institutions, their inherent principles of normative justification, and their concrete critique in the light of those very principles.

Given that this capacious project occupies more than three hundred pages of FR, I only give some flavor of the work here by indicating for each of the modern spheres of freedom analyzed: the specific aspect of individual freedom it institutionalizes; the values it serves and hence its normative justification; and its main limitations, injustices, misde-velopments, or pathologies. The summary follows Honneth's order of presentation: first, two spheres in which freedom is a mere possibil-ity – law and morality – and then the three central spheres of actual social freedom – personal relationships, the market economy, and democracy.

6.3.1   The legal sphere

Honneth begins with the legal sphere of subjective rights. When indi-viduals are granted rights, the law guarantees them a domain of action within which they need not be accountable to others, as long as they stay within the bounds set for lawful employment of one's individual rights. For instance, if I have a property right in my computer, I may use that computer in any way I want, subject only to the bounds of the lawful employment of property. I have the right to use it to play games or to write books; to process information or put it on a pedestal as a work of art; to lavish it with care or to smash it open as I please. Of course, I do not have the right to use my computer to steal the property of others – this limitation is the essence of the equal guarantee of sub-jective rights to all rights holders. The key to this property right for Honneth comes into view when we see that, by virtue of the subjective right to property, no one else may interfere with my rights to the com-puter. My property right then releases me from any obligations to others – any social expectations – that I may have had by simply pos-sessing the computer: obligations, say, to productively employ a socially valuable tool, to help others I have personal relationships with, or to contribute to overall social welfare. Therefore, the central function of subjective legal rights is to institutionalize a domain of *negative freedom* for individuals: it allows them to withdraw from the social roles and expectations they are embedded within and to take actions based solely upon contingent personal whims and desires.[5]

Legal freedom then institutionalizes negative freedom. But why is that valuable? As we saw in 6.2.2, there is little intrinsic value in being able to realize whatever contingent desires one happens to have; after all, those desires may be neither authentically one's own, nor autonomously formed, nor receive any uptake from the social world. So legal freedom can't be valuable simply because it allows us to withdraw from social obligations. Here Honneth turns away from the Hobbesian tradition of idealizing, as an end in itself, the situation of atomistic, egoistic, and rational personal utility maximizers, turning instead toward the perfectionist tradition within liberalism. John Stuart Mill, for example, argues for individual liberty (partly) on the grounds that it allows persons to try out various different approaches to life and find out which approaches in particular they find valuable and fulfilling. When subjective rights free us from our everyday interactive obligations, we are able to explore and experiment with a whole range of possible forms of the good life, enabling crucial processes of self-understanding and personal growth. Legal freedom is then justified as a sphere of freedom because it "guarantees individuals a space of private autonomy in which they can retreat from all existing role obligations and attachments in order to explore the meaning and aims of their individual lives" (FR: 72).

Even though the legal sphere clearly institutionalizes a sphere of individual action, Honneth does not count it as a real sphere of social freedom, but sees it as merely a potential sphere of freedom. In one sense, this claim follows simply from the definition of social freedom: since individuals who stand on their legal rights alone insist on withdrawing from their social roles and obligations, from intersubjective relations of recognition and mutual accountability, legal freedom is not realized in and through the "experience of commonality." But Honneth also argues that the sphere of subjective rights is essentially limited when it comes to realizing freedom. In essence, he claims that the sphere of legal freedom cannot, by itself, be a realm for self-realization. While it is true that legal freedom may allow a person to experiment with different conceptions of the good and explore various forms of life, those goods and forms of life ultimately must be evaluated in the light of the social roles and interactions they promote or block. Furthermore, we must step out of the distantiated, objectifying mode of insisting on our subjective rights and move back into the flow of social praxis in order to act on any resulting convictions or ideals. Ultimately, we can only fulfill ethical possibilities and achieve self-realization in and through ordinary social interactions with others; legal freedom at most enables us a temporary distance from these everyday obligations. In short, the freedom that legal rights secure cannot itself be a substantial form of freedom. This argument about the essential limitations of legal freedom can be recast in an older Honnethian idiom. According to recognition theory, there is no real ethical autonomy without intersubjectivity, and since subjective legal rights suspend intersubjective justifications and expectations – and the structures of recognition they embody – ethical autonomy is not possible purely from within the institutionalized sphere of legal action.

Of course, as long as participants understand and acknowledge this limitation of law, there is nothing inherently problematic about (reasonably just) legal relations. (I say "reasonably just" because Honneth insists that arbitrary or unjustifiable exclusion of some persons – say, minorities or women – from equal legal rights is a serious form of injustice.) However, Honneth is also worried about a deeper malaise that law can sometimes lead to: when legal freedom becomes socially pathological. Here he carries out a form of social diagnosis we investigated in chapter 4: that of situations where social actors systematically misunderstand the structure or point of the social institutions they find themselves participating in.

A word first on the fact that, in FR, Honneth systematically distinguishes between four different types of negative social developments. First, there are simple *limitations* of a type of freedom: here a form of freedom has only a limited role in social life, limited in the sense that it must operate within or alongside other complementary practices and exercises of freedom of different kinds. Second, a form of freedom may become *pathological*: "Social pathologies arise whenever some or all members of society systematically misunderstand the rational meaning of a form of institutionalized praxis" (FR: 113). According to Honneth, only the potential forms of freedom – negative legal freedom and reflexive moral freedom – may become socially pathological since they can come to seem falsely independent of supporting social institutions. By contrast, the social forms of freedom – realized in personal, market, and democratic relationships – cannot become pathological because such forms of freedom only exist where subjects can consciously realize their own ends in complementary relations with others. Limitations and social pathologies, further, are to be distinguished from "social *injustice*, which consists in an unnecessary exclusion from or restriction on opportunities to participate in social processes of cooperation" (FR: 86; emphasis added). Finally, a central focus of Honneth's theory is the detection of social *misdevelopments*, where actual social institutions or practices undermine or hollow out the principles of legitimacy historically developed within that specific sphere of social freedom. In short, misdevelopments occur where a social sphere falls short of or away from its inherent normative potential.

Returning specifically to law, modern societies are susceptible to social pathologies of legal freedom when actors mistakenly consider legal freedom as the very ideal of freedom itself, missing the way in which such freedom is essentially limited. Honneth gives a rich analysis of various manifestations of such a mistaken autonomization of legal freedom from its social contexts, and of the consequences it can have for social relations and for personal identity. To get just a flavor, consider his account of the movie *Kramer vs. Kramer* about a divorcing couple who increasingly regard both themselves and others only from the point of view of their legal suit. They calculate what to do, how to act, and what personality traits to cultivate, all based purely upon the hopes and expectations of how legal proceedings will regard those actions and traits. In instrumentalizing their own and others' personalities to strategic considerations of their legal battles, both Kramers increasingly lose touch with the flow and practice of the social lifeworld that law is supposed to afford merely a temporary respite from. The film is particularly poignant in its depiction of the deterioration of the protagonists' parental relationships with their single child, from originally being attuned to the child's needs and dependencies to later being oriented purely strategically toward what a judge might rule in divorce proceedings. It is important to note that Honneth does not regard such juridification of everyday life as caused simply by personal failings; instead, he considers it an artifact of tremendous social pressures to give priority to the medium of law over all other forms of conflict resolution, especially over those that are more interactive and intersubjective.

6.3.2 The moral sphere

The moral sphere of freedom according to Honneth institutionalizes reflexive freedom, in particular the autonomy version of reflexive freedom. The moral sphere is a domain where individuals can step back from their everyday lifeworldly entanglements in order to reflexively consider whether their interpersonal relations are justifiable from the point of view of universal morality. Working through the strengths and weaknesses of the versions of reflexive freedom articulated by Kant, Christine Korsgaard, and Habermas, Honneth argues that morality is not just a system of knowledge – concerning beliefs about what is right and wrong – but is also an interpersonal system of action, with norms, roles, and obligations that are based in the structure of intersubjective recognition. To be sure, morality is not as strongly institutionalized as law since moral rules of behavior are not as clearly delineated as legal rules and the sanctions for improper behavior are not carried out through coercive state measures. Nevertheless, morality is a system of action institutionalized through cultural norm patterns with real, if informal, sanctions. It allows individuals to retreat from the current demands of social life in order to reflectively examine the moral bona fides of those demands.

The central purpose of the moral sphere is allowing individuals to critically assess social demands, and so ultimately to reject those that cannot withstand reasoned scrutiny. This then enables the emancipation of individuals from their given ethical lifeworld. When moral freedom is considered as an intersubjective practice of reasoned discourse with others about collectively justifiable standards of behavior – as it is paradigmatically in Habermas's communicative model – the moral sphere allows for the transformation of that ethical lifeworld. For according to the communicative model of morality, we can only collectively determine which norms are truly universalizable by engaging in practices of reciprocal justification with others in a cooperative search for norms that could resolve conflicts consensually. Such universalizable norms then put limits on morally acceptable ethical ideals and forms of life, serving to weed out unjust or immoral ethical demands in a society's historically given way of life. Subject to relentless demands for moral justification, for instance, the male-only norms for professional work and careers were overcome – only eventually and only after much social struggle, of course. The sphere of moral freedom allowed women and men to step back from oppressive, patriarchal demands of eighteenth-century ethical life and to transform it to accord with universally justifiable standards of gender equality. Hence, according to Honneth, the crucial ethical value of the moral sphere – the worth of morality – is that it allows us to transform unacceptable elements of current ethical life through the public interpretation and transformation of moral norms.

As in the case with the legal sphere, Honneth analyzes the moral sphere as merely a potential domain of freedom. He argues that morality is essentially limited insofar as the moment of reflective detachment from social entanglements constitutively depends on being embedded within social contexts before detachment. Furthermore, the point of impartially examining norms is ultimately to connect back up with social practice, albeit a reformed and morally justified practice. "Just as was true of legal freedom, moral freedom essentially has the character of an interruption, a postponement. Whoever exercises moral freedom seeks to gain reflexive distance in order to reconnect to a social praxis, in a publicly justified way, that has faced him or her with unreasonable or irreconcilable demands" (FR: 112).

Here Honneth runs a version of an argument first famously made by Hegel against Kant's notion of moral reason. In essence, the contention is that there are limits to the detaching abstractions that Kantian moral autonomy theorizes as the essence of freedom. While it is certainly possible and appropriate, according to Honneth, to abstract from our own partial point of view to the impartial point of view of all those affected by contested norms, it is impossible to ignore the social meaning and motivating force of our relationships and attachments. Whether it is a process of applying the categorical imperative to maxims of action *à la* Kant or a process of justifying action norms before an unlimited communication community *à la* Habermas, the process of moral evaluation ultimately depends on our always already accepting the rules and practices of our given social world. In short, despite the pretensions of moral autonomy, individuals cannot morally self-legislate the whole social world; much of that social world must be accepted as meaningful and binding if our moral evaluation is to have any bite in the first place. For instance

> the meaning of friendship, constitutional norms, obligations between parents and their children – these are all institutional facts with normative substance which the moral discursive community, despite its combined efforts, cannot put aside....In other words, all moral discourse presupposes elementary forms of recognition that are so constitutive of the social environment that they cannot be questioned or suspended by its members. (FR: 112)

In sum, while the moral sphere enables a kind of freedom making possible the emancipatory transformation of the given social world, that freedom is itself constitutively limited by being embedded within and returning to the concrete, specific, and ethically substantive social world.

Unsurprisingly, Honneth believes the moral sphere is subject to social pathologies analogous to those evinced in the legal sphere, precisely where moral freedom is mistakenly understood to be autonomous from the social context it is embedded within. Honneth theorizes two main pathologies of moral freedom. On the one hand, there is the pathology of uninhibited moralism, captured most clearly in the figure of the moral saint. Rather than a means to repair ruptured or deficient forms of intersubjectivity, the moral saint sees morality as the final aim of her life. Such an individual ignores the facticity of everyday norms and takes herself as a legislator of the righteous world, thus fully disconnecting herself from the social relations she already finds herself within. It is important to note here that Honneth does not think that taking a moral stance automatically alienates one; only when it is taken to the extreme of ignoring one's own given identity and supporting social lifeworld. Moral saints ignore the fact that we always already find ourselves in a dense web of interpersonal relations, relations that we use as the starting point in deliberating morally about their acceptability. On the other hand, the sphere of moral freedom can become pathological when morality is taken as an excuse for the use of any means to achieve moral ends. The extant social world is seen as so fundamentally corrupt that, for instance, radical political terrorism is taken as morally justified to bring about the righteous world. Here, moral deliberation detaches itself from the social and institutional bases of extant society and the moral point of view is destructively considered to be autonomous from all socially given bonds of friendship, family, citizenship, and even fellow humanity. In its most extreme versions, morally justified terrorism is hard to distinguish from sociopathy.

6.3.3   The sphere of personal relations

One of the richest sections of FR concerns the first real sphere of social freedom Honneth analyzes: personal relations. While he considers three distinct kinds of personal relationships – friendship, sexual intimacy, and family – all three contribute to a distinct form of social freedom "in which two persons enable each other to consummate their own selves" (FR: 132). In personal relations, we achieve the distinctive freedom to fully become and understand ourselves through the confirmation of intimate others, whom we reciprocally confirm in their personality.

For instance, despite all of its changes over time, friendship continues to be the institutional setting within which individuals can safely explore and express their own intentions, desires, and feelings, having them shaped and confirmed in a space of reciprocity with, as Aristotle says, another self to oneself. My friend does not limit my freedom, but in fact allows me a safe space for my own ethical self-articulation. While my desires, feelings and intentions may be diffuse and unclear to me, by exploring them in the safe space of mutuality that the social institution of friendship enables, I can become clearer about who I am and who I would like to be. And I reciprocally accord the same space for self-exploration to my friend. The social roles and obligations that friendship institutionalizes thus enhance the freedom of both friends.

A similar space for self-exploration is opened up in relations of sexual intimacy and romantic love, the difference being that here my relationship to my body and bodily needs is the subject of self-exploration. In romantic love and sexual intimacy, we find a safe space for socially exploring bodily intimacy and the frailty of our bodies. Intimate relations ideally open the possibility for "a physical We, in which each person physically completes and expands the other" (FR: 148). They thus open a space for the realization of individuals' social freedom, where they can physically experience and understand their own needs, without the emotional threats of hurt or humiliation.

Family life, according to Honneth, essentially institutionalizes a community of solidarity between parents and children, allowing for the socialization of children into ethical life and the development of parents through their life course. In the system of roles and expectations of the family, each member supports and cares for the others in ways appropriate to their specific biological and maturational phases of life. Particularly in modern egalitarian families, "all... family members... represent equal partners in interaction who can each expect the degree of sympathy, affection and care they require in their respective life-stage" (FR: 164). Within families, children gain the social freedom for multiple aspects of basic socialization, maturation, and development, while parents gain the social freedom for their own maturation and development in distinct adult life phases. Because the social role obligations of care and support for family members are lifelong and interminable – as opposed to the potentially mutually terminable character of friendships and romantic relationships – families provide, according to Honneth's interesting reading, a kind of secular consolation, an easing of or relief from the solitude of life and the fear of death. Especially as individuals live ever longer lives, and children and parents eventually reverse their caretaking roles, the family becomes a site where we can grasp the rhythms of biological life in its various stages and come to terms with the uncontrollable nature of our biology.

Constituted by these three different kinds of relationships, the sphere of personal relations institutionally allows individuals to realize their inner natures – their needs, emotions, and personal characteristics – through being intersubjectively confirmed in their own distinctive personality. Because such personal relations are, according to Honneth, indispensable social conditions for individual self-realization, the social sphere of personal relations is normatively justified by facilitating the development of individuals' inner natures.

I have presented Honneth's conclusions about the sphere of personal relations in a schematic and summary way, although this is distinctly not the way they are developed. Rather, he engages in penetrating empirical, sociological, and especially historical analyses of changes in the nature and development of the social institutions of friendship, sexual intimacy, and family, paying particular attention to the profound changes in the interpersonal lifeworld of western societies over the last three centuries.

The extensiveness and detail of this empirical analysis is important for two reasons. The first is methodological: Honneth argues that it is only by engaging in careful social analysis of how ethical life is actually lived that one can normatively reconstruct the sphere under consideration. The idea is that social theory must articulate the moral grammar of relationships that competent members employ in negotiating the particular roles and obligations of a given sphere of freedom if theory is to grasp why that sphere is valuable to individuals for realizing their freedom. Such a normative reconstruction must not, however, look only at the totality of current existing social conditions; it must also attempt to distill out of the myriad and often rapid historical changes in patterns of interpersonal intimacy and private life a core of stable roles and obligations that gives personal relations ethical and moral importance.

Secondly, the normative reconstruction of personal relations as, essentially, "social relations in which our inner nature is set free by mutual confirmation" (FR: 132) allows Honneth to articulate an immanent standard for evaluating changes over time in that social sphere. The empirical and historical detail enables, in short, a *critical* social theory, one that can pass substantive judgments on what is progressive and regressive in these changes, and where we should look to more perfectly realize the social conditions of individual freedom. Of the three main spheres of social freedom that Honneth investigates – personal relations, market relations, and the democratic public sphere – he is most optimistic about personal relations as a well-developed and progressive sphere of freedom in contemporary societies. In large part, this is due to his reading of historical changes as largely dictated by the unfolding moral logic intrinsic to such relations.

In general, Honneth diagnoses three broad kinds of progressive changes. First, the institutions of personal relations became increasingly *generalized* or democratized over time, as the self-exploration they make possible spreads to groups of previously excluded or marginalized persons. Witness the social practices of friendship based upon mutual affection spreading beyond the aristocracy to the middle class; or the democratization of romantic love to the point that women and sexual minorities, not just heterosexual men, were allowed to freely explore their physical needs in safe and non-humiliating relations of intimacy; or the social recognition of the importance of intact family structures for all races, ethnicities, and economic classes. In each case we can see the logic of personal relations being subject to moral pressures to reduce unjustifiable inequality and exclusion. Second, especially in the case of the relationship between sexuality and marriage, we have witnessed a greater *differentiation* of the various institutional roles and expectations of friendship, romantic love, and family. Consider the myriad ways in which the "sexual revolution" of the late twentieth century fundamentally disentangled sexual relations from marital, procreative, and childcare relationships. In contemporary western societies, we now generally acknowledge that the inner relational logic of exploring our physical needs and that of creating a community of mutually caring solidarity are simply two different dynamics. Third, personal relations have become increasingly *mutual* in that they are dependent on the free acceptance of all participants of the norms and obligations of the relationship, rather than on power and status differentials according to individuals' ascribed identities. Such a mutualization of personal relationships is clear in the change from the ceremonial, instrumental acquaintances of the Middle Ages to the companionate friendships of modernity; in the gradual dissolution of the notion that sex was a right that men could demand from women regardless of their consent or desire; and in the gradual (and incomplete) transformation of family structures from the patriarchal model with its rigid, complementary, gender-specified obligations to the partnership model with its insistence that both parents share in child rearing and housework and that children are also supposed to be participants in family communications and negotiations.

Throughout his reconstruction of these and other changes, Honneth insists repeatedly on the centrality of changing gender relations and redefinitions of gender identity that have most profoundly resulted in moral progress: specifically, ever less androcentric and gender-oppressive interpersonal relations. The "we of personal relations" has become more democratic, more mutual, and more inclusive for persons, most especially women. Furthermore, all three of these changes have been caused, according to Honneth, by the driving force of the intrinsic moral logic of these forms of social freedom: the new relationship ideals are "inevitable, because the non-coercive power to assert a normative surplus exercises a permanent pressure that will sooner or later destroy any remains of traditional practices" (FR: 164).

Even though Honneth is most optimistic about the progress of personal relations, he does raise concerns about potential social problems and misdevelopments besetting the sphere. Thus he sensitively considers whether contemporary romantic love is threatened by pressures from ambitions for professional success, from increasingly insistent economic imperatives, and from dislocations caused by rapid globalization. And he is concerned that legal, political, and economic institutions have not done enough to support and facilitate the values realizable only in and through personal relationships. He recommends, among other measures, that gay marriage be legalized, that family care work receive social support, that work policies be adopted to allow for more flexible shifting between life stages of learning, working, and caring without financial difficulties, and that laws and redistributive polices give greater support to the family as a school for democratic virtues, that is, for the social cooperation and solidarity necessary for competent, democratic, and participatory citizenship.

6.3.4 The market sphere

The second real sphere of social freedom is that constituted by market-mediated interactions. In a significant sociological and historical deepening of the basic normative analysis first articulated in his earliest work and later sharpened in his debate with Fraser, Honneth argues that market relationships allow a form of social cooperation that is in the individual interest of all involved. According to this approach – labeled "moral economism" – markets distinctively enable the complementary realization of individuals' own aims by institutionalizing cooperation in a manner (ideally) responsive to two moral principles: meeting individual needs and recognizing individual achievement. The social freedom made possible by markets is thus institutionalized in two main arenas. First, there is the sphere of consumption within which freedom is realized in a mutual system for meeting needs, organized around the complementary roles of consumers and producers. Second, there is the sphere of the labor market where freedom is realized in a system of mutual, esteem-based recognition for individuals' distinctive and valued achievements in their roles as employees and employers. For Honneth, by tracing the expansion, development and change of market-mediated spheres of interaction over roughly three hundred years of capitalism, we can see that markets uniquely enable individuals' socially secured freedom by, on the one hand, meeting basic needs for food, shelter, clothing, and so on for ever greater numbers of people and in ever increasingly satisfactory ways and, on the other hand, facilitating social forms of esteem tied to the actual achievements of individuals in their distinctive and valued contributions to the system of social cooperation.

Even if, from one point of view, markets seem to be simply competitive systems that interlock egocentric interests of isolated subjects behind their backs – say, by the "invisible hand" of price signals – for Honneth, they must ultimately be judged according to implicit moral criteria of social cooperation. Markets, on this account, are distinctly *not* norm-free systems that coordinate action according to functional or purely economic imperatives. Instead, "economic processes of exchange…remain embedded in this frame of pre-market norms and values….There is an intrinsic connection between the conditions of competition on the market and the norms of the lifeworld" (FR: 190–1). As we have seen in chapter 5, this analysis of markets is not only at odds with Fraser's functionalist account, but also opposed, perhaps more fundamentally, to Habermas's sociological dualism, a dualism distinguishing sharply between functional and hermeneutic forms of social integration, that is, between systems and lifeworld. Honneth's moral economism rejects any conception of markets as essentially norm-free blocks of sociality. Consumer and labor markets are structured by the basic values they serve: meeting needs and recognizing achievement. That they serve those values – and thereby ultimately facilitate distinctive forms of individual freedom – is also what ultimately justifies markets from a normative perspective.

What evidence supports these significant claims for the inextricable embeddedness of markets in norms, and thus for the methodological inescapability of moral economism? How, for instance, might Honneth convince a traditional economist, a Marxist, or a systems theorist that moral economism is true, especially when all three are committed to some version of a contrary sociohistorical claim: namely, that markets increasingly detach themselves from any and all normative constraints, responding only to their own intrinsic imperatives and "iron" laws? Particularly in light of the apparently unstoppable powers of global markets to reshape any and all communities they come into contact with, Honneth's moral economism might seem hopelessly idealistic. Recall that in the exchange with Fraser ten years earlier, Honneth advanced two main arguments against the functional autonomy of markets: one formed around the claim that esteem orders have a determinative influence on wage and salary rates, and one formed around the normative preconditions for the existence of markets. If I read FR correctly, Honneth has more or less abandoned the first argument concerning esteem orders[6] – an argument that ran into serious trouble, as we saw in 5.2.2 – has deepened and subtly reformed the second argument about normative preconditions, and now implicitly advances a new, third argument from social history.

First, a few words about his reformulation of the preconditions argument. Recall that the basic idea is that if market institutions do not realize, at least to some tolerable extent, the implicit norms that justify them in the first place, then people will simply withdraw their consent from them and stop participating in them or in the legal and social practices needed to sustain them. Thus, to the extent that markets do actually continue to operate, there must be some at least minimal moral consent to them on the part of participants. Hence, from the evidence that markets continue to thrive, we can infer that they are morally embedded. Acknowledging the difficulty of empirically establishing that markets must be morally embedded, Honneth now explicitly recasts this argument as a form of *normative* functionalism: markets are only *freely consented to* when they are embedded in specific social relations that meet pre- or non-market moral criteria. So, for instance, if markets symmetrically and pervasively failed to meet large numbers of people's individual needs – say, left large populations destitute and hungry – and yet people continued to participate in them, we would be justified in saying that, although they acquiesced, they had not given their free consent to market institutions. Along with this reformulation of the argument, Honneth also significantly deepens it by showing the different kinds of consilient support it has received in thinkers as diverse as Hegel, Durkheim, Polanyi, and Parsons.

On my reading, FR also implicitly advances a new, much more extended argument for moral economism, an argument from actual social history. The idea here is that we can see that markets are in fact morally embedded once we carefully attend to all of the different ways that intellectual movements, legal and state reforms, and especially social struggles have invoked and employed the leading moral ideas of market cooperation in their attempts to socialize and domesticate the worst consequences and side-effects of capitalism. Tracing a wide range of diverse intellectual, political, legal, and social phenomena, especially over the last hundred and fifty years of capitalism, Honneth intends to show that these various movements and trends should be read as attempts to realize the normative potential implicit in market modes of social integration. While the force of the argument can only be appreciated by reading through the historical and sociological record Honneth advances, a few indications of the phenomena invoked can give at least some flavor of the argument.

Starting with the sphere of consumption,[7] Honneth traces many different intellectual and cultural critiques of markets stretching over at least three hundred years. One main focus is high culture: the intellectual accounts that seek to understand markets as necessarily embedded in normative frameworks and so as subject to critique when they do not sufficiently realize their inherent values: from Adam Smith, through Hegel, Durkheim, Polanyi, and Parsons, all articulate versions of moral economism. Honneth also considers strands of general popular culture that also presuppose a deep connection between markets and morals: eighteenth-century concerns about markets leading individuals to adopt greedy and purely strategic orientations, nineteenth-century indictments of markets for producing massive impoverishment and anarchistic boom–bust cycles, twentieth-century worries about the desiccated nature of purely consumerist identities, and twenty-first-century rejections of purely privatistic and competitive global capitalist individualism and the growth of socially conscious purchasing ideologies. Alternatively, consider a number of intellectual debates and concomitant social struggles over pre-market normative decisions that must be made in structuring markets. For instance, debates still rage over what should and should not be for sale as commodities (kidneys, sex, health care, computer algorithms?); over whether prices for, or distribution of, certain commodities (e.g., food, housing, clothing) should be determined by considerations of fairness or entirely by supply and demand; and over how extensive the satisfaction of luxurious desires should be in the light of religious, social, and ecological considerations.

Alongside such intellectual and cultural trends, Honneth points to the very great number of ways in which we can understand historic changes in state action, law, and regulation as evidence of the institutional constraint of markets so that they realize their inherent principles. Among others, he touches on state and legal functions, such as:

ensuring the legality of transactions; providing infrastructure; protecting consumers through inspections and product safety regulations; social welfare policies supporting the consumption of food, shelter, medicine, and education; social security; public health provisions; and regulations insuring the ecological and social sustainability of consumer markets. According to Honneth, all of these state activities implicitly acknowledge the structural advantage producers have over consumers and are intended to bring consumer markets in line with their implicit normative ideals, ideals of reciprocal and cooperative social labor to meet needs, constrained by considerations of the general good.

It would be wrong, however, to view political economic changes only from a state-centric perspective. For Honneth, it is crucial to see that state policies originated largely in response to determined social movements, struggling to force markets to realize their own ideals. Witness for instance, the importance of nineteenth-century bread riots and consumer boycotts for achieving state regulation of market prices for basic commodities and for state support of agricultural production. Alongside this "long march through the institutions" (FR: 215) of the state, Honneth also attends to various non-state forms of collective action aimed at realizing the value of meeting needs. Consider for instance the rise and prevalence of consumer cooperatives in the first half of the twentieth century, which socialized markets "from below." Recognizing that market-based distributions of many basic necessities were seriously deficient in actually meeting needs in an affordable way, individuals banded together into large purchasing cooperatives with the power to negotiate fair prices, distributing goods to their members according to principles of need rather than ability to pay current market prices. Such social movements show that the market is not understood by its participants as a purely individualistic sphere, but as a sphere of reciprocally enabled individual freedom, a sphere of social cooperation serving the general good.

The social history of labor markets and struggles over the conditions of capitalist production provides even clearer evidence that capitalism is morally embedded and can rightly be judged according to its inherent norms. In intellectual and general cultural domains, Honneth finds traces of the idea that labor is a critical site for the development of self-esteem through recognition of individual achievement in diverse discourses: in the nineteenth-century, worry about "the rabble" who have no access to esteem-generating jobs; in the rise of a distinctive class consciousness of wage laborers in the nineteenth and twentieth centuries; and in twentieth-century critiques of the emptiness and meaninglessness of fully mechanized industrial labor and concomitant calls for the humanization of labor. The history of state labor law and regulation also provides evidence for Honneth's thesis of moral economism.

Consider, for instance, minimum and living wage laws, mandated unemployment pay, rights to collective co-determination between management and organized labor, comprehensive education reforms and employment retraining programs, fiscal policies geared to promote full employment, occupational safety regulations, insurance against labor-ending contingencies, work-based pension systems, and so on.

Once again, it is quite clear that these transformations – which gradually domesticated and organized capitalist labor markets according to normative criteria – were largely made in response to the demands of social struggles, in particular those led by unions. Labor markets were embedded most successfully where (and during the time when) organized labor was able to ensure collective bargaining rights which offset the structural disadvantage that individual laborers are at vis-à-vis management when negotiating labor contracts. Such a domestication of the labor market was achieved, on Honneth's reading, by using a moral vocabulary shared between labor, management, and capitalists to justify the market, specifically invoking ideals such as the right to work, nonexploitative contracts, the dignity of labor, promoting the health and safety of workers, and cooperative determination of the conditions of labor. Social struggles carried the move to embed markets from above, that is, through the state and law, even as there were also moves by guilds and unions to act from below, for instance by providing insurance and retraining programs for members, as well as other forms of collective "self-help." Even in the face of twenty-first-century globalizing labor markets, Honneth finds some traces of moral economism in nascent international moves toward certification procedures for labor conditions, monitoring of labor contracts, and other attempts to force markets to live up to their implicit norms and values.

In sum, Honneth's new argument for the broad claims of moral economism – that capitalist markets are inescapably structured by normative content and so cannot be considered norm-free spheres integrated purely functionally – is neither conceptual nor normative, but empirical. In particular, the burden is shouldered by an in-depth sociological and historical reconstruction of about two centuries of economic history, attending to diverse attempts to institutionalize suitable moral constraints and conditions so that markets fulfill their inherent normative principles.

We can now summarize Honneth's account of the market sphere as a domain of social freedom. First, markets institutionalize individuals' freedom in two specific ways: by meeting needs and by providing a crucial location for self-esteem. Markets for consumer items fulfill individual needs by structuring complementary and reciprocal roles of consumers and producers. Markets for labor enable the development of healthy individual self-esteem through a reciprocal regime of recognition based on individuals' productive achievements in their complementary roles as employees and employers.

Second, what justifies the market domain as a sphere of social freedom is that it enables a form of social cooperation that is in the interest of all involved, one that serves the complementary realization of individuals' aims. The sphere of consumption is morally valuable to the extent that individuals' needs are met in a way consistent with the general good, and the sphere of labor is valuable to the extent that it allows self-realization through esteem-based mutual recognition. According to the thick and rich historical record Honneth develops, markets are not only organized around these two basic normative principles for, in order to fully realize social freedom within market arenas, we have progressively recognized over time that the spheres of consumption and labor need to be regulated according to further moral conditions: safety and environmental regulation of producers, promotion of accurate consumer information; reciprocal relations of solidarity across classes; respect for the dignity of others' work; equality of opportunity; rules of fair play in buying and selling; the security of a living wage; meaningful work and humane working conditions; reciprocal recognition of others as members of a cooperative community; and available arenas for discourse about and cooperative bargaining over the conditions of consumer and labor markets. In other words, Honneth finds rich normative content internally structuring market spheres, normative content that should be considered a historical elaboration of the central market values of meeting needs and enabling self-realization.

Finally, it is in the light of this normative content that Honneth proposes a number of diagnoses of the main limitations, injustices, and misdevelopments of the market sphere. He is especially concerned with economic transformations over the past two decades where social, geographical, and political changes have combined to increasingly disembed markets, a set of changes often summarized as "neoliberalism." Rather than consider the entire bill of particulars, it is perhaps sufficient to see that he is quite pessimistic about the current state of markets as spheres of social freedom, considering neoliberalism as a clearly regressive social misdevelopment, "one that hollows out and undermines the normative potential of the market" (FR: 177). Although his historical work has enabled him to reconstruct that normative promise through diverse historical and social phenomena over two centuries, Honneth is convinced that the economy cannot be understood as a sphere of social freedom in its contemporary configuration:

> There can be no doubt that the current economic system in the developed countries of the West in no way represents a "relational" institution and is thus not a sphere of social freedom. It lacks all the necessary

characteristics of such a sphere: It is not anchored in role obligations to which all could agree, and which interweave with each other in a way that allows subjects to view each other's freedom as the condition of their own freedom; it therefore lacks an antecedent relation of mutual recognition from which the corresponding role obligations could draw any validity or persuasive power. (FR: 176)

Honneth himself notices that this pessimistic diagnosis raises a prima facie challenge to his method of normative reconstruction, since such a method appears to require an appeal to evidence of moral progress, but here we have strong contrary evidence of regress. Even if we grant that progress need not be linear, continuous, or unidirectional, the evidence from the rapid disembedding of markets from normative constraints seems to undermine any faith in a claim to the progressive realization of the inherent normative content of market spheres. I return to this problem in 6.4.2.3.

6.3.5   The public political sphere

The third major sphere of real social freedom is the public political sphere. In the substantial final section of FR, Honneth systematically develops his theory of democracy, a theory grounded in the social freedom that democratic interaction enables for engaged citizens to improve the conditions of their lives through reciprocal, collective discourse and decision with other citizens. The following sections summarize that democratic theory (6.3.5.1), some of the themes of Honneth's reconstructive history of democracy (6.3.5.2), his account of the values of democratic social freedom (6.3.5.3), and his diagnosis of contemporary democratic promises and perils (6.3.5.4).

6.3.5.1   Theory of democracy   Honneth puts forward a political theory we might productively label as "radical deliberative democracy" in order to locate it among rival contemporary political theories. To begin, his theory focuses on *democracy* as the preeminent consideration when we are thinking about the public sphere and politics. The central question here is: How is collective self-rule possible? As specified by Honneth, it becomes: How can we collectively and legitimately control the social conditions essential to the realization of individual social freedom? This focus on democratic consociation distinguishes his theory from a large family of theories centered around individual liberal rights and putting justice for individuals at the center of politics: e.g., natural law, liberalism, social contractarianism, and libertarianism.

Secondly, Honneth joins a contemporary movement within democratic theory – led by thinkers such as Joshua Cohen, John Dryzek, James Fishkin, Jürgen Habermas, and David Held – that comprehends public processes of discussion, debate, discourse and deliberation between and amongst citizens and officials as the decisive processes of democracy. This distinguishes his theory from various models of democracy – whether aggregative, pluralist, minimalist or competitive elitist – which focus on voting and the government accountability as the key carriers of democracy. In particular, like Habermas, Honneth articulates a two-track model of deliberative democracy. On the one hand, in the "democratic public sphere," public opinions concerning collective matters arise through varied deliberative and contestatory processes carried by the interplay between social movements, non-governmental organizations, culture producers and disseminators, the mass media, and governmental actors. On the other hand, in the sphere of the "democratic constitutional state," the changing and revisable consensus arising from the public sphere should ideally be implemented by a responsive government. Democratic legitimacy then requires that the constitutional state act as an organ or agency of the public sphere by realizing in law and policy the consensus arrived at by "we the people" in a healthy process of collective debate and discussion in the public sphere.

Finally, I would say that Honneth's particular version of this two-track deliberative democracy is *radical* because, when considering the legitimacy of democracy, it places almost all the normative weight on the conditions and workings of the public sphere.[8] For Honneth – in contrast to traditional political theories and notably to Habermas's more recent work – the state is *not* the ultimate coordinating sphere of society; government, formal politics, and the production of law are not the keystones of the social arch. Rather, for Honneth's radical theory, not only should the democratic constitutional state take orders from, and ensure the protection of, the democratic public sphere; the democratic state is also theorized as founded by and upon the democratic public sphere (FR: 305). The legitimacy of the constitutional state is thus constitutively tied to the legitimacy of the democratic public sphere: it must sufficiently protect the public sphere and it must implement the consensus arrived at by the full public-sphere "we" of democracy.

6.3.5.2 Themes in the history of democracy Honneth provides a rich and insightful history of more than two hundred years of democratic ferment and change in order to support his key thesis that radical deliberative democracy is the inner meaning of the sphere of political freedom. Sketching five key themes can give some flavor of this history: an expanding public sphere; ambiguities of nationalism; the mass media; changes in the state; and transnational politics. The history begins in the late eighteenth century with the original development of a public space of opinion in which white male propertied elites could exchange information and opinions, debating and deliberating about culture and current events. As this nascent bourgeois literary sphere became more inclusive throughout the nineteenth century, developing into a properly democratic public sphere, a concomitant new and explosive principle of governmental legitimacy began to take root: "All acts of government... were to face up to the 'public opinion' that took shape in the discursive exchange of arguments within the forums of the public sphere" (FR: 256). Hence the public sphere became political, both in what it focused on and in its relations to political legitimacy. Another very significant change is the gradual increase in inclusiveness of the public whose opinion formation became so important. Here Honneth attends to the work of social movements in widening participation in the democratic public sphere during the nineteenth and especially the twentieth centuries, eventually including not just propertied white males, but also women, laborers, the economically dependent, ethnic, religious and racial minorities, and, most recently, sexual minorities. This expansion of the political "we" is regarded by Honneth as a clear indication of the historical realization of a central normative principle of democracy: *all* affected by collective decisions and actions must be included in public debates concerning those decisions and actions.

As a matter of contingent historical practice, the creation of an inclusive and active democratic "we" – one sufficiently motivated to put in the hard work of democratic consociation – was mostly effected in Europe through diverse practices of nationalism. Honneth gives a great deal of attention to the deep moral and political ambiguities of nationalism as it developed in concert with spreading democratization of the public sphere and government through the nineteenth and twentieth centuries – and as it sometimes metastasized and reacted cancerously back upon democracy itself. Even conceptually, nationalism fits uneasily with democracy. For while nationalism internally broadened the democratic "we" across at least class and gender cleavages and provided a demos with the participatory and solidaristic energies required for healthy democracy, it was also used persistently as an exclusionary cudgel against membership in "we the people" for members of ethnic, racial, and sexual minorities. Furthermore, an extremely virulent form of German nationalism was central to both the deep distortion of the public sphere and the terroristic tyranny loosed by the state in the National Socialist era. In fact, Honneth does not regard Nazism and its horrors as a misdevelopment or pathology of democratic social freedom, but something wholly outside social freedom. From the point of view of "our normative reconstruction of all the spheres of freedom institutionalized in liberal democratic societies, the period of National Socialist tyranny remains an 'Other' that cannot be integrated into this reconstruction" (FR: 321). At most, this Other of democracy reminds us that social freedom is a fragile achievement that must be actively maintained, rather than simply assumed as a fortunate deliverance of progressive history.

Another topic for deep historical reflection by Honneth is the changing nature and role of mass media over the last one hundred and fifty years. Following Dewey and Habermas, the democratic public sphere is understood in part as an epistemic community. The public sphere senses, collects, sorts, sifts, and disseminates knowledge, information, and opinion, especially on matters of public concern. It thus allows for collective learning processes that improve in rationality and accuracy to the extent that ever greater numbers and diversity of voices and sources are involved. Culture industries and the mass media both have crucial roles here, and Honneth investigates how their epistemic contributions have changed over time, especially as their underlying technologies and organizational structures have changed. As in the case of nationalism, Honneth is attuned to the ambiguities – the simultaneous promise and peril – involved in the various transformations of the mass media over its history.

A fourth set of themes in Honneth's history revolve around crucial changes in the organization and structures of the democratic constitutional state. He traces the roles of social movements in forcing a democratization of the state in the direction of increasing popular sovereignty. To begin with, there is the expanding circle of those eligible for active political citizenship, and further, an expansion of what is guaranteed by citizenship (from negative liberties, to positive political liberties, to social rights). He also attends to the gradual development and institutionalization of many democratic preconditions and ideals: a professionalized civil service; increasing state social and welfare policies; the constitutionalization of rights; the rule of law; the separation of governmental powers; and the increase of arenas for citizens to engage actively in legislations and governance.

A final set of themes links back to the questions of nationalism, but now considered from the perspective of global relations. The first half of the twentieth century was consumed with the dangers of national sovereignty in the international arena. For example, the creation of the League of Nations and the United Nations both arose out of the attempt to enforce moral limits on nationalistic aggression. And the second half of the twentieth century and the beginning of our own has witnessed a normatively disturbing disconnect between the national frame of democratic politics – at least as traditionally conceived – and the transnational communities of those affected by international policies and actions. Thus contemporary global problems raise once again the question of how it can be possible today to realize the central principle of democracy: that those affected have a say over the conditions of their coexistence and hence the conditions of their individual social freedom.

6.3.5.3   The values of democratic social freedom   A democratic public political sphere clearly fulfills Honneth's conception of a sphere of social freedom.[9] To begin with, one can only realize individual freedom in the broad public political context if one has the opportunity to participate in collectively constructing the rules, policies, and institutions that shape the public environment of one's actions. Furthermore, this is a real social and complementary form of individual freedom since political freedom is explicitly possible only through complementary cooperation with others whom one reciprocally recognizes as free and equal fellow citizens. Democratic freedom is, then, decidedly social, rather than individualistic: it simply can't be realized by withdrawing from intersubjective engagement with fellow citizens. In part, this requires epistemic engagement with others. The democratic public sphere can be seen as an organ of social thought, a medium for social cognition: only discussion and debate across the widest selection of affected persons can secure expectations of heightened rationality for public knowledge. But, in equal part, this requires a specific moral engagement with others, with a specific principle of reciprocal recognition: "All adult...members of society should now be capable of recognizing each other as equally entitled citizens within the nation-state, because the formation of a democratic will accorded the same weight to one citizen as it did to another" (FR: 261).

If the freedom of personal relations is realized in the complementary roles of friend, lover, or family member, and market freedom in the complementary roles of consumer and producer, democratic freedom is realized in the intermeshing roles of deliberative communicator, active citizen in and co-legislator of one's community. Accordingly, while personal relations provide individuals the social conditions needed to realize their inner natures, and market relations provide those needed to meet their needs, democratic relations provide the social conditions needed to reflexively improve those very social conditions. The democratic public sphere and constitutional state together (ideally at least) "constitute a form of social freedom by enabling individuals, in communication with all other members of society, to improve their own living conditions" (FR: 274). In short, democracy is a life of free and enriching communication and collective decision where we work together, cooperatively and in an experimental way, toward the consummation of our community. The sphere of democracy thereby realizes a diverse set of values, values which ultimately justify it as an irreplaceable sphere of modern life: maximal social freedom of each, equal citizenship of each, rational reflexive collective cognition under good informational conditions, and the self-determination of the community.

We can round out this consideration of the normativity of democratic social freedom by noting the seven main conditions Honneth identifies for a healthy and legitimate democracy in the contemporary world.[10] A first requirement is political rights: there must be legally reliable and constitutional guarantees, extended to all affected citizens, for both political expression and political participation, and in both the public sphere and the institutional organs of the state. Second, the political public sphere must bridge and transcend class and group cleavages that have historically excluded some. In the contemporary world, this second condition entails that a legitimate public sphere must span nation-state borders, as such borders are less and less relevant to delineating the set of those persons affected by various collective decisions and policies. Third, healthy democracy requires a responsible mass media that can provide useful information on public issues and social problems. (While Honneth believes that the current mass media does not fulfill this criterion, appearing more as an anti-journalistic, commercialized entertainment, it would be possible for the mass media to regain a productive role here, perhaps by leveraging new internet and online tools.) A fourth condition is citizen willingness to materially support face-to-face deliberations and active civil society organizations. Mere consultation of "public opinion" as revealed in opinion polls is not enough. Citizens must "be willing to resist the dis-solution of the public sphere by dividing up the necessary voluntary services needed for the material preparation and execution of actual events" (FR: 292). For, in the end, everyday moral behaviors and social practices are the real motor and medium for realizing democratic freedom since these behaviors and practices – not legislation, nor the franchise, nor the formal instruments of state governance – are the energizing elements of the wide public sphere, the normative key of real democracy. In turn, fifth, such energy comes from a political culture that would support dispositions to wide solidarity with disparate others and strong commitments to civic engagement even with those with whom one vehemently disagrees. Unfortunately, many actual attempts at such a political culture have been not only exclusionary but often dangerously so: witness the male-centered bourgeois public culture of the early nineteenth century, or the nationalistic fervor that gripped countries from the end of the nineteenth through the mid-twentieth centuries.

These five conditions are all central to what Honneth regards as the engine of healthy democracy: the democratic public sphere. But he does of course also recognize a sixth condition: a functioning, respon-sive, and effective democratic constitutional state that can make the collective decisions formed in the public sphere operative by modify-ing the conditions of social coexistence. "The members of society who supplement each other in their communicative exchange of views must feel that the products of their will-formation are effective enough to be practiced in social reality.... The social organ charged with guaranteeing the effectiveness of their convictions [is] the democratic constitutional state" (FR: 304).

Finally, I think we can safely say that a "democratic ethical life" is a seventh condition of democracy. What Honneth means by this phrase is an overall form of life in which the main spheres of social freedom – the different forms of personal relations, the market spheres of consumption and labor, and the democratic spheres of the public and the state – intermesh and support one another. For he is convinced that democratic public autonomy is impossible without complementary spheres which not only fulfill their own specific freedom-supporting functions, but also simultaneously nourish and promote the key virtues and characteristics required for active democratic citizenship.

> The political sphere of democratic will-formation can only do justice to its own normative claims of freely involving all participants if the latter learn that the social struggles to realize the demands of freedom institutionalized in the other spheres of action deserve support, because they represent the conditions of one's own freedom. The social system of democratic ethical life thus represents a complicated web of reciprocal dependencies. (FR: 330)

In short, democratic ethical life requires social freedom in all three spheres, where all three spheres are joined together in reciprocally reinforcing relations: "Free market participants, self-aware democratic citizens and emancipated family members – all of whom correspond to the ideals institutionalized in our society – mutually influence each other, because the properties of one cannot be realized without those of the other two" (FR: 330–1).

Radical deliberative democracy thus not only entails justice actualized in a well-functioning state directed by a vibrant democratic public sphere, but also a just cooperative economy and just forms of personal and family relations. Ultimately, Honneth's grand Hegelian vision in FR is that, by normatively reconstructing the practices and institutions of social freedom in the three spheres, we can come to see that all three spheres working together in a democratic form of ethical life is the substantive, justified conception of justice that social and political philosophers seek. For only a democratic ethical life – in this complex configuration of the different interconnected spheres of social freedom – fulfills the abstract criterion of justice animating all competing modern theories: "That which is 'just' is that which protects, fosters or realizes the autonomy of all members of society" (FR: 18).

6.3.5.4 Diagnosing contemporary democracy Clearly, this grand vision of a democratic ethical life – not to mention the narrower but still demanding vision of a functioning state operating as an organ of a vibrant, diverse, and broad public sphere – is an idealization, not an accurate descriptions of current reality. While Honneth reconstructs these idealizations from historical and contemporary social reality, he is fully aware that actuality falls well short. His diagnosis of the state of democracy today – more specifically democracy in today's core Europe – is in fact rather pessimistic, highlighting a number of significant insufficiencies, challenges, and perils. With respect to the all-important democratic public sphere, I have already noted Honneth's concerns about ambiguous tendencies in mass media and new communications technologies, encompassing both the perils of increasing commercialization, sensationalism, and anti-journalistic tendencies, and the potential promise of online communities for non-commodified and unmediated horizontal communications.

There are also the challenges of finding motivational replacements for the civic energy and solidarity-promoting functions played by nationalism. As Honneth stresses, democracy is demanding and requires real commitment: citizens need to see one another as worthy of trust and solidarity, and they must be concerned about the interests of all those affected. These motives were previously supplied by nationalism but, with the loss of national sovereignty and multicultural heterogeneity, traditional forms of European nationalism are declining or becoming dangerously reactionary. Civic apathy, disenchantment with politics, and individualistic depoliticization threaten the engine of democracy – the public political sphere – at the center of Honneth's radical deliberative democracy. At best, he holds out some hope for a European collective identity formed around past struggles for social freedom within the different spheres: around memories of, for example, the French Revolution, constitutional struggles, movements against horrible labor conditions, feminist struggles against oppressive female role obligations, and so on. The idea is that, perhaps, collective identification with such memories could then be the basis for contemporary, pan-European activist motivation and solidarity with others.[11]

Turning to the perils to democracy in the realm of the constitutional state, Honneth is particularly worried about liberal corporatism as a misdevelopment of governance structures. Under corporatism, the real bargaining and ultimate decisions are made by major economic players and politicians, out of sight of the public sphere, in a sort of nonconstitutional space outside of public legislative activity: "political decisions are increasingly removed from parliament or are only seemingly left up to the delegates, while secret deals with large economic groups are made in a space that, while close to government, cannot be democratically monitored" (FR: 325). He also diagnoses allied state misdevelopments as European politics becomes more and more like the American system of lobbyism, rent-seeking, and patronage.

In general, Honneth's diagnosis is a bit gloomy. On the one hand, democratic social freedom is fragile, demanding quite a bit of pro-social and pro-political energy on the part of citizens, and requiring a transnational political culture sensitive to the plight of all those affected by collective actions, whether heterogeneous co-nationals or globally dispersed and distant populations. On the other hand, disenchantment with politics and suspicion of elites grow by the day as formal political decision-making processes seem increasingly selective and sectional, biased in favor of organized but opaque rich and powerful interests. All of this is furthered by the weakening of national governments in the face of transnational and global forces and actors, in turn furthered by the concomitant disembedding of market processes from the normative constraints of social freedom. For instance, the best transnational hope for democracy – the European Union – is in fact, according to Honneth, increasingly integrated only through market freedoms understood on the model of negative property rights. The hope that Honneth holds out – more as an exhortation than a policy prescription or prediction of the future – is for the development of a common democratic culture that could integrate citizens politically across traditional borders and divisions, a common culture that could then underwrite massive social pressures to normatively re-embed market mechanisms and reinvigorate radical, transnational deliberative democracy.

6.4   Innovations and Critical Perspectives

Freedom's Right undoubtedly represents a new height of grand theorizing in the development of Honneth's critical social theory. As we have seen, it deepens and enriches his earlier focus on recognition by showing recognition's inner connection to a preeminent value of modernity: freedom. And it shows the complexity of freedom by developing an internally differentiated theory of social freedom, a conception that encompasses many of the diverse conceptions and aspirations of that value. Further, it is a methodologically sophisticated attempt to re-actualize a Hegelian tradition of social philosophy, even in the face of contemporary skepticism of both narratives of progress and grand sociopolitical theories. Despite such obstacles, Honneth presents a comprehensive, systematic, yet non-metaphysical theory of social organization and social institutions, one that can hold its own against competing accounts of the mechanisms of social integration and reproduction. Finally, all of this is achieved in the service of fulfilling the basic ideal of a critical social theory: an interdisciplinary social theory with emancipatory intent. In Honneth's case, such an emancipatory theory is realized through a history of the present, aimed at an insightful, critical, and utopian diagnosis of modernity's real achievements, worrisome misdevelopments, and destructive pathologies. In lieu of a comprehensive assessment, these concluding sections summarize FR's methodological innovations (6.4.1), and consider some critical issues that the normative (6.4.2) and socio-theoretic (6.4.3) components of the project face.

6.4.1   Methodological innovations

At the heart of Honneth's social theory is the insistence that social orders and institutions *must* be integrated and reproduced through values since their ongoing existence depends on the sense that participants have that they are legitimate. To the extent to which a given society has shared social practices and institutions that perdure, there must ultimately be some form of underlying normative consensus, even if only at a general level and on quite abstract values, among its members.[12] Taking a page from Hegel, Honneth then insists that the character – and justification – of this normative consensus should be analyzed as it has developed and changed in history through the agencies of various social actors, movements, struggles, and regimes of recognition. In particular, Honneth's distinctive social theory proposes to historically reconstruct the different spheres of society – personal, economic, and democratic – according to the specific values and forms of social freedom that each sphere characteristically realizes. Finally, this historical picture is given a developmental, directional reading, by considering changes in each of the spheres as driven by a kind of problem-solving logic, where progress is measured by the extent to which new practices and institutions solve problems inherent in older forms. For Honneth, as we have seen, progress is measured in part epistemically – in terms of increased discursive rationality – but also, and more fundamentally, normatively – in terms of increased inclusion and individualization.

This concrete social history is then integral to the analysis and justification of the moral ideals at the heart of the normative theory. Here again, Honneth's deep Hegelianism contrasts with competing conceptions of moral and political philosophy that start from abstract philosophical considerations and then attempt to apply ideal principles to less-than-ideal reality. Honneth's theory of justice sees its ideals as arising immanently out of social history – specifically as the ideals motivating leading social movements and struggles – and it considers the entire breadth of social reality as relevant to justice, rather than limiting its scope to law and the state alone. This strategy of identifying and justifying normative ideals immanently does not, however, foreclose the possibility of a strong critique of the present. For philosophical critique proceeds in the same way as everyday calls for social and political change: theorists and activists alike invoke the very ideals built into current institutions and practices, and point out the ways in which those institutions and practices do not or cannot fulfill their normative promise as currently configured. This is a process of drawing on the "normative surplus" inherent in social reality in order to critique that reality. Finally, as we have seen in 6.3.1, this complex normative-cum-social theory yields a number of different forms of critique of the present corresponding to different types of problems. Criticizing injustice corresponds to lack of equal opportunities for freedom; identifying limitations and diagnosing pathologies corresponds to situations where we fail to understand the ways in which individual legal and moral freedoms depend on accommodating forms of social freedom; and identifying misdevelopments corresponds to failures of social spheres to fully realize their inherent normative promise.

6.4.2   Normative issues

6.4.2.1   Only freedom?   Despite these achievements, there are potential problems which Honneth's new directions might face, and it is worth considering how he might address them. We have already seen (6.2.1 above) that the book's very strong opening claim – namely, that freedom is the single, preeminent value of modern social life – faces prima facie pushback from those who argue that modernity embraces a plurality of different and potentially incompatible values (e.g., Isaiah Berlin), as well as from those who would reject the claims to both singularity and preeminence made on behalf of freedom. What, for instance, of equality, human welfare and flourishing, human perfection, fairness, legitimacy, non-domination, collective self-rule, and so on? Perhaps there are multiple, competing, and incompatible values which cannot be prioritized (*à la* pluralism) or perhaps some one or a combination of these other modern values ought to be prioritized over freedom (*à la* competing moral or political philosophies).

On the one hand, Honneth sometimes flirts with the idea that all of these other values might be subsumed under freedom itself, seeing them as, for instance, mere elaborations or ornamentations of freedom: "As if by magical attraction, all modern ethical ideals have been placed under the spell of freedom: sometimes they infuse this idea with greater depth or add new accents, but they never manage to posit an independent, stand-alone alternative" (FR: 15). And more recently: "in modern societies, the idea of freedom has become the Archimedean point for legitimizing social order, insofar as it has come to form the background for all our normative obligations" (Honneth 2013b: 39). The problem with this argumentative strategy is that it requires broadening the notion of freedom to such an extent that it loses all distinctiveness as a value, becoming at most a kind of ill-defined honorific given to any ideal with a positive valence in modernity. (In Hegel's terms, this takes "freedom" into "the night in which all cows are black.")

On the other hand, I indicated that Honneth's argument may be implicit and launched by the whole book, that his actual reconstruction of western societies shows that freedom just is in fact the preeminent value. Assessing the success of this much more ambitious argument, then, can only be achieved in light of all of the relevant evidence, both that presented by Honneth's historical reconstructions and that which might be presented in favor of other alternative value reconstructions of modern, western societies.

6.4.2.2 Historical progress? Other worries revolve around Honneth's evaluative claims for the basically *progressive* character of modern western societies. Of course, his normative reconstructions of recent history are by no means triumphalist: consider, for instance his somewhat pessimistic assessments of the likelihood of overcoming contemporary misdevelopments in the economic and democratic spheres. And yet reasonable concerns might be raised in terms we might label as charges of promoting "Pollyannaish" and "Whiggish" history.[13]

The Pollyanna charge is simply that Honneth's overall story of moral progress is too optimistic given the brutal, destructive and horrific character of much of the nineteenth and especially the twentieth centuries. (We saw an analog of this charge back in 2.6.1, asking if Honneth's philosophical anthropology is overly optimistic.) This charge isn't easily formulated as an objection since Honneth's theory does not have the ambition to provide an overall assessment of modern western history. Instead, the project attempts to distill out of the vast domain of historical data only those that bear on a normative reconstruction of the ideals, practices, and institutions that have grown up and supported the development of the domains of social freedom. "In spelling out the normative implications of already institutionalized spheres of recognition we, as theoreticians, have to try to give the best possible interpretations of them in terms of moral progress" (Honneth and Marcelo 2013: 214). A claim that Honneth has missed accounting for, let us say, the horrors of the Holocaust, is a misplaced charge against a quite different intellectual project.

Nevertheless, one might be concerned about, as it were, the "attitudinal stance" of a Hegelian project that tries to reconstruct a story of progress – about the way such a project may appear to be too satisfied with the present and insufficiently cognizant of alternative stances from the point of view of outsiders, cynics, skeptics, or radicals. What, for instance might a queer theorist make of the moral principles distilled out of the reconstruction of heterosexual monogamy; a socialist of the morality of capitalism; an anarchist of the principles of constitutional democracy?[14] FR is certainly not a radical critique of the present calling for the overthrow of its basic practices and institutions, but an endorsement of its fundamental values, coupled with a call to correct our institutions and practices to fall better in line with their underlying ideals.

One also might level of charge of Whiggish history against an apparently Eurocentric account of inevitable progress toward increasing freedom. One potential problem here might be the picture of progress as more or less inevitable – in the Hegelian image, of the gradual and unstoppable unfolding of the inner content of the concept of freedom. Of course, Honneth is no defender of such an inevitability thesis. FR repeatedly stresses the developmental interruptions, discontinuities, and promising but untaken roads in history – contrary to any thesis of inevitable progress. In addition, the substantive diagnoses of contemporary pathologies, injustices, and misdevelopments should put paid to the suggestion that history is there painted as always progressive, never regressive. Nevertheless, one might reasonably wonder whether enough attention has been paid to the historical contingency and unpredictability of change.

Another general worry about Whiggish history is that it tends to idolize one's own current position as the proper goal of history. In the context of FR's focus only on the development of the so-called "WEIRD" societies – western, educated, industrialized, rich democracies – this becomes a worry that European and North American development is hypostasized as the single and sole telos of legitimate or worthy history. This then denigrates, at least by implication, any alternative social arrangements or developments found in non-western societies (Allen 2013). Even though the claim to cultural superiority is never endorsed, or even broached, as far as I can tell in Honneth's book, it seems nevertheless a plausible inference from the celebration of the practices and institutions of social freedom found therein.

These concerns are not merely ones of tone or focus, for to the extent to which Honneth aims methodologically to reanimate Hegel's project of an internal reconstruction of the progressive valence and direction inherent in the history of social freedom, he must deal with concerns about the philosophy of history. Of course, he intends to jettison Hegel's unconvincing metaphysical grounding of historical teleology in the self-unfolding of Reason/Spirit and replace this with an account of learning mechanisms built into social practices and institutions. Recall that the primary mechanisms of progress here are social struggles that push for change by exploiting surplus normativity – the difference between ideals implicit in social institutions and their actual realizations – and then the eventual consolidation of such improvements through rational assessment and reflective endorsement by participants.

Still, it is not clear how he might answer to concerns about teleological history as Whiggish, Eurocentric, and potentially culturally imperialistic. There seem to me to be at least two options, both of which have their own drawbacks. First, he could claim to be doing an internal reconstruction only of *our own* society's progress, whereby improvements or deteriorations are gauged only relative to previous states of that society, with no implications for cross-cultural comparisons. In this way, he could still maintain that freedom is our society's central and most worthy value, and that we have seen real progressive developments with respect to its realization in the various spheres of our social life. But he could scrupulously avoid any inference of cultural superiority or any claim that there is only one goal of moral history; social freedom has simply structured *our* history. The limitation of this approach – let's call it "conventionalism" – is that freedom, and the more specific forms of social freedom, seem to have little more claim on us, according to this approach, than that they are simply ours. Conventionalism looks like a groundless endorsement of our own values as worthy simply because they are the product of our own history. If so, critical social theory has become decidedly less critical: it could descend into an empty chauvinism coupled with an uncritical endorsement of the status quo, whatever that might be.

Alternatively, Honneth might argue in a more "objectivist" vein: that the various forms of social freedom are in fact superior to alternative values and different institutions realizing them – and it is only that superiority which could underwrite claims of real progress and diagnoses of real regress. Perhaps the standard for "objectively better" is a perfectionist account of human flourishing, or more likely for Honneth a specific philosophical anthropology of self-realization – in any case, something standing in the place of traditional value theory's reliance on inherent human nature. The philosophy of history would then have to explain explicitly its grounding in an account of human flourishing. Alternatively, the philosophy of history might be grounded in some form of transcultural claim to universal standards of rationality, such that progress is measured in terms of norms of rationality that are potentially operative in all cultures, even if the social conditions for their realization are not universally available.[15] At any rate, both forms of objectivism concerning freedom would still have to explain how one could avoid the implications of Eurocentrism or cultural imperialism, in addition to doing the philosophical work of supporting an account of human flourishing or universal rationality.[16]

6.4.2.3 Alternative teleologies? Objectivism might be ambitious, even daunting, in our anti-foundationalist, social constructionist, and generally skeptical philosophical times. But I would like to briefly sketch a case for why Honneth needs some form of objectivism in order to contend with a very serious problem that I believe FR's substantive diagnoses face – we might call this the problem of "alternative teleologies." It is perhaps easiest to see in terms of Honneth's diagnosis of economic misdevelopments, but I believe it is also structurally present in his diagnoses of current spheres of personal relations and democracy.[17]

Consider, then, FR's history and diagnosis of contemporary capitalism. In a nutshell, evidence is presented of a strong history of intellectual trends and social movements insisting on the inherently moral character of market capitalism, and fighting for necessary regulations and constraints on unbridled markets so that they realize their telos as spheres of social freedom. To be actual spheres of social freedom, markets would need to be relational institutions where individuals willingly take on their role obligations – as consumers and suppliers, as employees and employers – because those roles structure morally valid and persuasive relations of mutual recognition, within which individuals could realize their freedom in and through cooperation with others. According to the diagnosis of the last twenty years of market disembedding, however, actual markets today are not, according to Honneth, true domains of social freedom. Instead, current neoliberal regimes have witnessed the systematic detachment of markets from those moral constraints Honneth claims are inherent in them. In short, contemporary capitalism is a misdevelopment away from previously progressive trends, as the spheres of consumption and labor have become increasingly hollowed out of normative content and social promise, turning into fierce arenas for competition between warring, atomistic individuals who do not view others as co-facilitators of their own freedom.

According to this story, then, moral economism of the left-social-democratic variety is inherent in economic relations – as shown by the normative reconstruction of two centuries of history – but is currently on the rocks, battered by the misdevelopments of the recent disembedding of markets from morality.[18] This is, however, not the only story that might be plausibly told from the same evidence. An alternative version of moral economism – say, a libertarian version – might point to the recent disembedding of the market as the final triumph of the inherent normativity of market relations, the freeing of the individual from any constraints on personal liberty to buy and sell at will, and the achievement of individual esteem merely through one's superior income and wealth in comparison to others. Markets have been increasingly purified of their immoral redistributive, regulative, and nanny-state admixtures, and the pure risk-responsibility morality of unbridled individual contract rights has increasingly come to rule the roost. The market on the libertarian story is seen then as realizing fundamental moral values – but the values are quite different than those at the heart of the social freedom story. In particular, rather than a social conception of freedom, libertarianism reconstructs individual freedom to buy and sell at will as the normative goals of market relations. And, of course, the libertarian reconstruction is a story of triumph, while the social freedom story is, at best, one of temporary defeat, temporary misdevelopment.

Consider a third possible story, one put forth perhaps by neoliberal economists. Here, in contrast to the social freedom and libertarian models, the market is not seen as inherently moral or immoral – it is rather amoral. Markets are simply very efficient mechanisms coordinating production and distribution of goods, employing functional integration through price incentives. The neoliberal story is also a story of recent triumph, the triumph of removing exogenous moral content from the market. The recent disembedding of markets from moral constraints is a triumph of functionalist specialization: markets run best when they are responsive only to their own internal mechanisms and signals, rather than gummed up with social norms and moral fetters. Capitalism triumphs, on the neoliberal story, when economies are functionally differentiated from social integration.

Assuming that each of the alternative teleologies has sufficient historical evidence to make it plausible, which story is right and why? Honneth himself sometimes notes something like this problem: namely, that his diagnoses might lack the empirical evidence of actual social movements fighting against the proposed misdevelopments. Concerning, for instance, the problem of identifying social struggles against what he regards as regressive economic changes, he notes that "this misdevelopment...poses a problem for our normative reconstruction....we are faced with the difficult situation that we cannot longer rely on normative countermoves" (FR: 252) from those struggling to re-embed the market. But he never considers whether his normative diagnosis of the present political economy *as a misdevelopment* should be seriously questioned, given this problematic lack of empirical purchase. The only question is how the theorist can have access to the feelings of outrage that must surely be there – inarticulately, individually, unexpressed – because of the present misdevelopments.

Honneth raises a similar empirical worry about the difficulty of finding effective social struggles against supposed misdevelopments in the mass media toward celebrity sensationalism and the construction of virtual realities not corresponding to political realities.

> These virtualizing tendencies of traditional media pose a significant difficulty for our normative reconstruction; according to the criteria inherent in the democratic public sphere itself, these tendencies must be regarded as a misdevelopment because they no longer sufficiently inform the public, but rather produce reality self-referentially....It is quite difficult to separate reality from fiction and get a sober look at real social developments. (FR: 297)

But what if virtuality is the real normative telos of the public sphere, a sphere inherently concerned with spectacle and entertainment? How could we decide between the alternative normative reconstructions of the mass media as reporters or as entertainers? Again, the problem of alternative teleologies is normative: if there are competing reconstructions of the same historical evidence, how does critical theory decide which story articulates the correct normative analysis of the inner principles of a given social sphere?

At this point, I would contend, Honneth cannot employ a merely conventionalist account of historical progress. At points, he seems tempted this way. For instance, in the methodological introduction to FR, Honneth argues that the fact that persons do indeed continue to reproduce given social arrangements is evidence itself of their moral acceptability and hence of historical progress. "The fact that subjects actively preserve and reproduce free institutions is the theoretical evidence of their historical value" (FR: 59). In other words, the mere fact of existing institutions, which in turn rely on individuals accepting those institutions, appears to underwrite a claim to their moral rightness. Further evidence that Honneth is tempted to endorse conventionalism comes in his recent replies to critical reviews of FR, although that evidence is somewhat ambiguous.[19]

There are at least three major problems with this conventionalist account of moral progress. To begin with, it does not clearly decide between the alternative teleologies. The history of economic changes in our own societies is, simply, ambiguous. That history contains clear evidence of each of the three stories: struggles to embed markets in social relations, struggles to embed markets in libertarian individualism, and struggles to free economies of any moral interventions. Without more evidence than "this is the way we happen to do things around here," it is hard to see which should be used to assess progress or regress.

Second, conventionalism does not in fact favor the social freedom story since it is a story of defeat (misdevelopment) rather than triumph (progress). If anything, the increasing predominance of laissez-faire economic and policy regimes, disembedded from normative constraint, across the developed world over the last three decades points to the neoliberal teleology as the real progress. And the libertarian story is favored as progressive by evidence of the increasing spread of consumerist definitions of all conceptions of freedom, where freedom is seen as no more than an individual's choice between different product purchases, whether those are the consumer products realizing personal freedom or the politicians and policies realizing political freedom. In short, the neoliberal and libertarian stories seem more true to the social practices and institutions that are actually being reproduced. On the conventionalist approach, that is clear evidence that people find either neoliberalism or libertarian economism as in fact morally valid and convincing. By contrast, the social freedom story can point to much less evidence that it is getting sustained uptake by and support from individuals and groups. If ordinary folks simply no longer agree that social freedom is the basis of market legitimacy, then how can a conventionalist theory say that the move away from social freedom is normatively poor, a misdevelopment?

Third, it is simply insufficient for a critical social theory to claim that we can infer progress or even moral acceptability for social institutions from the mere fact of widespread individual compliance with the status quo. There may be any number of explanations for why individuals do (or do not) in fact continue to reproduce given social institutions. They may have no feasible alternatives; they may be unaware of alternatives; they may be forced to comply; they may find material incentives overwhelming; there may be rationality distorting ideologies or wealth-based asymmetries in communications; the structures of opportunity may be unfairly aligned with wealth disparities and class positions; and so on. Of course, individuals might also be convinced with good reason that their society's given economic institutions are morally justifiable and preferable. But compliance alone is not sufficient evidence to support this latter explanation of moral endorsement. In short, given the variety of explanations for ongoing compliance – many of them morally disreputable – compliance alone cannot warrant a claim for moral acceptability.[20]

In short, I would contend, on the basis of conventionalist internal historical reconstruction alone, there is no way to tell whether the social freedom teleology – including its story of long historical progress and recent misdevelopment – should in fact be favored over the alternative teleologies. Unfortunately, Honneth does not consider the libertarian and neoliberal alternative reconstructions (or any other alternatives), so we do not have the evidence in front of us even to compare the social freedom story with them. Furthermore, even if we could make an assessment about which story was most historically accurate, facts about social reality cannot alone settle the matter of whether the current arrangements represent, say, *moral* progress, stasis, or regress. For this assessment – which is at the heart of Honneth's diagnosis of the present – we need normative criteria which are justifiable independently of any current fact of given social consensus. In short, I would argue, Honneth needs some kind of trans-contextual universal standard – some form of moral objectivism – in order to underwrite his normative diagnoses and evaluations of the present. Perhaps this should be grounded in a philosophical anthropology of human flourishing; perhaps in a philosophical theory of universal communicative rationality; perhaps in some other way. But, in whatever way, a judgment that the recent disembedding of the market represents a misdevelopment requires a moral account of the way history *should* have gone, but did not – and this cannot be settled by historical facts alone.

6.4.3 Issues in social theory

6.4.3.1 Pluralism, heterogeneity, and globalism One way to think about the challenge of alternative teleologies is as a problem in normative theory: how exactly to justify a particular constellation of values in the light of the manifest value pluralism of modern heterogeneous societies. For the competing teleologies reflect competing conceptions of the good. There is, however, another way of seeing it: as a problem in social theory. Central to Honneth's methodology of normative-institutional reconstruction is the claim that there *must* be a fundamental society-wide consensus on at least basic values for existing social institutions and practices to perdure. The commitment to a kind of socio-theoretical value monism is not merely implicit, but is an explicit premise in Honneth's argument that a theory of justice is best realized in and through a social theory. "The *first* premise [is] that social reproduction hinges on a certain set of shared fundamental ideals and values.... The particularity of this model of society...is its claim that all social orders, without exception, must legitimate themselves in terms of ethical values and ideals worth striving for" (FR: 3–4).

The problem, however, is that this claim of an underlying value consensus as that which integrates social institutions simply seems belied by the facts of modern complex societies. One and the same society can contain so many disagreements, at such fundamental levels, across such different persons, with so many different kinds of intersubjective practices and forms of life – even as, for example, the economic institutions of consumer and labor markets exist and perdure across those differences.[21] Honneth himself acknowledges this problem, even as he appears to set it aside as a critical concern:

> Even the existence of "heterogeneous" societies marked by ethnic or religious diversity has little effect on this "transcendental" necessity of normative integration. Although in these societies ethical values need to be formulated in a more comprehensive and general manner so to make room for the ideals held by minority cultures, material reproduction and cultural socialization must comply with a set of shared norms. In this weak sense, every society embodies objective Spirit to a certain extent, because its institutions, social practices and routines reflect shared normative beliefs about the aims of cooperative interaction. (FR: 4)

Honneth's response to the problem of heterogeneity within a society seems then to be an abstractive move: granting diversity of substantive ethical commitments at a concrete level, nevertheless, at a sufficient level of generality it is possible to espy a societal consensus on more abstract and formal values and ideals. These abstract and formal values are then the essential, irreplaceable elements in the integration of those social institutions that normative reconstruction aims to elucidate. Although I am only flagging this concern here, without any sustained assessment, I do think that pluralistic heterogeneity is a real problem for Honneth's proposal to develop an action-theoretic social theory that is built around the integrating power of shared values and ideals.

Another allied social theoretic concern is whether such a social theory could be useful at all in analyzing transnational and global regimes, institutions, and practices. For here, the theorist needs to have an account of the shape, structural characteristics and typical causal dynamics of social entities – international nongovernmental organizations, trade alliances, transnational political regimes, international legal regimes, global governance organizations – which span different nations and quite different kinds of societies. Although such global practices and institutions do in fact exist and perdure, it seems simply unbelievable to ascribe their social integration to a shared consensus on fundamental values. In other words, at the global level, the type of Hegelian social theory proposed might be methodologically inadequate. The open question is, then, do we need a different kind of social theory to understand global social phenomena, or do we abandon the claim to the "transcendental necessity" of consensual normative integration for any and all institutions in the face of apparently contrary reality?

6.4.3.2 Idealism, power, structures, and systems The final concern I wish to raise here – without resolving – is one that has, in a sense, shadowed Honneth's project since its early days: what I'll call the problem of "socio-theoretic idealism." Begin with the problems of pluralism, heterogeneity, and globalism I just flagged: in each case, the deeper worry is that social integration – the fact that the actions of individuals intermesh with the large-scale regularities we call practices and institutions – is not sufficiently explained by reference to shared values, ideals, and meanings. In short, social integration may well occur through media that operate differently than cultural contents, contents which are in principle subject to rational scrutiny, reasoned critique, and reflective endorsement. These other media of integration might be as diverse as economic power, state coercion, class-specific ideology, invisible-hand-type functional imperatives, and nonconscious disciplinary socialization mechanisms. Whatever they are, however, the worry is that these media of integration operate differently than cultural values and ideals and are not subject to the same dynamics of change through rational insight and transformation.

We have seen this basic concern with socio-theoretic idealism several times: in the charges that recognition struggles are "merely symbolic" and ignore the pernicious power of the jargon of group authenticity (3.4.1 and 3.4.3); in the articulation of an account of ideological recognition to cope with oppressive forms of positive recognition (4.2.1); in concerns about recognitional monism limiting the etiological and therapeutic tasks of pathology diagnosis (4.3.1); and in Fraser's charge that economies cannot be accurately analyzed only in terms of recognition structures (5.2.2). Furthermore, the lack of a satisfactory theory of power has been a persistent theme of many sympathetic critics of recognition theory, represented most powerfully by Lois McNay and Danielle Petherbridge.[22] These concerns have not been assuaged by Honneth's latest book; if anything, they have been further accentuated by FR's explicit arguments in favor of an action-theoretic social theory, arguments intended to rebut all forms of systems theory (especially, but not only, with regard to the economy).

I am not arguing that Honneth ignores such less savory forms of social integration – recall that his first monograph aimed at "a systematic viewpoint from which the construction and maintenance of social power can be apprehended" (CoP: xi). But I am contending that the socio-theoretic *methodology* adopted in FR at the very least does not sufficiently highlight the interplay of idealist and non-idealist mechanisms of social integration. Because it is so focused on normatively reconstructing the deep value consensus that it hypothesizes as "transcendentally necessary" for social integration, it simply loses sight of what else might causally account for social integration: in particular, macro and micro structures and systems of power. Despite Honneth's evident concern with such topics, I wonder whether his methodological choice in favor of Hegel-inspired socio-theoretic idealism actually ends up obscuring phenomena that we need a critical theory to illuminate if it is to insightfully analyze manifold mechanisms of domination, exclusion, and oppression. Briefly, we can see three key ways this methodology may prove problematic.

The first problem is that idealism may yield inadequate explanations of the mechanisms reproducing social institutions and practices. We have already seen this problem with respect to the economy. Although much has changed in Honneth's account of political economy since the exchange with Fraser, FR is still committed to this basic argument scheme: markets could only operate if individuals consent to them; since markets do exist, individuals must be consenting to them; since there is consent, it must be based on individuals' basic agreement with the values that markets realize; those values should be reconstructed as those of social freedom; therefore, markets are, ceteris paribus, morally justified as enabling social freedom. A number of objections arise to this argument scheme. Couldn't individuals' consent be just another artificially manufactured product that markets produce, rather than a form of authentic endorsement of the values that markets supposedly realize? Couldn't raw, materialist power – say, the threat of starvation and premature death upon refusal of the market – be mistaken here for freely consented participation? Wouldn't labor and consumer markets continue to function even if participants didn't realize their social freedom in them by consciously and mutually acting as the conditions of one another's freedom? Can't economic systems become autonomous of normative control, running more or less automatically even when most societal members are opposed to them? Don't capitalist markets in fact operate between societies that both do and don't share the modern individualist values of social freedom? Isn't it the case that some societies may have markets more or less coercively forced upon them from without as a condition of survival in a global capitalist arena? If the answer to any of these questions is ever "yes," then, at least in some situations, the integration of markets is not occurring through value consensus. In such cases, more importantly, we need to have socio-theoretic access to the alternative mechanisms that are in fact responsible. We need, in other words, a theory of economic power and its sociological effects. Similar methodological problems beset the accounts of personal relations and democratic politics – think only of the multiple sources, dynamics, and effects of patriarchal and political power.

The second problem follows upon the first: socio-theoretic idealism may yield inadequate explanations of the causal dynamics of historical change. Consider, for instance, the surprising simultaneity of massive progressive changes in gender hierarchies in our societies over the last half-century, along with the stubborn perdurance of elements of patriarchal relations in that same time. For the former phenomenon, a story of normatively driven change seems appropriate: our society has achieved greater insight into the values of equal opportunity and the moral unacceptability of sex discrimination. However, it seems that moral enlightenment is not sufficient to explain the surprising perdurance, for example, of norms of masculinity and femininity that cause both women and men to maintain troubling gender hierarchies in their everyday practices. Here we need some account of the integrative power that reproduces unjust gender relations. Perhaps it is along materialist lines – as in accounts that stress the exploitative relations between men and women; perhaps it is along micro-political and psychoanalytic lines – as in accounts that stress the reproduction of individual's affective attachments to their own oppression through the power of gendered subjectivities.[23] Whatever the account – and there are many other contenders – it seems we need, at the least, to augment the account of historical change through culture changes with other accounts of change through the dynamics of power. Again, the basic problem with idealism is not so much that it is always wrong – clearly social practices and institutions can sometimes change and develop simply through changes in cultural ideas.[24] Rather, the problem is that there are diverse causal mechanisms underlying social changes, and Honneth's theory appears methodologically too monistic to capture that diversity.

Third, as we have seen in chapter 4 on social pathologies, a critical theory needs a more capacious account of diverse causal mechanisms of social integration in order to carry out its diagnostic, prognostic, and therapeutic tasks. Without repeating that discussion here, it is important to add that a methodological insensitivity to the structure and dynamics of different forms of social power means that critical theory may ignore some of the most important sources of oppression.[25] For individuals' moral consciousness – their reflective grasp of the values structuring social practices and institutions – may itself be tightly imbricated with mechanisms contributing to the continuation of oppressive, exclusionary, and exploitative social relations. From Rousseau's slaves who have become slavish through growing up under slavery, to Marx's critique of class-reinforcing ideology, to the first-generation Frankfurt School theorists' thesis of an authoritarian personality, to second- and third-wave feminism's uncovering of the perverse internalized endorsement of androcentric and patriarchal norms and practices by women themselves, it seems evident that there is a real need to attend to deep interrelationships between individuals' moral consciousness and the macro and micro structures of social power. Without that attention, critical theory cannot accurately diagnose the sources of important social pathologies, render convincing prognoses of the likelihood of overcoming them, or helpfully guide praxis to the most efficacious routes for social struggles against oppression.

For another example of this same problem, consider FR's diagnosis of current problems facing the democratic public sphere. It begins in a powerful analysis of the multiple and diverse causal factors contributing to widespread feelings of popular disenchantment with politics and increasing depoliticization of ordinary citizens: changes in mass news media toward sensationalism and entertainment; new communications and internet modalities that fragment the public; increasingly heterogeneous populations; the diminishment of national sovereignty and nation-state power; the increasing dominance of liberal corporatism; the detachment of regulatory regimes from democratic control and oversight; and the disembedding of markets from morality. But in the move to prognosis and therapy, Honneth seems to rest his hopes for progress on a revitalized, European-wide political culture and collective identity. There is a real question here, I think, of whether idealist social theory has proposed a culturalist remedy that is seriously out of line with the structural and material causes that have led to contemporary nation-states and transnational regimes being hijacked by economic interests and concentrated forms of social power. Is the hope for a shared, common, trans-European political culture an appropriate therapy in the face of such transformations in large-scale social power, or is it a therapy recommended because of an idealist socio-theoretic insistence that "the motor and the medium of the historical process of realizing institutionalized principles of freedom is...social struggles over the *appropriate understanding* of these principles and the resulting changes of behavior" (FR: 329; emphasis added)? Again, the point is not that changes in ideas can never drive successful emancipation – clearly they can. The question is whether a theory that methodologically restricts itself only to such cultural changes is up to the multiple tasks involved with diagnosing contemporary social pathologies where such pathologies are complexly causally interconnected not just with ideals, but also with structures and systems of power and material interests.

My sense, in the end, is that these are more problems of theoretical omission, oversight and often over-contrast with competing approaches – especially in the animus against forms of functionalism and systems theory – rather than insuperable structural difficulties with Honneth's new comprehensive social theory. In fact, I would suggest that the approach developed in FR may well be compatible with various theories of power, whether structural, materialist, discursive, psychodynamic, disciplinary, or even functionalist. As it stands now, however, *Freedom's Right* must face the reasonable charge that it is insufficiently attentive to the diversity of mechanisms of social integration and so surrenders some critical purchase on various causes of contemporary social pathologies. This is not then a call for rejection, but for further work in broadening and diversifying the basic social theory.

7

Concluding Speculations

Looking back at the elements of Honneth's theory considered in this book, we can see how they fit into a general mold of critical social theory, a mold shared not only by the Frankfurt School theorists but also by a broader range of critical theories including feminism, critical race theory, critical legal studies, postcolonial theory, queer theory, and post-structuralism. Broadly speaking, critical theories aim to describe, explain, and critically evaluate whatever contemporary social and political processes impede the goal of furthering human emancipation. The basic aim, broadly understood, is to comprehend in thought, as Marx puts it, the "struggles and wishes of the age" in a way that furthers progressive struggles and brings those wishes into reality. Thus any critical social theory will have to make use of research in the social sciences to get a basic understanding of the current situation and combine that with justified evaluative standards used to assess that situation, all in order to generate useful insights for society's change agents. In other words, most any critical social theory will be built out of some insight-producing combination of psychology, sociology, political science, economics history, and moral and political philosophy. Critical social theory is thus "interdisciplinary social theory with emancipatory intent."

Honneth's own critical social theory evinces a distinctive combination of elements, built around his focal interests in mutual recognition and social freedom. Therefore, its social psychology is developed in terms of an intersubjective account of individual subjectivity and identity development; its moral philosophy in terms of the legitimate expectations of persons for intersubjective recognition; its sociology in terms of social struggles for recognition and an account of the central social institutions enabling freedom; its political economy in terms of the moral infrastructure of consumer and labor markets; its history in terms of progressive development through social movements for expanded freedom and recognition; and its political philosophy of justice in terms of an analysis of the broad social conditions necessary for expanded social freedom for all persons. In addition to thereby fulfilling the general mold of a critical theory, Honneth also continues the distinctive inheritance of the Frankfurt School by carrying out the project of a diagnosis of social pathologies. As we have seen throughout, this involves using the critical social theory to highlight ways in which the present social ordering is defective or distorting, a perversion of the rational potential for undamaged sociality and for individuals' pursuit of the good life.

Instead of a backward-looking recapitulation as this book's conclusion, I offer here a forward-looking series of speculations about potential directions in which Honneth's broad research paradigm might or should go as it continues to deepen and develop. Speculating about the future is, of course, an endeavor fraught with large potentials for error. But these speculations are not just predictions. They are also express hopes for deeper explorations of barely outlined territory, and, air concerns that certain prominent objections be met head on. I offer the following seven thematic areas in part as guesses, in part as hopes, and in part as concerns – in whatever sense, they should be taken with a grain of salt.

The first area I anticipate further work in is securing the moral grounds of social critique. In particular, I detect a long-standing and still unresolved oscillation between two different forms of normative justification on Honneth's part: Hegelian historicism vs philosophical anthropology. FR tends more toward the former, with its focus on the reconstruction of normative principles immanent in the specific historical development of western social institutions. SfR tends more toward the latter, with its focus on the universal, transcultural claim that all humans depend on intersubjective recognition for the development and maintenance of their own identity. As Honneth puts it in a 2011 interview: "Basically, the anthropological impulse that drove my earlier work has taken a back seat to a more immanent 'grammatology' of modern recognition orders, such as Hegel sought to deliver" (Honneth and Willig 2012: 148). We have repeatedly seen throughout this book the promise and peril Honneth detects in both of these strategies, particularly in 3.3, 3.4, 4.3.2, 5.2.4, and 6.4.2. While Honneth understands himself as having moved more toward the historicist pole, it is clear he is still committed to certain universal claims about humanity simpliciter. Consider, for instance, his response in a 2010 interview to questions about how he might change or correct *Struggle for Recognition* today.

> I would try to keep the spirit of [SfR], which means to take inspiration from the early Hegel in order to develop a kind of social theory...But I

would try to avoid anthropological misunderstanding. In the book I have
a certain tendency to say that there are three stable forms of recognition
which are universal. The book has a certain ambivalence about this. I
could be much clearer in saying that the spheres of recognition are historically developed. That would be, I think, the main correction. Briefly
put, I would try to historicize the forms and spheres of recognition....
I would keep a certain anthropological idea, which is, let's say, a constitutive formal concept of recognition, namely, that human beings depend
on social forms of recognition in order to develop an identity and to gain
a certain understanding and a sufficient form of self-relation. I would
keep that. We cannot think of human beings as not being dependent on
some form of recognition.... This is the anthropological intuition. I also
think I would be much more historical about the different forms in which
this recognition can be established, in the different forms of relationship
in which it can be instantiated. (Honneth and Marcelo 2013: 210)

Even here, we can see oscillation between the two warring impulses
of history and anthropology. It should be no surprise to discover that
in a very recent article, these contending impulses are traced back to
Hegel and Kant respectively – while Honneth himself still stands
uneasily between them, attempting to overcome the charge of mere
conventionalism against historicism, while avoiding the worry about
empty metaphysical abstractions of anthropology (Honneth 2013a).[1]

Social theory is a second area where I hope for future development,
specifically a more capacious, differentiated, and *explanatory* theory of
social processes and changes. As I argued in 4.3.1, 5.2.2, 5.2.3, and 6.4.3,
there are limitations to social theoretic explanations that rely almost
exclusively on cultural contents – beliefs, norms, ideals, etc. – especially
when it comes to describing changes in society's political economy. On
the one hand, it is clear that Honneth decisively rejects the use of any
form of systems theory or functionalist theory, so that he refuses strategies like Habermas's combination of sociological functionalism and
hermeneutics, and Fraser's bi-causal explanations of injustice. On the
other hand, he also repeatedly acknowledges that cultural factors alone
cannot explain all economic dynamics, yet without really telling us
what does provide such explanation. While FR goes further in referring
to practices and institutions as well as culture, it pulls away from any
structural or functional explanations of major social processes and
changes. More work here would be welcome.

Third, I would urge Honneth to systematically develop a theory of
power, one that can be combined with the account of normatively
integrated social spheres he has already developed (see 6.4.3). My
guess is that whatever specifically Honnethian theory of power one
might be able to draw out of *Critique of Power*, that older theory would
be incompatible with his more recent social theory derived from Hegel.
Further, his earliest book was largely critical: Horkheimer and Adorno,

Foucault, and Habermas had all failed precisely where they had attempted to understand power-saturated complexes of society – such as the economy and state administrations – as purely technical, norm-free domains of strategic action.[2] But rejecting this notion does not yet tell us how to explain power operating within normatively integrated social spheres. It is perhaps here that another attempt to come to terms with post-structuralist social theory – in particular, the middle period work of Foucault and Judith Butler's theory of subjection – might prove to be quite worthwhile (Sinnerbrink 2011). I would add that this hope for an adequate theory of power is not merely an abstract theoretical demand for accurate social theory, but arises as a necessity for a truly critical social theory. Consider, for instance, how power relations centrally structure intersubjective recognition – e.g., between worker and employer, husband and wife, black and white, citizen and stateless, servant and master, and so on – and how recognition relationships themselves serve to reproduce differential and unequal power between persons (Allen 2010; McNay 2008). In short, critical social theory needs an accurate and illuminating account of the sources of oppression, domination, exploitation, and exclusion – and of the causal dynamics of those sources.

Issues of power are also connected to another persistent theme of diverse critics of Honneth's. Bluntly, his work has been seen as overly optimistic in its treatment of social recognition and freedom (see 2.6.1, 3.4.1, 5.2.3, 6.4.2). Hence a fourth wish is for increased attention to negative or destructive phenomena associated with recognition and freedom. Consider, to begin, the ways in which intersubjective recognition can itself contribute to oppression (Markell 2003; McNay 2008). For instance, there is a clear connection between androcentric esteem and the subordination of women – e.g., recognizing women for being good housewives. Or the connection between neoliberal respect and the dismantling of the welfare state – paeans to the self-made man have an elective affinity with the state's increasing individualization of responsibility and privatization of services. To be sure, Honneth has attempted to address such concerns (Honneth 2012j), but I would wish for more in-depth and extended consideration of such issues. Consider, further, the dark or negative sides to individual development through intersubjective socialization (Butler 1997, 2008; Lear 2008). One potent result of socialization is the development of deep affective ties to certain forms of subjectivity. There are real concerns about an overly optimistic picture of intersubjective socialization when the resulting subjectivities are themselves damaging or destructive, or when the resulting affects are on the aggressive rather than the sociability side of the spectrum. Finally, increased insight would surely arise through more attention to contemporary phenomena of conflict, dissent, and disruption. While Honneth has addressed some forms of recent class conflict within

Europe (Honneth 2012a), I would wish for additional attention to such contemporary conflicts as the Occupy movement, the Arab Spring, ecological protests, animal rights protests, indigenous rights movements, religious–secularist conflicts, militant and neofascist movements, and so on. What light would Honneth's theory shed on such diverse conflicts?

A fifth area in which I fully expect to see continued research is the diagnosis of social pathologies and social misdevelopments. Given the impressive empirical work Honneth is shepherding at the Institute for Social Research, and his own conception of critical theory as diagnostic social philosophy, I am confident we will see much more exciting work here. Speculatively, we might hope for analyses that are able to show how certain social phenomena should be understood specifically as social pathologies or misdevelopments: for instance, increasing economic inequality and impoverishment; increases of and changes in the nature of psychopathology and its diagnosis; the rigidification of social conflicts into irreconcilable factions; the increasingly precarious nature of employment, health care and social security, family life, and provision of basic goods; and, increases in silent suffering from social atomization, individual isolation and anomie.

Sixth, I would hope to see further work in what we might call "applied" recognition theory, on the analogy with what is called "applied ethics" in Anglo-American philosophy. The idea here is to take the normative and conceptual tools supplied by the central theory – in this case, Honneth's theories of recognition and social freedom – and use them to analyze and morally assess contemporary social issues, including the evaluation of potential remedies. Possible topics here are quite diverse; consider only the range of issues treated in a recent collection of essays springing from recognition theory (O'Neill and Smith 2012): immigration (Cox 2012); relations between nation-states (Heins 2012); ethno-nationalist conflict (O'Neill 2012); multinational citizenship and voting rights (Owen 2012); laws of religious expression (Seglow 2012); the division of labor and modern work (Smith 2012); the legal categorization of crime (Yar 2012); and contemporary marriage and marital law (Zurn 2012). One can easily imagine that many such projects in applied social research, combining empirical and normative analyses of contemporary social issues, could be launched from Honneth's most recent theory of the institutions of social freedom.

In the final area, I would hope for a critical social theory that goes beyond its current categorial borders. What I mean here is that, as currently structured, Honneth's critical social theory is limited in a number of ways that prevent it from analyzing many pressing ecological and global issues. Perhaps most evidently there seems very little room for issues like ecology, climate change, and humans' relation to other forms of life within categories structured centrally on inter-human relations and institutions. It is not at all clear, for instance, how the various forms of intersubjective recognition and the different principles of social freedom are directly relevant to the multitude of quite pressing questions about, for instance, how to restructure our societies in order to avoid catastrophic environmental damage, or what an equitable distribution of mitigation costs across affected populations might be, or what we owe to future generations in terms of environmental stewardship, or how we should relate to other species or to inanimate nature. To be sure, there is hypothetical room in a social freedom framework for considering any enabling or constraining conditions relevant to individuals' opportunities for freedom, and environmental conditions might be considered under such a heading. But this bare place-marker in the theory is a long way from direct consideration of central problems of the age caused by our societies' industrial and capitalist development.

Naturally, environmental questions bleed over into questions of global justice – another set of questions that Honneth's theory is currently ill-equipped to address.[3] What do members of rich, developed nation-states owe to citizens of impoverished nations? What constitutes justice in border, immigration, emigration and citizenship policies; who should have a say in which affairs of what locales; how do we best structure international security institutions? Are there ways to legitimately constrain the ill effects of rapid global capital flows? Are there any prospects for making global capitalism consistent with social democratic ideals? Are human rights best guaranteed through nation-state or international institutions? Are democratic public spheres and democratic constitutional regimes viable and desirable above or below the level of the nation-state? How do nascent antiglobalization protests fit into all of these questions? These and many allied questions have not been systematically treated; and on account of internal, theoretical reasons, I think.

To begin with, although Honneth has written a bit on international relations between nation-states (Honneth 2012k) and on transnational issues of cultural integration within the European Union (FR: 332–5), the general structure of both his recognition theory and his theory of social freedom is more or less nationally or culturally bounded. Recall that his analysis centrally supposes that social integration occurs through a general background consensus on some abstract norms and ideals. An implication of this view, though never explicitly thematized as such, is that the boundaries of any given society are drawn around this consensus; groups of people with fundamentally distinct norms and values constitute distinct societies. Honneth's social theory is centrally focused on the structure and dynamics internal to "our" society but gives little attention to understanding the relationships between societies. The unaddressed empirical questions are significant: for example, how exactly are we to understand the evident social integration we do witness transnationally – for instance, in the United Nations or in global capital markets – if social integration is supposed to occur largely through a shared background consensus? The normative questions are equally formidable: how exactly, for instance, are we to understand the content and justification of norms relevant to global conflicts, norms we cannot reconstruct internally out of shared practices and institutions?

One theorist surely cannot cover all pressing topics. But the absence of Honneth's distinctively critical social theoretic outlook on such issues means, in a sense, that the field is occupied largely by those doing work in the mold of applied ideal political philosophy. This means our theories of global justice are stuck with its attendant limitations, including a focus only on formal systems of law and national state apparatuses, while ignoring everyday social practices, attitudes, and institutions. We ignore thereby the domain of the social at the global level, even though the social is, according to Honneth, more consequential for the realization of freedom than the domains of law and the state. As Honneth puts this latter point in his domestic analysis:

> The motor and the medium of the historical process of realizing institutionalized principles of freedom is not the law, at least not in the first instance, but social struggles over the appropriate understanding of these principles and the resulting changes of behaviour. Therefore, the fact that contemporary theories of justice are guided almost exclusively by the legal paradigm is a theoretical folly. We must instead take account of sociology and historiography, as these disciplines are inherently more sensitive to changes in everyday moral behaviour. (FR: 329)

The "struggles and wishes of our age" are, however, *environmental* and *global* struggles and wishes. Capturing them in thought – specifically in an interdisciplinary social theory with emancipatory intent – will, I believe, require expanding Honneth's critical social theory through new categories and modes of analysis adequate to new perils and promises.

Notes

Chapter 1   Introduction

1 Much of this biographical information comes from websites, all accessed most recently January 6, 2014: Honneth's page at the Institut für Sozialforschung (the Institute for Social Research, home of the Frankfurt School of critical social theory), http://www.ifs.uni-frankfurt.de/mitarbeiter_in/axel-honneth/; Honneth's faculty page in the Philosophy Department at Goethe University, Frankfurt am Main, http://www2.uni-frankfurt.de/44526981/Honneth_Axel; and Honneth's faculty page in the Philosophy Department at Columbia University, New York, http://philosophy.columbia.edu/directories/faculty/axel-honneth.

2 This book also takes advantage of the fact that two excellent scholarly monographs already focus intently on Honneth's earlier work, especially in philosophical anthropology (SAaHN), in contemporary European social theory (for instance, the essays collected in *The Fragmented World of the Social*), and his dissertation and post-dissertation work on theories of power (CoP). Jean-Philippe Deranty has written a substantial treatise attempting both a systematic reconstruction and an immanent critique of Honneth's corpus (and the secondary literature on it) from its beginning up through about 2008 (Deranty 2009). By showing how Honneth's theory of recognition systematically fulfills the multiple tasks of a critical social theory, Deranty intends to simultaneously push Honneth away from an understanding of recognition overly indebted to Habermas's theory of rational communication and toward a more substantial, interactionist theory of intersubjectivity inspired by materialist phenomenology. Danielle Petherbridge has published an important study attempting a "genealogy" of Honneth's critical social theory by reinterpreting Honneth's own interpretations of Foucault, Habermas, Hegel, Marx, Mead, and Winnicott. She intends to rehabilitate insights she believes Honneth had in his earlier work on philosophical anthropology and theories of power, but which were unfortunately circumvented in his mature theories of recognition and

democracy (Petherbridge 2013). While Deranty systematically treats Honneth's theory of recognition – the core of Honneth's own paradigm in my estimation – both Deranty's and Petherbridge's volumes were written too early to treat Honneth's theory of social freedom as developed in his recently published second magnum opus: *Freedom's Right*. The book before you is centered on Honneth's theories of recognition and of social freedom.

3 Although I will often shorten the phrase "critical social theory" to "critical theory," this should not be confused with the use of "critical theory" to designate aesthetic theories focused specifically on literature. The kind of theory Honneth develops is first and foremost a theory of *society* and is quite different in structure and content from, for example, theories of novelistic form or the definition of literary genres.

4 In 1985, Honneth defined a critical social theory as a "theory in which the intention of a philosophically guided diagnosis of the time is combined with an empirically grounded social analysis" (CoP: 3). As we will see especially in chapter 4, Honneth has remained remarkably faithful to this definition in the three decades since. In focusing on the specific task of *social diagnosis*, Honneth's definition is less generic than my stipulation of merely having an "emancipatory interest."

5 Karl Marx, September 1843 letter to Arnold Ruge, translation from https://www.marxists.org/archive/marx/works/1843/letters/43_09-alt.htm, accessed January 8, 2014.

6 Some of what I omit here is nevertheless quite important for Honneth: the twentieth-century tradition of philosophical anthropology (especially Plessner, Gehlen, and Elias); the grand sociological theorists (most especially Durkheim, but also Parsons, Simmel, and Weber); American pragmatism (especially Mead and Dewey); phenomenology (especially Sartre and Merleau-Ponty, but also Heidegger); hermeneutics and philosophy of language (especially Gadamer and Wittgenstein); English social anthropology and cultural history (especially E. P. Thompson and Barrington Moore); and feminism, especially second-wave debates centered around equality and difference and the ethics of care.

7 Honneth's sustained interpretations of Kant are decidedly fewer than those of Hegel (Honneth 2007a, 2007d, 2009b). Honneth traditionally hosts an annual picnic in a park and soccer game for participants in his seminar. Soccer players can join the Kantian or the Hegelian team; Honneth usually joins the latter.

8 Hegel himself was indebted to Fichte's earlier moves making Kantian philosophy more intersubjective. Honneth acknowledges Fichte's importance, especially for the theme of intersubjective recognition but, beyond an essay on the 1796 *Foundations of Natural Right* (Honneth 2003), has not systematically worked through Fichte's writings.

9 Paul Ricoeur famously claimed that "Three masters, seemingly mutually exclusive, dominate the school of suspicion: Marx, Nietzsche, and Freud" (Ricoeur 1970: 32).

10 Two essays directly treat Freud (Honneth 2009a, 2012b). SfR relies substantially on the object relations theories of Donald Winnicott and Jessica Benjamin, and dialogues with psychological research in various schools and traditions have been critical to Honneth's work. Among others, see especially R and Honneth 1995a, 1999, 2012d, 2012f, 2012l.

11 Honneth has attended most to the work of Adorno, though that attention is quite ambivalent. A significant portion of Honneth's first monograph is on Adorno (CoP: 32–103), though he came later to replace that reading of Adorno with quite a different one (Honneth 2009c).

12 The Institute's comprehensive website is very informative: http://www.ifs .uni-frankfurt.de.

13 Two essays announcing research programs give clear indications of how Honneth intends to fulfill the empirical aims of critical social theory's diagnosis of the present: (Hartmann and Honneth 2012 [2004]; Honneth and Sutterlüty 2011).

14 See 5.2.5 and 6.4 for fuller discussions.

15 For Marx, for Lukács, and for the members of the Frankfurt School before World War II, the immanent transcendent was to be found in the conditions of labor. They were the key to understanding the basic organization of capitalist society and its attendant pathologies, as well as harboring the revolutionary promise for overcoming those pathologies. That project foundered on the shores of the resilience of capitalism and the loss of hope for proletarian revolution in the advanced societies of the West. After the war, pessimistic diagnoses from Adorno and Horkheimer (and sometimes Marcuse) seemed to reduce the immanent transcendent to the barely aflicker embers of authentic, fully subjective aesthetic experiences (Horkheimer and Adorno 2002). Habermas, coining the term "emancipatory interest," locates it in "the only thing whose nature we can know we can know: language. Through its structure, autonomy and responsibility are posited for us" (Habermas 1971: 314). He proceeded to develop a systematic and comprehensive critical social theory around a theory of linguistic intersubjectivity and communicative action (Habermas 1984, 1987).

16 While I believe that the different emphases on language and on recognition are the core of the difference between Habermas and Honneth, it should also be pointed out that that there are many methodological and substantive disagreements beyond this. For instance, Honneth rejects the functionalist analysis of economies and bureaucratic power that Habermas employs, and Honneth focuses more on everyday social practices, mores, and institutions as the sites of social integration in contrast with Habermas's focus on law and the constitutional state.

17 Honneth's mature political philosophy thus has striking parallels with the work of British political theorist David Miller who also insists that normative political philosophy and empirical social research must be systematically interrelated (Honneth 2012i).

18 This difference in scope is also reflected in the fact that, while both Habermas and Honneth endorse a method of normative reconstruction – an analysis arising from the values and norms immanent in contemporary society – the former reconstructs constitutional democracy while the latter reconstructs all of the various spheres of social freedom (FR: 345, n. 1).

Chapter 2 Individuals' Struggle for Recognition

1 While Honneth is influenced by philosophical anthropology – see his and Joas's enlightening overview of the twentieth-century German tradition in

SAaHN – he is not presenting a comprehensive theory of the essence of human nature. Nor is he presenting a full theory of all the aspects of individual human development. The aim is more modest: an account of the development of a practical sense-of-self.

2 For an insightful reading of Fichte's account of recognition, see Bernstein 2010.

3 Deranty, one of Honneth's most astute critical expositors, in fact urges him to back away from this radical intersubjectivism, and to incorporate various insights about subjectivity and subjective experience from various traditions: historical materialism (especially Feuerbach and early Marx), American pragmatism, and existential and embodied phenomenology (Heidegger and Merleau-Ponty); see the summary in Deranty 2009: 467–79.

4 An important history and conceptual analysis of psychoanalytic approaches to recognition is in Wildt 2010.

5 Relying on more recent infant development work than Winnicott, Meehan (2011) rightly warns that the fusion of identities is never complete and that it is quite differently structured for parent and for child; Honneth agrees (Honneth 2011: 393).

6 Exemplary here is John Rawls's social contract theory of justice which states as one of its foundational assumptions that the individuals contracting together into a just society are

> rational and mutually disinterested. This does not mean that the parties are egoists, that is, individuals with only certain kinds of interests, say in wealth, prestige, and domination. But they are conceived as not taking an interest in one another's interests.... Moreover, the concept of rationality must be interpreted as far as possible in the narrow sense, standard in economic theory, of taking the most effective means to given ends. (Rawls 1971: 13–14)

7 William Blackstone, in his canonical summary of English common law, explains the doctrine of coverture: "By marriage, the husband and wife are one person in law: that is, the very being or legal existence of the woman is suspended during the marriage, or at least is incorporated and consolidated into that of the husband: under whose wing, protection, and cover, she performs every thing;... her condition during her marriage is called her *coverture*" (Blackstone 1979: 430) (spelling modernized). Various significant components of coverture persisted in common-law legal systems through the late twentieth century.

8 Honneth's account of the proper objects of esteem recognition have changed somewhat over time. While in the early 1990s (e.g., SfR) he focused on traits and abilities as the objects of esteem, by the early twenty-first century (e.g., RoR) he focuses attention on individual's achievements as the main object of esteem. Among other reasons for the change is his later emphasis (e.g., in FR) on the relationships between social esteem, a democratic division of labor, and a just capitalist economy. I will return to these themes in chapter 6. For now, I will retain traits, abilities, and achievements, particularly since it seems to me that the more capacious definition enables one to sensibly compare esteem across both pre-modern and modern societies.

9 In Mead's account, society's esteem order is largely constructed around the division of labor and the prestige attached to different occupations.

In contrast, Hegel's conception of the esteem order focuses on what he calls "ethical life," the complex set of ideas, mores, and institutions that surround and support modern social interaction. Objecting that both of these pictures are limited only to modern societies, Honneth's concept of esteem order is intended to apply to many different societies over time.

10 Varga and Gallagher (2011: 252–5) present useful links between current research in psychology and Honneth's conception of antecedent recognition.

11 This is probably the most significant area of difference between Honneth's original and later discussions of this type of recognition. In the earlier "Invisibility," Honneth goes so far as to suggest that elementary gestural expressions actually embody a direct perception of the intrinsic moral worth of another as a free and intelligent being (Honneth 2001a: 121–6). By contrast, in *Reification* Honneth is at pains to stress that this primordial form of recognition does not have an intrinsic connection to the broader, differentiated normative order of recognition expectations outlined in the other three forms of recognition.

12 This table modifies and updates the one found at SfR: 129. Because antecedent recognition is not a normative relationship, it does not make sense to understand its negative or perverted forms, strictly speaking, as forms of *disrespect*, ways of wrongly or unjustly treating others. Hence, although the following summary chart places reification in the disrespect row corresponding to antecedent recognition, it is better understood as a forgetting of recognition, that is, a pathology of sympathetic engagement.

13 See also Owen 2008; Varga and Gallagher 2011.

14 A deeper but more limited objection might focus only on one form of self-relation and claim that it does not require intersubjective recognition. For instance, using the example of Frederick Douglas before his emancipation from slavery, McBride argues that Honneth is wrong to say that one's own self-respect depends upon respect recognition from others (McBride 2013: 63–70). McBride suggests that claims about practical identity should not be justified through empirical psychology; Honneth, I believe, would disagree.

15 As Honneth himself has acknowledged, he was not clear about many of these conceptual matters in SfR, only gaining such clarity through critical exchanges with sympathetic commentators (Honneth 2002a; Ikäheimo 2002, 2010; Laitinen 2002). The current Honnethian analysis of recognition is well presented in Ikäheimo and Laitinen 2007.

16 Does this then mean that recognition is socially relative, that any form of intersubjective regard is true or false, good or bad, appropriate or inappropriate as long as it accords with the prevailing standards of one's own society? Here Honneth endorses a developmental account of social progress that is intended to rebut the worry about social relativism. On the connection between moderate value realism and progress, see also Honneth 2012j: 79–85. This topic is treated at length in the next chapter.

17 Although versions of this concern are raised and responded to in the 2002 articles in *Inquiry* (Honneth 2002a; Ikäheimo 2002; Kauppinen 2002; Laitinen 2002), a particularly powerful version is developed by Markell through a consideration of similar ambiguities in Mead's account of the relationship between the "me" and the "I" (Markell 2007). Honneth's response to

Markell is consistent with the position represented in this paragraph (Honneth 2007h: 350–1 and 54–6).

Chapter 3   Social Struggles for Recognition

1 Hobbes clearly thinks only some people will invade to gain glory. Unfortunately, Hobbes's insights here into the role of a kind of intersubjective struggle for recognition have, to my knowledge, gone entirely unremarked upon in the recognition literature.
2 While there may be struggles to establish the social conditions necessary for antecedent self-affirmation, I do not analyze any here since the negative form of reification, at least as analyzed by Honneth, is so rare and socially pathological. Recall that paradigm cases of social reification – where persistent praxis is combined with ideological schemata so that participants forget their antecedent recognition of the very human personhood of others – are industrialized mass murder and genocide.
3 I tend to draw examples from recent United States' movements, but only because of personal familiarity. Similar examples can be found throughout the world and across a greater span of time.
4 The marital rape exception was but one component of the broader judicial doctrine known as "coverture," whereby women lost their legal personality to their husband upon marriage. In the United States, the marital rape exception is no dusty relic from hundreds of years ago: "not until 1984... did a New York appellate court overturn that state's marital rape exemption – then other states followed" (Cott 2000: 211). By 1993, all fifty states had acknowledged marital rape as a legal crime, though thirty-three of those states still allow some exceptions from culpability only for spouses, usually on the theory that forced sexual intercourse is somehow less serious or wrong when perpetrated against someone you are married to (Burgess-Jackson 1998; Ryan 1995).
5 An interesting variation on "Take Back the Night" marches are the "SlutWalk" protests, begun in Toronto Canada in 2011 and copied elsewhere, that pointedly attempt to change the excuses for rapists, no longer making it acceptable for sexual violators to refer to the appearance or dress of women as somehow exculpatory.
6 The United Nations Convention against Torture and Other Cruel, Inhuman or Degrading Treatment or Punishment. Notably, the United States ratified this treaty in 1994, though its twenty-first-century practices of "enhanced interrogation" and "extraordinary rendition" of persons with supposed connections to terrorism have clearly violated international obligations.
7 For a particularly powerful account of how universal demands of justice apply to gender relations, especially concerning family structures, child-raising practices and legal relations of marriage, see Okin 1989.
8 Although I focus here on recent self-esteem struggles, their prospects and problems are not new. Consider, for instance, the similarity between Young's politics of difference and the strategies of uplifting and differentiating black culture forwarded at the beginning of the twentieth century by thinkers like W. E. B. Du Bois and Alain Locke. Particularly interesting is Locke's call in

1916 for American blacks to develop healthy practical identities on two tracks simultaneously: both a cosmopolitan, universalist "primary race consciousness" (i.e., as belonging to the human race), as well as a "secondary race consciousness" of the specific cultural achievements of black culture. While the former is aimed at the social bases of self-respect – fully equal legal rights – Locke recommends the latter precisely in order to create adequate social bases for the motivation and self-esteem of blacks amidst the new forms of oppression in post-Reconstruction era America (Locke 1992: especially 84–104).

9 Honneth has made this same point about anchoring theory's normative aspirations in actual social processes throughout his career, from his famous 1981 article critiquing Habermas's theory of class conflict (Honneth 1995g), to his 1985 book on the critical theories of power (CoP), to his extended exchange from 2003 with Nancy Fraser (RoR), to his 2011 book on social freedom (FR).

10 Honneth's commitment to this proviso – the requirement that no particular comprehensive doctrine or ethical way of life can legitimately demand that individuals surrender their individual rights or their physical or emotional integrity – is shared with a broad family of liberal theories, ranging historically from Locke to Kant to Mill, and prominently represented in contemporary political philosophy (Habermas 1994; Kymlicka 1995: 152–72; Rawls 1996: 58–66). Guarantees for individual exit from, for instance, patriarchal groups, and equal treatment before the law are central ways of institutionalizing this priority relationship (Okin 1989).

11 Cooke presents interesting reflections on, for instance, the differences between the slow-food movement's claims about how all people should eat, and the more restricted claims of support for Welsh language communities (Cooke 2009).

12 McBride 2013: 134–63 stresses the ineliminable character of struggles for recognition given endemic conflicts of normative interpretations under conditions of value pluralism.

13 I have made similar arguments with respect to disputes between "radical," "egalitarian," and "difference" feminist theories (Zurn 1997).

14 In SfR Honneth argued that, while respect's developmental potential lay in the dimensions of "generalization" and "de-formalization," esteem's developmental potential lay in the dimensions of "individualization" and "equalization." It seems to me that in more recent writings he has dropped these distinctions, preferring to apply the two criteria of individualization and inclusion across love, respect, and esteem. So I will not make the distinctions Honneth did earlier, for instance in the chart at SfR: 129.

15 McBride insists that recognition is a material resource, in part because respect and esteem can be converted into other resources like money and power (McBride 2013). This leads him to treat recognition as a good that the state should distribute. But, after an exhaustive search reveals no possible legitimate principle of justice for state distribution of esteem, he concludes that only respect can be distributed: everybody ought to receive rights. This result then narrows McBride's recognition politics essentially to only a liberal rights universalism. In concert with Honneth and with Young 1990a, I'd say that recognition should not be treated as stuff to be

distributed in the first place, and I do not think that the topic of justice is exhausted by considering what the state can legitimately coercively distribute.

16 This is also stressed in chapter 1 of McBride 2013.

17 Alexander and Lara 1996 make a similar point about "the darker possibilities that the search for esteem might imply" (134), but attribute the problem to insufficiently textured analyses of the notions of community and solidarity in Honneth (133–6).

Chapter 4   Diagnosing Social Pathologies

1 I have developed this analysis at greater length, and with more pointed critical intent, in Zurn 2011. Honneth has endorsed the notion of second-order disorder as a useful way of organizing his pathology diagnoses (Honneth 2011).

2 Honneth argues that the hyperboles, suggestive metaphors, and oxymoronic phrases used to describe the social world in the later works of Horkheimer and Adorno should be understood as potentially useful strategic exaggerations and distortions (Honneth 2007g, 2009c). He also uses examples from literature and film throughout FR.

3 The difficulties inherent in extending the metaphor of pathology from individual biological organisms – where it is relatively easy to articulate standards of health – to societal phenomena occupies much of the interesting work in Honneth 2007f.

4 An exemplary early attempt at such epidemiologies are the various projects investigating phenomena associated with the "authoritarian personality," carried out by Frankfurt School members in the 1940s while they were in exile in the United States (Adorno et al. 1950).

5 Another more general methodological issue has recently been clarified. In response to queries about what kind of a causal social theory he might be inclined toward – Adorno-inspired physiognomies, grand unified social theory, or more modest individual pathology-specific causal accounts – Honneth has endorsed the third option: different kinds of social phenomena have different kinds of causal explanations that are individually appropriate to them (Honneth 2011; Zurn 2011).

6 His accounts of moral freedom pathologies, by contrast, do not yet strike me as *social* pathologies since the phenomena he cites seem to be the failings of isolated individuals and where those failings have no discernible social causes (FR: 113–20).

7 It is worth noting that Geuss then develops this thought into a specific argument concerning reification: namely, that Honneth has smuggled moral content into his critique, even though the critique of reification is supposed to be non-moral. I think this specific argument is based on a misunderstanding: antecedent recognition is a non-moral relationship (see 2.5). Whatever general qualms Geuss has about moral philosophy would be better directed at Honneth's accounts of love, respect, and esteem recognition.

8 There may remain here a concern about whether cashing out the very notion of human flourishing in terms of self-realization, as Honneth does,

itself precludes certain conceptions of the good, e.g., conceptions that would reject self-realization in general as a worthy end of human life (Zurn 2000).

9 Nancy Fraser, for instance has frequently claimed that relying on the empirical results of psychology imperils Honneth's theory since it is then subject to falsification of particular results in those domains (Fraser 2000).

Chapter 5 Recognition and Markets

1 Three excellent books on recognition theory put Fraser, Honneth, and Taylor front and center in the canon (McBride 2013; McNay 2008; Thompson 2006), while also giving attention to other contemporary theorists important to recognition debates such as Seyla Benhabib, Jessica Benjamin, Pierre Bourdieu, Judith Butler, Jürgen Habermas, Maria Pia Lara, Patchen Markell, James Tully, Iris Marion Young, and Slavoj Žižek.

2 This tendency to equate recognition and identify politics is more pronounced in Fraser's earlier articles on recognition (Fraser 1995, 1997a, 2000, 2001), but it is also evident in her RoR exchange with Honneth. Elsewhere, I have criticized Fraser for falsely attributing an "authenticity model" of struggles for recognition to Honneth, whereby such struggles are always taken to be jingoistic calls by cultural groups for valorization of their group differences. This is decidedly not Honneth's view (Zurn 2003b: 529–31). This attribution was also a necessary ingredient leading to Fraser's influential – but now abandoned – thesis of an inevitable dilemma between the group balkanization of recognition politics and the societal homogenization of redistributive politics (Fraser 1997a; Zurn 2004).

3 See also Honneth 2007h: 75–7.

4 This 1998 essay on Dewey is the main focus of my critique, based on some of Fraser's arguments, of Honneth's attempt to integrate a theory of distributive justice into his recognitional accounts of critical theory, social justice, and democracy (Zurn 2005). For responses to such critiques of Honneth's theory, see Deranty 2010; Schmidt am Busch 2010. The present chapter tackles most of the issues raised in my earlier article, but in a less technical manner. It also focuses on Honneth's political economy as presented in RoR, which is slightly different in emphasis and details than the earlier Dewey essay.

5 See Fraser 1995, 1997a, 1997b, 1997c, 1998, 2000, 2001. I have developed my own critiques of Fraser's program for a "bivalent" social theory comprehending both issues of recognitional and distributive justice, but on different socio-theoretic registers, in Zurn 2003a, 2003b, 2004. For a comprehensive collection of articles on Fraser's theory, see Fraser 2008.

6 Fraser's first chapter in the book is a revised and expanded version of her Tanner Lectures on Human Values, delivered in 1996 (Fraser 1998).

7 The importance of Honneth's insistence on a "lifeworldly" theory of political economy, in explicit contrast with Habermas's functionalist theory of the economy, is rightly stressed in Smith 2011.

8 See 3.3.1 for the two criteria of societal progress: inclusion and individualization.

9 There is no mention of the distribution of resources or material goods in Taylor's influential essay on the politics of recognition (Taylor 1994), only how individual rights are "distributed" in liberal constitutional regimes. Of the six eminent commentators considering Taylor's account of contemporary politics, only Anthony Appiah and Jürgen Habermas mention class struggles, and only in passing at that.

10 One might think that recognition theory has displaced economic questions because it has not proposed ideal principles for any just distribution of resources, something akin to Rawls's difference principle. But surely this is not the only way of grappling with questions of economic justice. Honneth's practice has been to consider actually existing capitalism as a historically specific form of social organization that has given rise to determinate injustices and social pathologies.

11 For instance, one might argue that Honneth simply underappreciates the extent to which capitalism fundamentally structures all aspects of society, including its recognition order, an order which performs deep ideological functions (Wild 2013).

12 This and the previous quote are my translations; corresponding passages can be found in the German *Umverteilung oder Anerkennung* on 183 and 285.

13 Although Honneth does talk as though his first argument from the reigning recognition order is not properly interpreted in strong terms, a careful reading of his response shows that he actually reinterprets the recognition order argument in terms of the second normative preconditions argument:

> My concept of a "recognition order," which…aims at this stratum – the epoch-specific grammar of social justice and injustice. Such a conception is, of course, not sufficient to explain the dynamics of developmental processes in contemporary capitalism. But it is meant only to make clear the normative constraints embedded in such processes because subjects face them with certain expectations of recognition….I continue to assume that even structural transformations in the economic sphere are not independent of the normative expectations of those affected, but depend at least on their tacit consent. (RoR: 250)

14 It should be noted, by the same token, that Fraser's theory is also missing such a suitably detailed account of capitalist political economy that would be needed to underwrite her counter-thesis that economic factors constitute their own autonomous power for structuring social injustice. There is some secondary literature which begins to at least suggest forms of heterodox economic theory that might be used by Honneth to fill in the lacuna I indicate in the main text (Deranty 2010). I have tried to avoid getting bogged down here in a long-running methodological debate that forms the background to the Honneth–Fraser exchange (Smith 2011). This is the debate about how to comprehend specifically economic phenomena that was sharpened by Habermas's 1970s' and 1980s' sociological theory (Habermas 1984, 1987), a debate between proponents of functionalist systems theory (like Habermas, and apparently Fraser), and proponents of action-theory (like Honneth).

15 In Habermas's terms, capitalist modernity is marked by the structural decoupling of systemic forms of integration from social forms of integration.

16 Honneth might respond to this entire line of critique in this way: it is not the point of social theory to advocate for any particular remedies or take sides on political questions. Advocacy is the domain of the citizen; social explanation is the domain of the theorist. Hence it is simply misleading to criticize the theory of recognition for providing insufficient strategic guidance. This would be in line with a strict separation between theory and praxis, one that Honneth has recently come close to endorsing (Honneth and Marcelo 2013: 212–14). Nevertheless, even Honneth acknowledges: "It's complicated. It is a very thin line between what I take as being adequate for Critical Theory and what I take to be the too direct political involvement of theory" (214). The difficulty is that critical social theory is not mere value-free explanatory social science; it is rather thoroughly imbued with normative content from the get-go and assumes its basic orientation from the point of view of morally progressive social change. Questions of strategic guidance inherently straddle the line between theory and praxis.

17 I have levied critiques similar to Fraser's against Honneth's teleological approach (Zurn 2000), attempted more nuanced and in-depth evaluative comparisons of Fraser's and Honneth's normative strategies (Zurn 2003b), and levied a set of critiques against Fraser's own preferred approach (Zurn 2003a). In this brief section, we are just tasting some of the deeper philosophical controversies between them, and only focusing on Fraser's critiques of Honneth. However, some of Honneth's crucial responses are that Fraser's own theory of participatory parity suffers from serious defects as well. I share some of Honneth's reservations about Fraser's normative theory, but will not pursue those here.

18 It should be noted that Honneth's strategy of arguing for a universally valid but formal conception of the social conditions of the good life has a number of affinities with Martha Nussbaum's project of developing a theory of human capabilities as a universally justifiable form of weak perfectionism.

19 In a penetrating discussion of Honneth's reliance on experienced feelings of disrespect, Thompson argues that there is no easy way to reconcile the tension between the immanence of unmediated feelings and the need for transcendence of ideologically or traumatically distorting emotional experiences (Thompson 2006: 165–85). I argue below that the tension can be resolved.

Chapter 6 Social Freedom and Recognition

1 I avoid here an attempt to reconstruct Honneth's understanding of Hegel, much less Hegel's own thought. However, it is worth noting a significant change over time in Honneth's general assessment of Hegel. In his 1990s' work, especially SfR, Honneth clearly preferred only the early Hegel; the

work of the last fifteen years, however, especially PoIF, *The I in the We*, and FR, also usefully employs Hegel's mature work. Honneth himself explains this change clearly:

> Whereas in *The Struggle for Recognition* I had still assumed that only Hegel's Jena lectures contained coherent elements of a theory of recognition, after more intensive study of his mature writings I came to realize how wrong I had been. I no longer believe that Hegel sacrificed his initial intersubjectivism in the course of developing a monological concept of spirit; rather, Hegel sought throughout his life to interpret objective spirit, i.e. social reality, as a set of layered relations of recognition. On the basis of this reassessment I sought to make Hegel's *Philosophy of Right* fruitful for the development of a theory of recognition. Much stronger than in his early writings, we find the groundbreaking notion that social justice is to be defined in terms of the requirements of mutual recognition, and that we must take our point of departure in historically developed and already institutionalized relations of recognition. (*The I in the We*: vii–viii)

2 These are not Honneth's examples, nor does he argue against negative freedom on the basis of such ideal-typical counterexamples. But I think they capture the essence of his more extended arguments in a compact, familiar way.

3 Honneth acknowledges that Habermas and Apel's discourse theory of reflexive freedom has an ineliminable social component – namely the intersubjective justification of norms – and so is quite close to social freedom. But he argues (mistakenly I think) that discourse theory does not really require historically concrete and accommodating social institutions for real freedom (FR: 42–3).

4 This mechanism of progress allows Honneth to escape from Hegel's unconvincing metaphysical grounding of a historical teleology in the self-unfolding of Reason/Spirit. It does leave him with a new burden of normative justification for the institutions themselves, however, as we will see in 6.4.2.

5 I refer here to subjective rights since Honneth recognizes that modern legal freedom comes in two quite different forms. Subjective rights allow individuals to do things free from the interference of others, while political rights enable individuals to engage in collective self-rule with others. The latter establish an actual domain of social freedom – democracy – treated later in FR and here at 6.3.5.

6 In certain passages, Honneth appears to return to this idea, for example: "wage levels are a symbolic expression of the measure of social esteem of a given instance of labor" (FR: 246). Yet I interpret such passages as only reporting an experiential connection often felt by labor market participants between pay scales and self-esteem, rather than as shouldering an argumentative burden in favor of moral economism.

7 The focus on the sphere of consumption is itself a significant expansion of Honneth's moral economism from his earlier work, where the focus was almost entirely only on labor markets and the world of work. The influence of Hegel's *Philosophy of Right* is evident here.

8 I am not claiming that Honneth's theory is a version of "radical democracy," where that label refers to a family of "agonistic" political theorists stressing

ineliminable political conflict and often indebted to post-structuralist suspicions of reason: e.g., Wendy Brown, William Connolly, Ernesto Laclau, Chantal Mouffe, Antonio Negri, Sheldon Wolin. There are similarities, however, especially in a shared attention to insurgent social movements as the real engine of democratic change.

9 I would say as clearly a domain of social freedom as the sphere of personal relations, and more clearly than the economic sphere. For in both the personal and democratic spheres, as opposed to the economic, the success of an individual's actions is obviously tied to receiving appropriate uptake from others engaged in a complementary project, and all in a context of reciprocal recognition among participants.

10 I draw this list from the five necessary conditions of social freedom in the public sphere summarized at FR: 289–93, plus the requirement of a responsive democratic constitutional state. The seventh condition is drawn from a concluding discussion of democratic ethical life (FR: 329–35).

11 Honneth doubts that a culture of "constitutional patriotism," promoted prominently by Habermas and others as a replacement for nationalism, has the substance and motivating power needed to nourish solidarity and civic commitment.

12 Honneth has long been insisting that social institutions can only continue to exist if there is some form of participant consent to them. Consider the concluding clause of his 1985 book, where he claims that "social organizations" ought to be understood "as fragile constructions that remain dependent for their existence on the moral consensus of all participants" (CoP: 303). What is new in FR is that this claim is elaborated into a complex social theory that explains how the various spheres of freedom are differentiated, integrated, and reproduced over time.

13 One can imagine that John Grey, a relentless critic of the idea of progress might level all of the charges collected here, and more. For a flavor, consider the first section of essays in Grey 2004.

14 From my own "attitudinal stance," the sections of the book on the family are those I find most worrisomely optimistic, especially FR: 161–76. My sense is that they are overly suffused with the warm glow of inevitable moral progress in family relations, and unfortunately insensitive to the ways in which the family sphere has been and continues to be a school of androcentric oppression (Okin 1989), and a reliable reproducer of heterosexism, racism, xenophobia, stunted emotions, and fraught intersubjective relations – Brink 2013 develops these concerns about FR at greater length. For some of my concerns about the contemporary institution of marriage, as well proposed remedies, see Zurn 2012.

15 This is basically the strategy of Habermas's critical theory: universal, transcultural standards of rationality are built into communicative uses of language, even as they have not been fully realized in the course of more-or-less progressive western history (Habermas 1984).

16 This problematic surrounding conventionalism and various forms of objectivism is deeply related to concerns canvassed earlier in this book: in discussing Honneth's grounding of the idea of a "formal conception of ethical life" in 3.3 and 3.4; in considering the problems of grounding claims about social pathologies in 4.3.2; and in evaluating Fraser's critique of teleological

moral theories as inherently sectarian in 5.2.4. Many years ago I argued that Honneth had basically three options for grounding his normative claims: (1) piggybacking on Habermas's language-based arguments for the universality of moral standards; (2) rationally reconstructing features of social rationality that are taken to be universal across cultures; or (3) relying on a universalist account of inherent human nature (Zurn 2000). It is now clear that the first option is not of interest to Honneth. My sense is that he has not yet settled decisively between the second and third options, but is still actively grappling with the problem (Honneth 2013a).

17 Brink 2013 contains some analogous considerations about alternative teleologies of personal relations, especially from the point of view of conservative views of the family.

18 The argument that follows about alternative teleologies is deeply inspired by critiques made in Claassen 2013. Whereas Claassen takes them to be probative about the debate between philosophical constructivists (like Kant and Rawls) and reconstructivists (like Hegel and Honneth), I pursue them in order to argue that Honneth ought to adopt an objectivist over a conventionalist form of reconstructionism.

19 Honneth's ambiguous summary of FR's mostly favors conventionalism:

> It is a requirement on the (in principle corrigible) validity of any particular normative reconstruction that it should know itself *to be tied to those particular* emancipatory promises of modern societies which it treats as already institutionalized and thus, *within* this historical context, as *universally authoritative*. But granted the *acceptance* of the relevant principles, the reconstructive method then claims to *objectively trace* the developmental trajectories along which those principles come to be actualized. (Honneth 2013b: 39, all emphases added)

The central idea in this and other passages (e.g., 37) seems to be conventionalist: namely, that the moral ideals that are the markers of progress are only justified immanently to a particular society. The "objectivity" referred to pertains only to the factual, historical claims of the reconstruction.

20 This is not just a problem in normative theory, but a problem in social theory as well: see 6.4.3.2 below.

21 Jansen 2013 uses considerations of both pan-European heterogeneity and globalization to raise normative and socio-theoretic questions about whether modern democracy requires as much of a homogeneous collective identity as Honneth hypothesizes in his theory of democracy.

22 McNay 2008; Petherbridge 2013. But also see the essays collected in Brink and Owen 2007b, especially Bader 2007; Brink and Owen 2007a; Rössler 2007; Young 2007; Allen 2010; and the essays collected in Petherbridge 2011, especially Ferrara 2011; Renault 2011; Smith 2011; Zurn 2011. The McNay and Petherbridge monographs in particular go beyond a mere critical analysis of Honneth's theory to develop their own accounts of the relationship between recognition and the social structures and microstructures of power. McNay elaborates Bourdieu's account of embodied habitus in order to analyze gendered power. Petherbridge turns to Honneth's earliest work on Foucault in order to analyze the way power mediates subject-formation and agency.

23 For two different insightful materialist accounts stressing exploitation, see Hartsock 1983; Pateman 1988; for an account that stresses the relationship between Foucaultian power and psychodynamics, see Butler 1997.

24 This would seem to be the case with the rather quick disappearance of the honor code and its associated practices of dueling at the beginning of the nineteenth century, at least if Appiah's account is correct (2010).

25 This worry is sometimes expressed as the contention that a theory *insensitive* to oppression is thereby *complicit* with oppression. This charge has been made repeatedly against recognition theories in general; see Markell 2003; McNay 2008; Oliver 2001. Honneth himself, as noted in 4.2.1, is quite aware of the potential problem and explicitly develops his account of ideological recognition to deal with it. Before accepting such critiques, however, one would be well advised to see whether the generic "recognition theory" attacked therein actually corresponds in detail to that developed by Honneth, and whether the latter has resources for distinguishing appropriate from inappropriate recognition (as I have argued it does). If so, then insensitivity to oppression will not automatically transform into complicity with oppression.

Chapter 7 Concluding Speculations

1 A video of this lecture is available at http://www.youtube.com/watch?v =UuSSLA8_0cE, accessed January 25, 2014.

2 Danielle Petherbridge argues that Honneth originally derived important insights from Foucault's microphysics of power, but that his more recent work (at least before FR) has surrendered many of these insights. She too endorses the need for a more fully developed theory of power (Petherbridge 2013).

3 Heins 2008 and Schweiger 2012 provide good starts.

References

This reference list only details works actually referred to in this book, hence not all of the essays in the collections are listed. Dates in square brackets indicate publication of German original.

Honneth Books

SAaHN (1988), Co-authored with Hans Joas, *Social Action and Human Nature*, trans. Raymond Meyer (Cambridge: Cambridge University Press).
[1980], *Soziales Handeln und menschliche Natur: anthropologische Grundlagen der Sozialwissenschaften*. Frankfurt am Main: Campus Verlag.
CoP (1991), *The Critique of Power: Reflective Stages in a Critical Social Theory*, trans. Kenneth Baynes. Cambridge, MA: The MIT Press.
[1985], *Kritik der Macht: Reflexionsstufen einer kritischen Gesellschaftstheorie*. Frankfurt am Main: Suhrkamp Verlag.
SfR (1995), *The Struggle for Recognition: The Moral Grammar of Social Conflicts*, trans. Joel Anderson. Cambridge, UK: Polity Press.
[1992], *Kampf um Anerkennung*. Frankfurt am Main: Suhrkamp Verlag.
PoIF (2010), *The Pathologies of Individual Freedom: Hegel's Social Theory*, trans. Ladislaus Löb. Princeton, NJ: Princeton University Press.
[2001], *Leiden an Unbestimmtheit. Eine Reaktualisierung der Hegelschen Rechtsphilosophie*. Stuttgart: Reclam.
RoR (2003), Co-authored with Nancy Fraser, *Redistribution or Recognition? A Political-Philosophical Exchange*. New York: Verso.
[2003], *Umverteilung oder Anerkennung: Eine politisch-philosophische Kontroverse*. Frankfurt am Main: Suhrkamp Verlag.
R (2008), *Reification: A New Look at an Old Idea*, trans. Joseph Ganahal. Oxford: Oxford University Press.

[2005], *Verdinglichung: eine anerkennungstheoretische Studie*. Frankfurt am Main: Suhrkamp Verlag.

FR (2014), *Freedom's Right: The Social Foundations of Democratic Life*, trans. Joseph Ganahal. Cambridge, UK: Polity Press.

[2011], *Das Recht der Freiheit: Grundriß einer demokratischen Sittlichkeit*. Berlin: Suhrkamp Verlag.

Honneth Essay Collections

(1995 [1990]), *The Fragmented World of the Social: Essays in Social and Political Philosophy*, trans. Charles W. Wright. Albany, NY: SUNY Press.

(1995a), "Decentered Autonomy: The Subject after the Fall," 261–71.

(1995b), "Domination and Moral Struggle: The Philosophical Heritage of Marxism Reviewed," 205–19.

(1995c), "Embodied Reason: On the Rediscovery of Merleau-Ponty," 150–7.

(1995d), "The Fragmented World of Symbolic Forms: Reflections on Pierre Bourdieu's Sociology of Culture," 184–201.

(1995e), "Integrity and Disrespect: Principles of a Conception of Morality Based on the Theory of Recognition," 247–60.

(1995f), "The Limits of Liberalism: On the Political-Ethical Discussion Concerning Communitarianism," 231–46.

(1995g), "Moral Consciousness and Class Domination: Some Problems in the Analysis of Hidden Morality," 205–19.

(1995h), "Rescuing the Revolution with an Ontology: On Cornelius Castoriadis' Theory of Society," 168–83.

(1995i), "A Structuralist Rousseau: On the Anthropology of Claude Lévi-Strauss," 135–49.

(1995j), "Work and Instrumental Action: On the Normative Basis of Critical Theory," 15–49.

(2007 [2000]), *Disrespect: The Normative Foundations of Critical Theory*. Cambridge, UK: Polity Press.

(2007a), "Between Aristotle and Kant: Recognition and Moral Obligation," 129–43.

(2007b), "Decentered Autonomy: The Subject after the Fall," 181–93.

(2007c), "Democracy as Reflexive Cooperation: John Dewey and the Theory of Democracy Today," 218–39.

(2007d), "Is Universalism a Moral Trap? The Presuppositions and Limits of a Politics of Human Rights," 197–217.

(2007e), "The Other of Justice: Habermas and the Ethical Challenge of Postmodernism," 99–128.

(2007f), "Pathologies of the Social: The Past and Present of Social Philosophy," 3–48.

(2007g), "The Possibility of a Disclosing Critique of Society: The Dialectic of Enlightenment in Light of Current Debates in Social Criticism," 49–62.

(2007h), "The Social Dynamics of Disrespect: On the Location of Critical Theory Today," 63–79.

(2009 [2007]), *Pathologies of Reason: On the Legacy of Critical Theory*, trans. James Ingram. New York: Columbia University Press.

(2009a), "Appropriating Freedom: Freud's Conception of Individual Self-Relation," 126–45.

(2009b), "The Irreducibility of Progress: Kant's Account of the Relationship Between Morality and History," 1–18.

(2009c), "A Physiognomy of the Capitalist Form of Life: A Sketch of Adorno's Social Theory," 54–70.

(2009d), "A Social Pathology of Reason: On the Intellectual Legacy of Critical Theory," 19–42.

(2012 [2010]), *The I in We: Studies in the Theory of Recognition*, trans. Joseph Ganahal. Cambridge, UK: Polity Press.

(2012b), "Disempowering Reality: Secular Forms of Consolation," 232–38.

(2012c), "Dissolutions of the Social: The Social Theory of Luc Boltanski and Laurent Thévenot," 98–118.

(2012d), "Facets of the Presocial Self: Rejoinder to Joel Whitebook," 217–31.

(2012e), "From Desire to Recognition: Hegel's Grounding of Self-Consciousness," 3–18.

(2012f), "The I in the We: Recognition as a Driving Force of Group Formation," 201–16.

(2012g), "Labour and Recognition: A Redefinition," 56–74.

(2012h), "Organized Self-Realization: Paradoxes of Individualization," 153–68.

(2012i), "Philosophy as Social Research: David Miller's Theory of Justice," 119–34.

(2012j), "Recognition as Ideology: The Connection betweeen Morality and Power," 75–97.

(2012k), "Recognition between States: On the Moral Substrate of International Relations," 137–52.

(2012l), "The Work of Negativity: A Recognition-Theoretical Revision of Psychoanalysis," 193–200.

Other Honneth Works

(1979), "Communication and Reconciliation: Habermas' Critique of Adorno." *Telos* 39: 45–61.

(1999), "Postmodern Identity and Object-Relations Theory: On the Seeming Obsolescence of Psychoanalysis." *Philosophical Explorations* 2(3): 225–42.

(2001a), "Invisibility: On the Epistemology of 'Recognition.'" *Proceedings of the Aristotelian Society* 75 (supplement): 111–26.

(2001b), "Recognition or Redistribution? Changing Perspectives on the Moral Order of Society." *Theory, Culture & Society* 18(2–3): 43–55.

(2002a), "Grounding Recognition: A Rejoinder to Critical Questions." *Inquiry* 45(4): 499–519.

(ed.), (2002b), *Befreiung aus der Mündigkeit: Paradoxien des gegenwärtigen Kapitalismus.* Frankfurter Beiträge zur Soziologie und Sozialphilosophie, Frankfurt am Main: Campus Verlag.

(2003), "Die transzendentale Notwendigkeit von Intersubjektivität: Zum Zweiten Lehrsatz in Fichtes Naturrechtsabhandlung," *Unsichtbarkeit: Stationen einer Theorie der Intersubjektivität.* Frankfurt: Suhrkamp Verlag, 28–48.

(2007h), "Rejoinder," in Bert van den Brink and David Owen (eds), *Recognition and Power: Axel Honneth and the Tradition of Critical Social Theory.* New York: Cambridge University Press, 348–70.

(2011), "Rejoinder," in Danielle Petherbridge (ed.), *Axel Honneth: Critical Essays: With a Reply by Axel Honneth.* Leiden: Brill Academic Publishers, 391–421.

(2012a), "Brutalization of the Social Conflict: Struggles for Recognition in the Early 21st Century." *Distinktion: Scandinavian Journal of Social Theory* 13(1): 5–19.

(2013a), "The Normativity of Ethical Life." *Freedom's Right: A Symposium on Axel Honneth's Political Philosophy.* New York: Stony Brook University. Unpublished lecture. Available at www.youtube.com/watch?v=UuSSLA8_0cE

(2013b), "Replies." *Krisis: Journal for Contemporary Philosophy* 2013(1): 37–47.

Honneth, Axel, and Marcelo, Gonçalo (2013), "Recognition and Critical Theory Today: An Interview with Axel Honneth." *Philosophy & Social Criticism* 39(2): 209–21.

Honneth, Axel, and Sutterlüty, Ferdinand (2011), "Normative Paradoxien der Gegenwart – eine Forschungsperspektive." *WestEnd: Neue Zeitschrift für Sozialforschung* 8(1): 67–85.

Honneth, Axel, and Willig, Rasmus (2012), "Grammatology of Modern Recognition Orders: An Interview with Axel Honneth." *Distinktion: Scandinavian Journal of Social Theory* 13(1): 145–9.

Other Works Cited

Adorno, Theodor W., et al. (1950), *The Authoritarian Personality.* New York: Harper & Brothers.

Alexander, Jeffrey C., and Lara, Maria Pia (1996), "Honneth's New Critical Theory of Recognition." *New Left Review* I(220): 126–36.

Allen, Amy (2010), "Recognizing Domination: Recognition and Power in Honneth's Critical Theory." *Journal of Power* 3(1): 21–32.

Allen, Amy (2013), "The Ineliminability of Progress?" *Freedom's Right: A Symposium on Axel Honneth's Political Philosophy*. New York: Stony Brook University.

Anderson, Joel (2011), "Situating Axel Honneth in the Frankfurt School Tradition," in Danielle Petherbridge (ed.), *Axel Honneth: Critical Essays: With a Reply by Axel Honneth*. Leiden: Brill Academic Publishers, 31–57.

Anderson, Joel, and Honneth, Axel (2005), "Autonomy, Vulnerability, Recognition, and Justice," in Joel Anderson and John Christman (eds), *Autonomy and the Challenges to Liberalism: New Essays*. New York: Cambridge University Press, 127–49.

Appiah, Kwame Anthony (1994), "Identity, Authenticity, Survival: Multicultural Societies and Social Reproduction," in Amy Gutmann (ed.), *Multiculturalism: Examining the Politics of Recognition*. Princeton, NJ: Princeton University Press, 149–63.

Appiah, Kwame Anthony (2010), *The Honor Code: How Moral Revolutions Happen*. New York: W. W. Norton & Company.

Bader, Veit (2007), "Misrecognition, Power, and Democracy," in Bert van den Brink and David Owen (eds), *Recognition and Power: Axel Honneth and the Tradition of Critical Social Theory*. New York: Cambridge University Press, 238–69.

Barry, Brian (2001), *Culture and Equality: An Egalitarian Critique of Multiculturalism*. Cambridge, MA: Harvard University Press.

Benhabib, Seyla (1986), *Critique, Norm, and Utopia: A Study of the Foundations of Critical Theory*. New York: Columbia University Press.

Benhabib, Seyla (2002), *The Claims of Culture: Equality and Diversity in the Global Era*. Princeton, NJ: Princeton University Press.

Benjamin, Jessica (1988), *The Bonds of Love: Psychoanalysis, Feminism and the Problem of Domination*. New York: Pantheon.

Bernstein, J. M. (2010), "Recognition and Embodiment (Fichte's Materialism)," in Hans-Christoph Schmidt am Busch and Christopher F. Zurn (eds), *The Philosophy of Recognition: Historical and Contemporary Perspectives*. Lanham, MD: Lexington Books, 47–87.

Blackstone, William (1979), *Commentaries on the Laws of England: A Facsimile of the First Edition of 1765–1769*, IV vols (I). Chicago: University of Chicago Press.

Brink, Bert van den (2013), "From Personal Relations to the Rest of Society." *Krisis: Journal for Contemporary Philosophy* 2013(1): 23–7.

Brink, Bert van den, and Owen, David (2007a), "Introduction," in Bert van den Brink and David Owen (eds), *Recognition and Power: Axel*

Honneth and the Tradition of Critical Social Theory. New York: Cambridge University Press, 1–30.

Brink, Bert van den, and Owen, David (eds) (2007b), *Recognition and Power: Axel Honneth and the Tradition of Critical Social Theory*. New York: Cambridge University Press.

Burgess-Jackson, Keith (1998), "Wife Rape." *Public Affairs Quarterly* 12(1): 1–22.

Butler, Judith (1997), *The Psychic Life of Power: Theories in Subjection*. Stanford, CA: Stanford University Press.

Butler, Judith (2008), "Taking Another's View: Ambivalent Implications," in Martin Jay (ed.), *Reification: A New Look at an Old Idea*. New York: Oxford University Press, 97–119.

Claassen, Rutger (2013), "Justice: Constructive or Reconstructive?" *Krisis: Journal for Contemporary Philosophy* 2013(1): 28–31.

Connolly, Julie (2010), "Love in the Private: Axel Honneth, Feminism and the Politics of Recognition." *Contemporary Political Theory* 9(4): 414–33.

Cooke, Maeve (2009), "Beyond Dignity and Difference: Revisiting the Politics of Recognition." *European Journal of Political Theory* 8(1): 76–95.

Cott, Nancy F. (2000), *Public Vows: A History of Marriage and the Nation*. Cambridge, MA: Harvard University Press.

Cox, Ruth (2012), "Recognition and Immigration," in Shane O'Neill and Nicholas H. Smith (eds), *Recognition Theory as Social Research: Investigating the Dynamics of Social Conflict*. New York: Palgrave Macmillan, 192–212.

Deranty, Jean-Philippe (2009), *Beyond Communication: A Critical Study of Axel Honneth's Social Philosophy*. London: Brill Academic Publishers.

Deranty, Jean-Philippe (2010), "Critique of Political Economy and Contemporary Critical Theory: A Defense of Honneth's Theory of Recognition," in Hans-Christoph Schmidt am Busch and Christopher F. Zurn (eds), *The Philosophy of Recognition: Historical and Contemporary Perspectives*. Lanham, MD: Lexington Books, 285–317.

Descartes, René (1993), *Meditations on First Philosophy*, trans. Donald A. Cress. Indianapolis, IA: Hackett.

Dewey, John (1984), *The Public and Its Problems*, ed. Jo Ann Boydston (The Later Works of John Dewey, 1925–1953 (2: 1925–1927). Carbondale: Southern Illinois University Press.

Dworkin, Ronald (2000), *Sovereign Virtue: The Theory and Practice of Equality*. Cambridge, MA: Harvard University Press.

Emerson, Ralph Waldo (1979), "Self-Reliance." *The Collected Works of Ralph Waldo Emerson* (II, Essays: First Series). Cambridge, MA: Harvard University Press, 25–51.

Feinberg, Joel (1970), "The Nature and Value of Rights." *The Journal of Value Inquiry* 4: 243–57.

Ferrara, Alessandro (2011), "The Nugget and the Tailings. Reification Reinterpreted in the Light of Recognition," in Danielle Petherbridge (ed.), *Axel Honneth: Critical Essays: With a Reply by Axel Honneth*. Leiden: Brill Academic Publishers, 371–90.

Ferrarese, Estelle (2009), " 'Gabba-Gabba, We Accept You, One of Us': Vulnerability and Power in the Relationship of Recognition." *Constellations* 16(4): 604–14.

France, Anatole (1925 [1894]), *The Red Lily*, tr. Winifred Stephens. New York: Dodd, Mead.

Fraser, Nancy (1995), "Recognition or Redistribution? A Critical Reading of Iris Young's *Justice and the Politics of Difference*." *The Journal of Political Philosophy* 3(2): 166–80.

Fraser, Nancy (1997a), "From Redistribution to Recognition? Dilemmas of Justice in a 'Postsocialist' Age," *Justice Interruptus: Critical Reflections on the "Postsocialist" Condition*. New York: Routledge, 11–40.

Fraser, Nancy (1997b), "Heterosexism, Misrecognition, and Capitalism: A Response to Judith Butler." *Social Text* 15(3 and 4): 140–50.

Fraser, Nancy (1997c), *Justice Interruptus: Critical Reflections on the "Postsocialist" Condition*. New York: Routledge.

Fraser, Nancy (1998), "Social Justice in the Age of Identity Politics: Redistribution, Recognition, and Participation," in Grethe B. Peterson (ed.), *The Tanner Lectures on Human Values* (19). Salt Lake City: University of Utah Press, 1–67.

Fraser, Nancy (2000), "Rethinking Recognition." *New Left Review* 3: 107–20.

Fraser, Nancy (2001), "Recognition without Ethics?" *Theory, Culture & Society* 18 (2–3): 21–42.

Fraser, Nancy (2008), *Adding Insult to Injury: Nancy Fraser Debates her Critics*. New York: Verso.

Freud, Sigmund (1961), *Civilization and Its Discontents*, trans. James Strachey. New York: W. W. Norton & Company.

Geuss, Raymond (2008), "Philosophical Anthropology and Social Criticism," in Martin Jay (ed.), *Reification: A New Look at an Old Idea*. New York: Oxford University Press, 120–30.

Gitlin, Todd (1995), *The Twilight of Common Dreams: Why America is Wracked by Culture Wars*. New York: Metropolitan Books.

Grey, John (2004), *Heresies: Against Progress and Other Illusions*. London: Granta Books.

Habermas, Jürgen (1971), *Knowledge and Human Interests*, trans. Jeremy J. Shapiro. Boston, MA: Beacon Press.

Habermas, Jürgen (1984), *The Theory of Communicative Action. Volume 1: Reason and the Rationalization of Society*, trans. Thomas McCarthy. Boston: Beacon Press.

Habermas, Jürgen (1987), *The Theory of Communicative Action. Volume 2: Lifeworld and System: A Critique of Functionalist Reason*, trans. Thomas McCarthy. Boston: Beacon Press.

Habermas, Jürgen (1992), "Individuation through Socialization: On George Herbert Mead's Theory of Subjectivity." *Postmetaphysical Thinking: Philosophical Essays*. Cambridge, MA: The MIT Press, 149–204.

Habermas, Jürgen (1993), "On the Pragmatic, the Ethical, and the Moral Employments of Practical Reason." *Justification and Application: Remarks on Discourse Ethics*. Cambridge, MA: The MIT Press, 1–17.

Habermas, Jürgen (1994), "Struggles for Recognition in the Democratic Constitutional State," in Amy Gutmann (ed.), *Multiculturalism* (2nd edn). Princeton: Princeton University Press, 107–48.

Hartmann, Martin, and Honneth, Axel (2012 [2004]), "Paradoxes of Capitalism: A Research Programme." *The I in We: Studies in the Theory of Recognition*. Cambridge, UK: Polity Press, 169–90.

Hartsock, Nancy C. M. (1983), *Money, Sex, and Power: Toward a Feminist Historical Materialsim*. Boston, MA: Northeastern University Press.

Hegel, G. W. F. (1977), *Phenomenology of Spirit*, trans. A. V. Miller. New York: Oxford University Press.

Hegel, G. W. F. (1991), *Elements of the Philosophy of Right*, ed. Allen W. Wood, trans. H. B. Nisbet (Cambridge Texts in the History of Political Thought). New York: Cambridge University Press.

Heins, Volker (2008), "Realizing Honneth: Redistribution, Recognition, and Global Justice." *Journal of Global Ethics* 4(2): 141–53.

Heins, Volker (2009), "The Place of Property in the Politics of Recognition." *Constellations* 14(4): 579–92.

Heins, Volker (2012), "The Global Politics of Recognition," in Shane O'Neill and Nicholas H. Smith (eds), *Recognition Theory as Social Research: Investigating the Dynamics of Social Conflict*. New York: Palgrave Macmillan, 213–30.

Hochschild, Arlie Russell, and Machung, Anne (2003), *The Second Shift* (updated edn). New York: Penguin Books.

Horkheimer, Max (1992), "Traditional and Critical Theory." *Critical Theory: Selected Essays*. New York: Continuum, 188–243.

Horkheimer, Max, and Adorno, Theodor W. (2002), *Dialectic of Enlightenment: Philosophical Fragments*, trans. Edmund Jephcott. Stanford, CA: Stanford University Press.

Ikäheimo, Heikki (2002), "On the Genus and Species of Recognition." *Inquiry* 45(4): 447–62.

Ikäheimo, Heikki (2010), "Making the Best of What We Are: Recognition as an Ontological and Ethical Concept," in Hans-Christoph Schmidt am Busch and Christopher F. Zurn (eds), *The Philosophy of*

Recognition: Historical and Contemporary Perspectives. Lanham, MD: Lexington Books, 343–67.

Ikäheimo, Heikki, and Laitinen, Arto (2007), "Analyzing Recognition: Identification, Acknowledgement, and Recognitive Attitudes towards Persons," in Bert van den Brink and David Owen (eds), *Recognition and Power: Axel Honneth and the Tradition of Critical Social Theory.* New York: Cambridge University Press, 33–56.

Jansen, Yolande (2013), "The 'Us' of Democratic Will-Formation and Globalisation." *Krisis: Journal for Contemporary Philosophy* 2013(1): 32–6.

Kauppinen, Antti (2002), "Reason, Recognition, and Internal Critique." *Inquiry* 45(4): 479–98.

Kymlicka, Will (1995), *Multicultural Citizenship: A Liberal Theory of Minority Rights.* New York: Oxford University Press.

Laitinen, Arto (2002), "Interpersonal Recognition: A Response to Value or a Precondition of Personhood?" *Inquiry* 45(4): 463–78.

Laitinen, Arto (2010), "On the Scope of 'Recognition': The Role of Adequate Regard and Mutuality," in Hans-Christoph Schmidt am Busch and Christopher F. Zurn (eds), *The Philosophy of Recognition: Historical and Contemporary Perspectives.* Lanham, MD: Lexington Books, 319–42.

Lear, Jonathan (2008), "The Slippery Middle," in Martin Jay (ed.), *Reification: A New Look at an Old Idea.* New York: Oxford University Press, 131–43.

Locke, Alain LeRoy (1992), *Race Contacts and Interracial Relations: Lectures on the Theory and Practice of Race,* ed. Jeffrey C. Stewart. Washington, DC: Howard University Press.

MacIntyre, Alasdair (1989), *Whose Justice? Which Rationality?* Notre Dame, IN: University of Notre Dame Press.

Markell, Patchen (2003), *Bound by Recognition.* Princeton, NJ: Princeton University Press.

Markell, Patchen (2007), "The Potential and the Actual: Mead, Honneth, and the 'I,' " in Bert van den Brink and David Owen (eds), *Recognition and Power: Axel Honneth and the Tradition of Critical Social Theory.* New York: Cambridge University Press, 100–32.

Marshall, T. H. (1950), *Citizenship and Social Class.* London: Cambridge University Press.

McBride, Cillian (2013), *Recognition.* Cambridge, UK: Polity Press.

McNay, Lois (2008), *Against Recognition.* Cambridge, UK: Polity Press.

Meehan, Johanna (2011), "Recognition and the Dynamics of Intersubjectivity," in Danielle Petherbridge (ed.), *Axel Honneth: Critical Essays: With a Reply by Axel Honneth.* Leiden: Brill Academic Publishers, 89–123.

Mill, John Stuart (1978), *On Liberty,* ed. Elizabeth Rapaport. Indianapolis, IN: Hackett.

Neuhouser, Frederick (2010), *Rousseau's Theodicy of Self-Love: Evil, Rationality, and the Drive for Recognition*. New York: Oxford University Press.

O'Neill, Shane (2012), "The Politics of Ethno-National Conflict Transformation: A Recognition-Theoretical Reading of the Peace Process in Northern Ireland," in Shane O'Neill and Nicholas H. Smith (eds), *Recognition Theory as Social Research: Investigating the Dynamics of Social Conflict*. New York: Palgrave Macmillan, 149–72.

O'Neill, Shane, and Smith, Nicholas H. (eds) (2012), *Recognition Theory as Social Research: Investigating the Dynamics of Social Conflict*. New York: Palgrave Macmillan.

Okin, Susan Moller (1989), *Justice, Gender, and the Family*. New York: Basic Books.

Okin, Susan Moller and respondents (1999), *Is Multiculturalism Bad for Women?*, eds Joshua Cohen, Matthew Howard, and Martha C. Nussbaum. Princeton, NJ: Princeton University Press.

Oliver, Kelly (2001), *Witnessing: Beyond Recognition*. University of Minnesota Press.

Owen, David (2008), "Recognition, Reification and Value." *Constellations* 15(4): 576–86.

Owen, David (2012), "Recognition as Statecraft? Contexts of Recognition and Transformations of State Membership Regimes," in Shane O'Neill and Nicholas H. Smith (eds), *Recognition Theory as Social Research: Investigating the Dynamics of Social Conflict*. New York: Palgrave Macmillan, 173–91.

Pateman, Carole (1988), *The Sexual Contract*. Stanford, CA: Stanford University Press.

Petherbridge, Danielle (ed.) (2011), *Axel Honneth: Critical Essays: With a Reply by Axel Honneth*. Leiden: Brill Academic Publishers.

Petherbridge, Danielle (2013), *The Critical Theory of Axel Honneth*. Lanham, MD: Lexington Books.

Rawls, John (1971), *A Theory of Justice*. Cambridge, MA: Harvard University Press.

Rawls, John (1996), *Political Liberalism* (paperback edn). New York: Columbia University Press.

Renault, Emmanuel (2011), "The Theory of Recognition and Critique of Institutions," in Danielle Petherbridge (ed.), *Axel Honneth: Critical Essays: With a Reply by Axel Honneth*. Leiden: Brill Academic Publishers, 207–32.

Ricoeur, Paul (1970), *Freud and Philosophy: An Essay on Interpretation*, trans. Denis Savage. New Haven, CT: Yale University Press.

Rössler, Beate (2007), "Work, Recognition, Emancipation," in Bert van den Brink and David Owen (eds), *Recognition and Power: Axel Honneth and the Tradition of Critical Social Theory*. New York: Cambridge University Press, 135–63.

Ryan, Rebecca M. (1995), "The Sex Right: A Legal History of the Marital Rape Exemption." *Law and Social Inquiry* 20(4): 941–1001.

Sandel, Michael J. (1982), *Liberalism and the Limits of Justice*. New York: Cambridge University Press.

Schlesinger Jr, Arthur M. (1992), *The Disuniting of America*. New York: W. W. Norton & Company.

Schmidt am Busch, Hans-Christoph (2010), "Can the Goals of the Frankfurt School be Achieved by a Theory of Recognition?", in Hans-Christoph Schmidt am Busch and Christopher F. Zurn (eds), *The Philosophy of Recognition: Historical and Contemporary Perspectives*. Lanham, MD: Lexington Books, 256–83.

Schweiger, Gottfried (2012), "Globalizing Recognition: Global Justice and the Dialectic of Recognition." *Public Reason* 4(1–2): 78–91.

Seglow, Jonathan (2012), "Recognition and Religious Diversity: The Case of Legal Exemptions," in Shane O'Neill and Nicholas H. Smith (eds), *Recognition Theory as Social Research: Investigating the Dynamics of Social Conflict*. New York: Palgrave Macmillan, 127–46.

Sinnerbrink, Robert (2011), "Power, Recognition, and Care: Honneth's Critique of Poststructuralist Social Philosophy," in Danielle Petherbridge (ed.), *Axel Honneth: Critical Essays: With a Reply by Axel Honneth*. Leiden: Brill Academic Publishers, 177–205.

Smith, Nicholas H. (2009), "Work and the Struggle for Recognition." *European Journal of Political Theory* 8(1): 46–60.

Smith, Nicholas H. (2011), "Recognition, Culture and Economy: Honneth's Debate with Fraser," in Danielle Petherbridge (ed.), *Axel Honneth: Critical Essays: With a Reply by Axel Honneth*. Boston: Brill Academic Publishers, 321–44.

Smith, Nicholas H. (2012), "Work as a Sphere of Norms, Paradoxes, and Ideologies of Recognition," in Shane O'Neill and Nicholas H. Smith (eds), *Recognition Theory as Social Research: Investigating the Dynamics of Social Conflict*. New York: Palgrave Macmillan, 87–108.

Sullivan, Andrew (1996), *Virtually Normal: An Argument about Homosexuality*. New York: Vintage Books.

Taylor, Charles (1989), *Sources of the Self: The Making of the Modern Identity*. Cambridge, MA: Harvard University Press.

Taylor, Charles (1994), *Multiculturalism: Examining the Politics of Recognition*, ed. Amy Gutmann. Princeton, NJ: Princeton University Press.

Thompson, Simon (2005), "Is Redistribution a Form of Recognition? Comments on the Fraser–Honneth Debate," *Critical Review of International Social and Political Philosophy* 8(1): 85–102.

Thompson, Simon (2006), *The Political Theory of Recognition: A Critical Introduction*. Cambridge, UK: Polity Press.

Varga, Somogy, and Gallagher, Shaun (2011), "Critical Social Philosophy, Honneth and the Role of Primary Intersubjectivity." *European Journal of Social Theory* 15(2): 243–60.

Warner, Michael (2000), *The Trouble with Normal: Sex, Politics, and the Ethics of Queer Life.* Cambridge, MA: Harvard University Press.

Whitebook, Joel (2001), "Mutual Recognition and the Work of the Negative," in William Rehg and James Bohman (eds), *Pluralism and the Pragmatic Turn: The Transformation of Critical Theory, Essays in Honor of Thomas McCarthy.* Cambridge, MA: The MIT Press, 257–91.

Wild, David B. (2013), "Recognising Capital and the Politics of Theory." Unpublished dissertation. Macquarie University.

Wildt, Andreas (2010), "'Recognition' in Psychoanalysis," in Hans-Christoph Schmidt am Busch and Christopher F. Zurn (eds), *The Philosophy of Recognition: Historical and Contemporary Perspectives.* Lanham, MD: Lexington Books, 189–209.

Yar, Majid (2012), "Recognition as the Grounds of a General Theory of Crime as Social Harm?," in Shane O'Neill and Nicholas H. Smith (eds), *Recognition Theory as Social Research: Investigating the Dynamics of Social Conflict.* New York: Palgrave Macmillan, 109–26.

Young, Iris Marion (1990a), "Displacing the Distributive Paradigm." *Justice and the Politics of Difference.* Princeton, NJ: Princeton University Press, 15–38.

Young, Iris Marion (1990b), *Justice and the Politics of Difference.* Princeton, NJ: Princeton University Press.

Young, Iris Marion (2007), "Recognition of Love's Labor: Considering Axel Honneth's Feminism," in Bert van den Brink and David Owen (eds), *Recognition and Power: Axel Honneth and the Tradition of Critical Social Theory.* New York: Cambridge University Press, 189–212.

Zurn, Christopher F. (1997), "The Normative Claims of Three Types of Feminist Struggles for Recognition." *Philosophy Today* 41 (Supplement): 73–8.

Zurn, Christopher F. (2000), "Anthropology and Normativity: A Critique of Axel Honneth's 'Formal Conception of Ethical Life.'" *Philosophy & Social Criticism* 26(1): 115–24.

Zurn, Christopher F. (2003a), "Arguing Over Participatory Parity: On Fraser's Conception of Social Justice." *Philosophy Today* 47 (Supplement): 130–44.

Zurn, Christopher F. (2003b), "Identity or Status? Struggles over 'Recognition' in Fraser, Honneth, and Taylor." *Constellations* 10(4): 519–37.

Zurn, Christopher F. (2004), "Group Balkanization or Societal Homogenization: Is there a Dilemma between Recognition and Distribution Struggles?" *Public Affairs Quarterly* 18(2): 159–86.

Zurn, Christopher F. (2005), "Recognition, Redistribution, and Democracy: Dilemmas of Honneth's Critical Social Theory." *European Journal of Philosophy* 13(1): 89–126.

Zurn, Christopher F. (2011), "Social Pathologies as Second-Order Disorders," in Danielle Petherbridge (ed.), *Axel Honneth: Critical Essays:*

With a Reply by Axel Honneth. Leiden: Brill Academic Publishers, 345–70.

Zurn, Christopher F. (2012), "Misrecognition, Marriage and Derecognition," in Shane O'Neill and Nicholas H. Smith (eds), *Recognition Theory as Social Research: Investigating the Dynamics of Social Conflict*. New York: Palgrave Macmillan, 63–86.

Index